D0880218

FICTION AND REPETITION

FICTION
AND
REPETITION
Seven English Novels

J. HILLIS MILLER

HARVARD UNIVERSITY PRESS
Cambridge, Massachusetts

Printed in the United States of America

10 9 8 7 6 5 4 3 2

Library of Congress Cataloging in Publication Data

Miller, J. Hillis (Joseph Hillis), 1928–
Fiction and repetition.

Includes index.
1. English fiction—History and criticism.
2. Repetition in literature.
3. Fiction—Technique. I. Title.
PR830.R53M5 823'.009 81-6733
ISBN 0-674-29925-6 (cloth) AACR2
ISBN 0-674-29926-4 (paper)

ACKNOWLEDGMENTS

THIS BOOK has been a good while in the making. It is a pleasure to acknowledge here the various sorts of indebtedness I have incurred along the way.

The book was originally conceived during my tenure of a Fellowship from the John Simon Guggenheim Memorial Foundation. Since then work on it has continued with the help of a Fellowship at the Center for the Humanities, Wesleyan University, a Fellowship from the Council of Humanities at Princeton University, a Senior Fellowship from the National Endowment for the Humanities, and, most recently, during a triennial leave from Yale, a Carnegie Fellowship at the University of Edinburgh and a month at the Bellagio Study and Conference Center of the Rockefeller Foundation. For the free time provided by all of these and for the generous provision of research leaves from Johns Hopkins and Yale I am profoundly grateful.

Early versions of parts of this book, since extensively revised, were published in *The Interpretation of Narrative,* ed. M. W. Bloomfield, Harvard English Studies, I (Harvard University Press, 1970); in *The Shaken Realist,* ed. Melvin J. Friedman and John B. Vickery (Louisiana State University Press, 1970); in *Forms of Modern British Fiction,* ed. Alan Warren Friedman (University of Texas Press, 1975); as the introduction to The New Wessex Edition of Thomas Hardy's *The Well-Beloved* (Macmillan, 1975); and in *Notre Dame English Journal* (April 1980). I thank the editors of these publications for allowing me to regather this material for revision and inclusion here. A few words from the original manuscript of *Tess of the d'Urbervilles* which differ from the published versions appear in the chapter on that novel. I thank the Keeper of Manuscripts of the British Library for allowing me to examine the manuscript and the Trustees of the late Miss E. A. Dugdale for allowing me to reproduce these words.

My greatest debt is to students and colleagues who have listened to me talk about fiction and repetition and whose responses to what I have said have greatly aided my thinking about this topic. I want particularly to thank the participants in three Summer Seminars for College Teachers sponsored by the National Endowment for the Humanities. In addition, I owe special debts to students and colleagues at Johns Hopkins, Yale, Zürich, Princeton, and Edinburgh, and at the School of Criticism and Theory at the University of California at Irvine. These are the sorts of debts one does not ever pay off.

Deer Isle, Maine
July 31, 1981

CONTENTS

FICTION AND REPETITION

1
TWO FORMS OF REPETITION

A LONG WORK LIKE A NOVEL is interpreted, by whatever sort of reader, in part through the identification of recurrences and of meanings generated through recurrences. I say "in part" because there are of course many types of literary form which generate meaning in novels. These include, for example, the straightforward sequence of unrepeatable events in the order in which they occurred or are retold. The story as such, event following event, tends to arouse passionate human responses. These responses might in one sense be thought of as the "meaning" of the novel. This book for the most part suspends such other sources of meaning in order to focus on the contribution to meaning of the various forms of recurrence in novels. That these forms are various or even disparate I would agree, but insofar as they all involve one instance which then in one way or another reappears in another instance they are all cases of the same identifiable problem of repetition.

Take, for example, *Tess of the D'Urbervilles,* one of the novels read in detail in a later chapter in this book. The first instance of the color red in the novel may be passed over as trivial or as merely representational. It is not unlikely that Tess would have a red ribbon in her hair. When the reader encounters the third, the fourth, and the fifth red things, red begins to stand out as a salient motif, repeated in sequence, like those words Tess meets on walls or fences painted by the itinerant religious man, each word oddly followed by a comma: "THY, DAMNATION, SLUMBERETH, NOT," or "THOU, SHALT, NOT, COMMIT ——."[1]

A number of different forms of repetition may be identified in *Tess,* as in realistic novels generally. On a small scale, there is repetition of verbal elements: words, figures of speech, shapes or gestures, or, more subtly, covert repetitions that act like metaphors, as the cigar-smoking Alec d'Urberville is said to be "the blood-red ray in the spectrum of [Tess's] young life" (ch. 5), while the sun's rays coming into her room in a later episode are said to look like that phallic-shaped garden flower called "red-hot poker" (ch. 14). On a larger scale, events or scenes may be duplicated within the text, as Tess's life is made up of reenactments of the "same" event involving the same cluster of motifs: somnolence, the color red, some act of violence done or received. Motifs from one plot or character may recur in another within the same text, as 'Liza-Lu, Tess's sister, seems at the end of the novel destined to reenact another version of Tess's life. A character may repeat previous generations, or historical or mythological characters, as Tess's violation repeats the violence done to long-dead peasant girls by Tess's male ancestors, or as her death repeats the crucifixion of Christ or the prehistoric sacrifices performed at Stonehenge. Finally, an author may repeat in one novel motifs, themes, characters, or events from his other novels. Hardy published *Tess* in 1891, the first version of *The Well-Beloved* in 1892, *Jude the Obscure* in 1895, and the second version of *The Well-Beloved* in 1897. An earlier title of *Tess of the d'Urbervilles* was *Too Late Beloved* or *Too Late, Beloved.* The similarity in titles indicates the way the two novels echo each other thematically and formally. The three adjacent novels are at least as much bound together as, say, adjacent poems in one of Hardy's collections of lyrics. The second version of *The Well-Beloved* may have been motivated or to some degree influenced by the writing during the intervening years of *Jude the Obscure.* (I discuss *The Well-Beloved* in detail in Chapter 6.)

A novel is interpreted in part through the noticing of such recurrences. This book is an exploration of some of the ways they work to generate meaning or to inhibit the too easy determination of a meaning based on the linear sequence of the story. The reader's identification of recurrences may be deliberate or spontaneous, self-conscious or unreflective. In a novel, what is said two or more times may not be true, but the reader is fairly safe in assuming that it is significant. Any novel is a complex tissue of repetitions and of repetitions within repetitions, or of repetitions linked in chain fashion to other repetitions. In each case there are repetitions making up the structure of the work within itself, as well as repetitions determining its multiple relations to what is outside it: the author's mind or his life; other works by the same author; psychological, social, or historical reality; other works by other authors; motifs from the mythological or fabulous past; elements from the purported past of the characters or of their ancestors; events which have occurred before the book begins. In all these kinds of recurrence the questions are the following: What controls the meaning these repetitions create? What methodological presuppositions will allow the critic, in the case of a particular novel, to control them in his turn in a valid interpretation?

In each chapter of this book I attempt to answer these questions for one novel, exploring as fully as possible the working of repetition in it. I have listed the ways a novel represents social or psychological reality as a mode of repetition. As such, it comes up as a topic here and there in the chapters of this book, but my primary focus here is not on the problems of "realism." Moreover, this book is not a work of theory as such, but a series of readings of important nineteenth- and twentieth-century English novels. The readings are more concerned with the relation of rhetorical form to meaning than with thematic paraphrase, though of course it is impossible in practice to separate these wholly. The focus of my readings is on the "how" of meaning rather than on its "what," not "what is the meaning?" but "how does meaning arise from the reader's encounter with just these words on the page?" I try to attend to the threads of the tapestry of words in each case rather than simply to the picture the novel makes when viewed from a distance. This necessitates my focus on details of language in each novel. In order to investigate the kind of repetition involved in the relation between two novels by the same author, I consider two novels by Thomas Hardy and two by Virginia Woolf, though each chapter is meant to stand on its own as an interpretation of that particular work from the point of view of my topic. Taken together the chapters indicate something of the range of ways repetitive structures work in the English novel of the Victorian and modern periods. Each novel has been chosen because it is of special interest and excellence in itself, both among other novels by the same author and among nineteenth- and twentieth-century English novels generally. Each has also been chosen as the best text I know in nineteenth- and twentieth-century English fiction to explore the mode of repetition in question in that chapter: irony and repetition, for example, in the chapter on *Henry Esmond;* or a certain form of immanent repetition in *Tess of the d'Urbervilles.* All these types of repetition occur elsewhere in other novels, but my choice of these may be justified in the same way the French ethnographer Marcel Mauss justifies his close study of certain primitive societies rather than others. The societies he has chosen to study, says Mauss, "represent truly the maximums, the excessive, which make it possible to see better the facts than where, not less essential, they remain small and involuted."[2] To put this in terms of one of my categories of repetition, all realistic novels in one way or another are ironical texts, but in *Henry Esmond* irony is a major and pervasive characteristic of the narrative style throughout.

I do not claim that my seven readings represent an exhaustive repertoire of the kinds of repetition in nineteenth- and twentieth-century English fiction or in realistic fiction generally. Each novel is to some degree unique, and there are over forty thousand Victorian novels alone. It is my hypothesis that all modes of repetition represent one form or another of the contradictory intertwining of the two kinds of repetition I will identify in this chapter. All the novels I have studied in detail confirm this hypothesis, but that still leaves open the question of how many it would take to prove the case. Would the ways of reading novels exemplified here work for other novels by the same authors, or for other novels by other authors of the same period, or by authors of different periods or countries? Are my readings "exemplary"? That could be determined certainly only by doing more readings, but the diversity of modes of repetition among my seven novels would suggest that it would be well to expect to find as much difference as similarity in further examples, even in further novels by the same authors.

The specificity and strangeness of literature, the capacity of each work to surprise the reader, if he can remain prepared to be surprised, means that literature continually exceeds any formulas or any theory with which the critic is prepared to encompass it. The hypothesis of possible heterogeneity of form in literary works has the heuristic value of preparing the reader to confront the oddnesses of a given novel, the things in it that do not "fit." The seven readings here have attempted to identify the anomalous in each case and to begin to account for it. This means of course attempting in one way or another to make the unlawful lawful, but the law that emerges will necessarily differ from the one presupposed in readings that assume a good novel is necessarily going to be homogeneous or organic in form.

The history of Western ideas of repetition begins, like our culture generally, with the Bible on the one hand and with Homer, the Pre-Socratics, and Plato on the other. The long centuries of Biblical hermeneutics whereby the New Testament was seen in one way or another as repeating the Old are still presupposed in the use of Biblical types in *Henry Esmond* or *Adam Bede.* The modern history of ideas about repetition goes by way of Vico to Hegel and the German Romantics, to Kierkegaard's *Repetition,* to Marx (in *The Eighteenth Brumaire*), to Nietzsche's concept of the eternal return, to Freud's notion of the compulsion to repeat, to the Joyce of *Finnegans Wake,* on down to such diverse present-day theorists of repetition as Jacques Lacan or Gilles Deleuze, Mircea Eliade or Jacques Derrida.[3]

The two alternative theories of repetition are set clearly against each other in a passage in Gilles Deleuze's *Logique du sens.* Deleuze opposes Nietzsche's concept of repetition to Plato's:

> Let us consider two formulations: "only that which resembles itself differs," "only differences resemble one another" [*"seul ce qui se ressemble diffère," "seules les différences se ressemblent"*]. It is a question of two readings of the world in the sense that one asks us to think of difference on the basis of preestablished similitude or identity, while the other invites us on the contrary to think of similitude and even identity as the product of a fundamental disparity [*d'une disparité de fond*]. The first exactly defines the world of copies or of

> representations; it establishes the world as icon. The second, against the first, defines the world of simulacra. It presents the world itself as phantasm.[4]

What Deleuze calls "Platonic" repetition is grounded in a solid archetypal model which is untouched by the effects of repetition. All the other examples are copies of this model. The assumption of such a world gives rise to the notion of a metaphoric expression based on genuine participative similarity or even on identity, as when Gerard Manley Hopkins says he becomes Christ, an "afterChrist," through the operation of grace.[5] A similar presupposition, as Deleuze recognizes, underlies concepts of imitation in literature. The validity of the mimetic copy is established by its truth of correspondence to what it copies. This is, so it seems, the reigning presupposition of realistic fiction and of its critics in nineteenth- and even in twentieth-century England. This theory of repetition still has great force. To many it seems the normative one.

The other, Nietzschean mode of repetition posits a world based on difference. Each thing, this other theory would assume, is unique, intrinsically different from every other thing. Similarity arises against the background of this "disparité du fond." It is a world not of copies but of what Deleuze calls "simulacra" or "phantasms." These.are ungrounded doublings which arise from differential interrelations among elements which are all on the same plane. This lack of ground in some paradigm or archetype means that there is something ghostly about the effects of this second kind of repetition. It seems that X repeats Y, but in fact it does not, or at least not in the firmly anchored way of the first sort of repetition. An example would be the way Henchard, in Hardy's *The Mayor of Casterbridge,* thinks, during his wanderings at the end of his life, that he returns to the spot where he sold his wife in the scene that opens the novel. In fact, as the narrator tells us, with Hardy's characteristic insouciant ironic cruelty, he has not correctly identified the place.

A passage in Walter Benjamin's "The Image of Proust" ("Zum Bilde Prousts") will help to specify further the distinction between the two kinds of repetition. If Penelope unwove by night what she wove by day, Proust's writing, says Benjamin, was the reverse of this. It wove by night and unwove by day. The distinction is between the rational, willed, intentional remembering of the daytime, and that kind of involuntary memory which Benjamin calls forgetting. The first kind of memory constructs a lucid pattern from which the "life" has disappeared, like a dry historical recital of facts. The second kind of memory constructs an imaginary life, "lived life," as dreams make for us a strangely powerful affective "memory" of things which never happened as such. The originality of Benjamin's insight here is his recognition of the constructive, fictive, falsifying aspect of Proust's involuntary affective memory. This "memory" creates, for the one who experiences it, as Marcel's narration creates for him, a vast intricate network of lies, the memory of a world that never was. This world is posited on the negative work of forgetting. The paragraph in Benjamin's essay is of great concentration and beauty:

> We know that in his work Proust did not describe a life as it actually was, but a life as it was remembered by the one who had lived it. And yet even this statement is imprecise and far too crude. For the important thing for the remembering author is not what he experienced, but the weaving of his memory, the Penelope work of recollection [*Eingedenkens*]. Or should one call it, rather, a Penelope work of forgetting? Is not the involuntary recollection, Proust's *mémoire involuntaire,* much closer to forgetting than what is usually called memory? And is not this work of spontaneous recollection, in which remembrance is the woof and forgetting the warp, a counterpart [*Gegenstück*] to Penelope's work rather than its likeness [*Ebenbild*]? For here the day unravels what the night has woven. When we awake each morning, we hold in our hands, usually weakly and loosely, but a few fringes of the tapestry of lived life, as loomed for us by forgetting. However, with our purposeful activity and, even more, our purposive remembering each day unravels the web and the ornaments of forgetting. This is why Proust finally turned his days into nights, devoting all his hours to undisturbed work in his darkened room with artificial illumination, so that none of those intricate arabesques might escape him.[6]

The relevance of Benjamin's oppositions to an understanding of repetition lies in the fact that a different form of echoing occurs in each form of memory-work. The tapestry of memory in each case is woven on the basis of the experience of recurrence, but the two forms of recurrence differ. Daylight, willed memory works logically, by way of similarities which are seen as identities, one thing repeating another and grounded in a concept on the basis of which their likeness may be understood. This corresponds to Deleuze's first, Platonic form of repetition. (The reader will note that in saying "corresponds to" I am using the form of relation which I am discussing. Repetition cannot be analyzed without using it, in forms of language which inevitably turn back on themselves and lose their lucid or logical transparency. Benjamin "repeats" Deleuze. In which way? According to which mode of repetition is my own tapestry being woven here?)

The second, involuntary form of memory, which Benjamin calls the "Penelope work of forgetting [*Penelopewerk des Vergessens*]," is woven also out of similarities, but these are called by Benjamin "opaquely similar [*undurchschaubar ähnlich*]." These similarities he associates with dreams, in which one thing is experienced as repeating something which is quite different from it and which it strangely resembles. ("It was a sock, but it was my mother too.") This repetition is not grounded. It arises out of the interplay of the opaquely similar things, opaque in the sense of riddling. How is a mother like a sock? This repetition is the true mode of Proust's novel. It corresponds to Deleuze's second, Nietzschean form of repetition. Benjamin, accordingly, writes of "Proust's frenetically studying resemblances, his impassioned cult of similarity [*Ahnlichkeit*]." "The true signs of [the dream's] hegemony [*Herrschaft*]," he continues, "do not become obvious where [Proust] suddenly and startlingly uncovers similarities in actions, physiognomies, or speech mannerisms. The similarity of one thing to another which we are used to, which occupies us in a wakeful state, reflects only vaguely the deeper resemblance of the dream world in which everything that happens appears not in identical but in similar guise, opaquely similar to one another [*nie identisch, sondern ähnlich: sich selber undurchschaubar ähnlich*]."[7]

In explaining what he means by "opaque similarity," Benjamin has recourse to an emblem which is an example of what he is trying to define. The defined enters once more into the definition, disqualifying that definition, as in my own language here, according to a necessity of this second form of repetition. If the similarity is not logical or wakeful, but opaque, dreamlike, it cannot be defined logically, but only exemplified. The example will then only present again the opacity. Another necessity of the second form of repetition, "exemplified" by both Deleuze and Benjamin, is its dependence on the first, grounded, logical form. Each form of repetition calls up the other, by an inevitable compulsion. The second is not the negation or opposite of the first, but its "counterpart," in a strange relation whereby the second is the subversive ghost of the first, always already present within it as a possibility which hollows it out. If logical, daylight resemblances depend on a third thing, on a principle of identity which precedes them, the opaque similarities of dream are baseless, or, if based at all, then based on the difference between the two things. They create in the gap of that difference a third thing, what Benjamin calls the image [*das Bild*]. The image is the meaning generated by the echoing of two dissimilar things in the second form of repetition. It is neither in the first nor in the second nor in some ground which preceded both, but in between, in the empty space which the opaque similarity crosses. Freud's early discovery of the hysterical trauma is an example of this. In such traumas the first experience ultimately generating hysterical symptoms is presexual in that the child does not understand its sexual meaning. A much later trivial event repeats some detail of the first and brings it back into mental life, now reinterpreted as a traumatic sexual assault. The trauma is neither in the first nor in the second but between them, in the relation between two opaquely similar events.[8]

Benjamin invents a brilliant emblem of this relation. It is like a sock which is also an empty sack, but also at the same time a gift inside the sack, filling it, but also a sock again. The emblem turns on the oppositions, or rather counterparts, of inside/outside; full/empty; waking/dream; remembering/forgetting; identity/similarity; container/thing contained. These pairs have structured Benjamin's interpretation of Proust in their strange function not as polar opposites but as differences which remain differences but can turn into one another, as in the transformations in Benjamin's parable of the sock:

> Children know a symbol [*ein Wahrzeichen*] of this world [of dreams]: the stocking which has the structure of this dream world when, rolled up in the laundry hamper, it is a "bag" and a "present" at the same time. And just as children do not tire of quickly changing the bag and its contents into a third thing—namely a stocking—Proust could not get his fill of emptying the dummy, his self [*die Attrappe, das Ich*], at one stroke in order to keep garnering that third thing, the image [*das Bild*] which satisfied his curiosity—indeed, assuaged his homesickness [*Heimweh*]. He lay on his bed racked with homesickness, homesick for the world distorted in the state of resemblance [*der im Stand der Ähnlichkeit entstellten Welt*], a world in which the true surrealist face of existence [*das wahre surrealistische Gesicht des Daseins*] breaks through.[9]

The ratios established here are peculiar. They are peculiar in not being based on *ratio* in the sense of reason, *logos, Grund*. The oddness lies partly in the fact that the figure of the sock is an example of what it is supposed to clarify. It lies also partly in the difficulty of following out exactly what stands for what when the emblem is applied. Unexpected meanings emerge when the reader articulates the equivalences established by the "symbol" [*Wahrzeichen*]. When the stocking is rolled up inside itself in the laundry hamper it becomes alternately two other things. These seem stark opposites but at the same time are felt to be opaquely similar. Each is clearly another form of the same object. The stocking is both the empty bag, sign of an absence, and at the same time the precious contents of that bag, a present. As a present it is an object of value which is passed from one person to another and establishes the reciprocal interchange of gift-giving and gift-receiving between them. Such an interchange is a fundamental property of signs, for example of all those signs Proust assembles and gives to his readers in *A la recherche du temps perdu*. The obscurity of the similarity between the bag and the present lies in the fact that one cannot see through the similarity to its ground. This is true because the ground, namely the sock, is, literally, the possibility of being two apparently opposite things, both the container and what is contained, both the empty bag and the present. The opacity remains even when the bag and its contents are transformed into the third thing, namely a stocking, by being turned outside in again. From oneness to twoness, from figure to literal ground, the relation is continuously reversible. Each state of the object is both the literal ground of the other and the figure of it.

In Benjamin's application of his parable, Proust himself, surprisingly, is not the third thing, the self recovered through the activity of involuntary memory, as many interpretations of Proust would have it. Proust is the empty bag, hollow, void, a dummy (*eine Attrappe*), out of which he emptied all his memories in order to produce a third thing born of the opaque similarity between empty self and its inert contents, namely the image. The "image" here corresponds to the stocking itself. The stocking/image is both the most literal thing around, what the object "really is," and at the same time something wholly figurative. The word *Bild* in German means both "image," in the sense of picture or representation, and "figure," in the sense of figure of speech, trope. Benjamin's difficult concept of the image is worked out more fully in his theory of allegory in *Ursprung des deutschen trauerspiels.*[10] The image/sock is both the self and the "third thing" which arises from the relation of obscure repetition between the first two things, as the "image" in Proust is not in any single thing but arises out of the relation woven by the "forgetting" of two things, the first madeleine dipped in tea, for example, and its repetition in the second. The self in this process is not a source but a function, and an empty one at that. It is a negative element in a system.

Readers of Benjamin's essay on Goethe's *Elective Affinities* will remember his firm rejection there of biographical interpretations of literature. The real experiences of an author are "empty or ungraspable," and "the only rational correlation [*Zusammenhang*] between author and work lies in the evidence that the latter has discarded the former."[11] The self of the author is not the explanatory origin of the work. That origin, or rather the apparent origin, metaleptically reversing cause and effect, is another, more genuine self. This self is made by the work. The self exists only in the work and in the work's detachment from the "real life" of the author. Proust did not, in Benjamin's interpretation of him, seek to recuperate his selfhood through his writing. He sought rather to escape from that self through the image into a world for which he was homesick, the world "distorted in the state of resemblance." The home from which he was exiled could be reached only through the kind of image born of the clashing of two dissimilars which characterizes the second form of repetition. If Proust's remembering was a form of forgetting, his homesickness too was the counterpart and not the likeness of ordinary longing for home. To it apply exactly those phrases used by Walter Pater to describe "aesthetic poetry": "The secret of the enjoyment of it is that inversion of home-sickness known to some, that incurable thirst for the sense of escape, which no actual form of life satisfies, no poetry even, if it be merely simple and spontaneous."[12] Such a homesickness can only be assuaged by the image born of ungrounded recurrences, like Benjamin's figure of the sock.

Thomas Hardy will provide a final example of the interaction of the two forms of repetition. A passage from *The Well-Beloved* describes the hero's habit of seeing Rome as a repetition of his native peninsula, Portland Bill, "the Isle of Slingers" as it is called in the novel:

> The unconscious habit, common to so many people, of tracing likes in unlikes had often led him to discern, or to fancy he discerned, in the Roman atmosphere, in its lights and shades, and particularly in its reflected or secondary lights, something resembling the atmosphere of his native promontory. Perhaps it was that in each case the eye was mostly resting on stone—that the quarries of ruins in the Eternal City reminded him of the quarries of maiden rock at home.[13]

"To discern, or to fancy he discerned"—the alternation between the two forms of repetition I am distinguishing is neatly stated in these phrases. For Hardy each rock, tree, person, event, or story is different from all the others. For him, nothing repeats in nature; nothing happens more than once for an individual person; nor is there repetition from person to person, nor from generation to generation. Nevertheless, there is a strong inclination for people in Hardy's world to trace likes in unlikes. This is as true for the narrators of his novels as for the characters. Such tracing follows in the lines of the new the lines of the old, seeing the old again in the new. This habit is "unconscious," spontaneous and unrationalized. It seems to be a primary aspect of perception, not something projected, but something there in the act of seeing itself.

The result of this habit is double. On the one hand, Hardy's narrators see things in figure. They call attention to repetitions which are likenesses in the unlike. The narrator of *The Well-Beloved,* for example, sees the sequence of Jocelyn Pierston's loves as duplications of one another. Such a vision sees things in their metaphors, or rather, it sees things as metaphors, as the transportation of the same pattern from one episode or event in the narrative to another. At the same time, Hardy's characters, Jocelyn, for example, are also driven by unconscious habit to make the linguistic mistake of seeing one person or situation in their lives as repeating an earlier person or situation. The mistake is linguistic because it sees things and persons not in their substantial uniqueness but as signs pointing back to earlier things or persons, "standing for" them. Such a character makes the fundamental error of taking figures of speech literally. He lives his life as metaphor, that is, as mistake. He imposes an interpretation on what he encounters which makes his life take, or seem to take, the form of a series of repetitions. The "unconscious" human state of illusion is the cause of repetition. It is the cause which drives the characters to live as they do and to understand their lives as they do. At the same time it is the cause which leads the narrator to interpret the story he tells as a sequence of repetitions when in fact nothing repeats, and each person, event, or thing remains stubbornly closed in on itself, as itself.

The knowledge that this double operation is an error is not, in Hardy's novels, brought in from the outside by the reader. It is provided by the narrator. It is even presented explicitly by the protagonist when he or she, often shortly before death, finally understands the errors in interpretation which have made him or her suffer so. The narrator demystifies his own reading of life as well as that of the characters. He gives the reader the information necessary not only to understand the way the characters dwell in illusions, but also to know why his reading of the story he tells has taken the form it has taken. This insight does not constitute total understanding or total liberation, for reasons I shall try to define in my chapters on Hardy.

In the passage from *The Well-Beloved,* the reader can see both the affirmation of the human habit of seeing likes in unlikes and the demystification of this habit. This exposing of illusion is as much performed by the narrator's dry ironic tone of detachment as by what he explicitly says. "Likes in unlikes"—this already tells the reader that Rome and the Isle of Slingers are not in fact alike. Moreover, the beguiling appearance of resemblance lies not so much in what is visible, the primary object of sight, as in "reflected or secondary lights," that is, in something already deflected or transported away from its source, carried over to another place, like a metaphor. This displacement produces "something resembling" a figurative similarity, not an identity. The final sentence figures this identity in difference in the fact that both Rome and the Isle of Slingers are mostly stone, though it is ruins in one case, the latest of the late, and "maiden rock" in the other, stone virgin, uncut, not yet marked or shaped, the earliest of the early. The irony lies in the fact that as a civilization modern England, where the maiden rock is quarried, is far later than ancient Rome. On the other hand, readers of the novel will know what further irony there is in calling Portland stone "maiden rock," since it is made of oolite, "egg-stone." It is the bones of millions of sea-creatures dead for eons and eons, immeasurably older in its grain than any Roman ruin, maiden only in that it has not been touched by human hands, just as the Slingers were living on Portland and the nearby mainland long before the Romans came. Late and early reverse and then reverse again, and this makes problematic the order of primary and secondary which is at stake in this or any other repetitive series. Of Rome and the Isle of Slingers it can be said that each precedes and yet also follows the other.

In Hardy's work a form of what I am calling the first kind of repetition is embodied in the characters and in one side of the narrator's discourse. This form is the personification, concretely presented in the lives and minds of the characters, of the basic metaphysical beliefs which have been instinctive to mankind for millennia: belief in origin, end, and underlying ground making similarities identities, belief in the literal truth of the trope of personification or prosopopeia. The latter projects character and makes it seem real, as the ancient Greeks saw persons in every tree, river, or spring. The novel as a genre might in fact be defined as the preservation, in a skeptical age, of these primitive beliefs.

Just such a definition of the novel is given by Nietzsche in a curiously comic passage in *The Birth of Tragedy*, in which Plato is named as the creator of a new genre, the novel:

> If tragedy had absorbed into itself all the earlier types of art, the same might also be said in an eccentric sense [*in einem exzentrischen Sinne*] of the Platonic dialogue which, a mixture of all extant styles and forms, hovers midway between narrative, lyric, and drama, between prose and poetry, and so has also broken the strict old law of the unity of linguistic form . . . The Platonic dialogue was, as it were, the barge on which the shipwrecked ancient poetry saved herself with all her children: crowded into a narrow space and timidly submitting to the single pilot, Socrates, they now sailed into a new world, which never tired of looking at the fantastic spectacle of this procession. Indeed, Plato has given to all posterity the model [*das Vorbild*] of a new art form, the model of the *novel*—which may be described as an infinitely enhanced Aesopian fable.[14]

If the Platonic dialogue and its many children, that multitude of novels it fathered, preserved the primitive beliefs present in earlier forms of literature, both the Platonic dialogues and the novels they begot also at the same time deconstructed these beliefs. In that sense they were eccentric, outside the spiritual center of the old art and destructive of it. Socrates, with his eternal questions and his corrosive irony, earned the hemlock as a man putting in danger the illusions sustaining political order. He is the model, then, for the other, demystifying side of novels, as well as for the beliefs they preserve. Socrates is the precursor of such a narrator as the storyteller in Hardy's *The Well-Beloved.* That narrator preserves and lovingly records Jocelyn's illusions, while at the same time he shows them to be illusions. He replaces belief in the first form of repetition with an affirmation of the second, ungrounded kind, the kind arising from unlikeness. Or perhaps it might be better to say that Hardy's narrator demonstrates the necessary inherence, one in the other, of the two forms.

This intertwining of the two kinds of repetition is in one way or another exemplified by the seven novels I interpret here. This does not mean that there are not some novels or other texts entirely ordered according to one or the other of the forms of repetition. Whether or not this is the case could only be determined, as I have said, by more analyses of more novels, but my examples would suggest that each form of repetition inevitably calls up the other as its shadow companion. You cannot have one without the other, though each subverts the other. The difference between one text and another from this point of view is in the varying modes of the intertwining. Anti-Platonism is present in Plato; the metaphysical antagonist is by no means expelled from Nietzsche's language; and both Benjamin's Marxism and his Jewish Messianism in other writings work against the grain of his brilliant expression of the "second" form of repetition in the passage I have discussed. Even Gerard Manley Hopkins, cited above as a believer in the "first" mode of repetition, which surely he is, develops in his concept of the "underthought" in Greek tragedy a brilliant model for that kind of heterogeneous form I find in one way or another in my seven English novels. As I have elsewhere tried to demonstrate, his theory of language in "The Wreck of the Deutschland" and in other writings is not compatible with his theological overthought.[15] His overthought is an example of the first theory of repetition, his underthought of the second. Underthought is still underthought, and it would be a mistake to make too much of its presence in Hopkins, but the fact that it is indubitably there, along with his Christian affirmations, is a striking example of the way it seems to be impossible to have one form of repetition without the other, even though one form or the other may no doubt be dominant in a given writer. The passages discussed in this preliminary chapter are not solutions to the problem of the way repetition works in fiction but miniature exemplifications of it. The discussions are also exemplifications of the mode of interpretation to be used on a larger scale in the essays which follow.

The relationship between the two forms of repetition defies the elementary principle of logic, the law of noncontradiction which says: "Either A or not-A." In all the novels read here both forms of repetition are in one way or another affirmed as true, though they appear logically to contradict each other. It would appear that a repetitive chain must be either grounded or ungrounded. In my novels, however, as I shall try to show, the repetitive series is presented as both grounded and ungrounded at once. This book is an attempt to explore the consequences of this for the reading of the novels in question. The heterogeneity of these texts lies in the fact that both forms of repetition are present, though the two forms can be shown to be incompatible. The hypothesis of such a heterogeneity in literary and philosophical texts is a working principle of that form of criticism called "deconstruction." "Instead of a simple 'either/or' structure," writes Barbara Johnson, "deconstruction attempts to elaborate a discourse that says *neither* 'either/or' *nor* 'both/and' nor even 'neither/nor,' while at the same time not totally abandoning these logics either. The very word 'deconstruction' is meant to undermine the either/or logic of the opposition 'construction/destruction.' "[16] The relation between the two forms of repetition in my seven novels is an example of this alogic or of this other logic. Insofar as the existence in works of literature of structures of language which contradict the law of noncontradiction is a major point of controversy in current discussions of this form of criticism, my focus on an important mode of such "alogical" structures may contribute to elucidation of the issues involved.

I have elsewhere attempted to discuss the kind of criticism necessary to take account of the heterogeneity of works of literature and to identify my relationship to it.[17] One characteristic of my own criticism is a desire to account for the totality of a given work, a desire which, insofar as it is not simply constitutional, is probably an inheritance from the New Criticism. Certainly it is possible to be satisfied with a partial or approximate reading of a given work. Many good critical essays stop short of claiming to account for the whole, though most indicate at least implicitly what such an accounting would be like. My training has led me to presuppose that the best critical essays are those which more or less overtly confront the question of what a total reading of the work at hand would be. The readings in this book assume that the demand for a total accounting is implicit in the effort of interpretation, even when it is evaded or minimized.

I came to literature from science and mathematics, and have come to the kind of criticism practiced here by way of the New Criticism and the sort of "criticism of consciousness" written by Georges Poulet, Marcel Raymond, Albert Béguin, and others. This means that my relation to "deconstruction" is necessarily different from that of the large group of young critics who have received their primary training in the new mode and to whom it seems to be almost as natural as a mother tongue, or at any rate as a first second language. For me it is a third or fourth second language. I would not have tried to learn it if it had not seemed necessary to account for important features of literary form which slip through the nets of those other languages of criticism. It seemed to me when I began the study of literature, as it still seems to me now, that one of the most obvious characteristics of works of literature is their manifest strangeness as integuments of words. Poets, novelists, and playwrights say things which are exceedingly odd by most everyday standards of normality. Any way of interpreting literature would need to account for that oddness. Henry James, in his well-known advice to the aspiring novelist, told him to try to be one of those people on whom nothing is lost. James was speaking of "life," but the one thing most needed for the literary critic too is to be one of those on whom nothing is lost, though in the critic's case it is the anomalous in literature rather than in life which must not be missed. A critical hypothesis, it may be, has more or less value as it facilitates or inhibits this noticing.

Twentieth-century thought—in linguistics, in psychology, in biology, in ethnology and sociology, in atomic physics, and in astrophysics—has been characterized by this recognition that the realms of man and nature are stranger than we had thought, along with the unceasing attempt to find out the laws of this strangeness and so make the unfamiliar familiar. Language, the human psyche, genetics, the workings of "primitive" societies, the interior of the atom, the nature of the stars, have shown unexpected anomalies. To understand them has in one way or another required ways of thinking and of formulating interpretations which defy or seem to defy elementary principles of logic and geometry. Among those things which are turning out to share this peculiarity is literature. Much in many works of literature seems unaccountable by traditional standards of coherence and unity. This book attempts to identify and to account for one form of this unaccountability.

The New Criticism has great value in its assumption that every detail counts, but the accompanying presupposition that every detail is going to count by working harmoniously to confirm the "organic unity" of the poem or the novel may become a temptation to leave out what does not fit, to see it as insignificant or as a flaw. So-called criticism of consciousness has great power as a mode of criticism. In the hands of a master critic like Georges Poulet, it can facilitate recognition of the diversity of an author's work by way of the presupposition that the "consciousness" of an author moves dialectically through a series of adventures. Even so, the intimate grain of an author's language tends to disappear in the thematic or paraphrastic use of citations to construct a model of those adventures. Insofar as such criticism presupposes a unified consciousness as the *point de départ* of those adventures and as their persisting ground and end, the anomalous within the work of an author, those features which do not fit the presupposed unified consciousness, may be passed over. The assumption that a work may be heterogeneous seems to me of great value in preparing the critic to take note of elements in a work which are manifestly "important" but cannot easily be accommodated within either of the theories of unity I have mentioned. The shift back from "consciousness" to "language" as the category to be investigated allows in principle a closer look at what is actually there on the page and at the transaction between reader and word from which meaning emerges. It will be evident from the readings here that I think more is gained by talking about the words of the work, its rhetorical texture, than by talking about the reader as such and his responses. The thing all readers share is those words on the page. Civilized dialogue or even controversy about the meanings of a literary work is most aided by sticking to the words as the things to be accounted for.

If I say, "The novel is a representation of human reality in words," that definition contains the possibility of three different kinds of discourse about fiction, each of which has its validity or necessity, none of which can be kept wholly separate from the others. If I emphasize "human reality" in the definition, then I shall be likely to ignore the fact that I know the fiction is only a fiction, willingly suspend my disbelief, speak of the characters as if they were "real people," and work out the "meaning" of their story in terms of ethical values, judgments of good and bad, happy and unhappy, and so on. If I emphasize "representation" in the definition, I shall focus on the conventions of storytelling in a given case as vehicles of meaning. From this focus there may be developed a full-fledged "phenomenological" criticism of fiction. This will concern itself with the assumptions the novelist makes about the kind of consciousness of himself and of others the narrator has or the characters have, or with the temporal structures of consciousness the novel expresses, or with the elaborated emotional responses the story as a sequence of represented events arouses in the reader. Finally, if I remember that a novel is a representation of human reality "in words," I may focus on local features of style, the "rhetoric of fiction," taking "rhetoric" not as modes of persuasion but in its other meaning as the discipline of the workings of tropes in the most inclusive sense of that word: all the turnings of language away from straightforward referential meaning. Though, as I have said, no one of these forms of discourse about fiction can be practiced in full isolation from the others, the kind of "rhetorical" criticism of fiction attempted in this book explores the ways in which the third feature of novels, the fact that they are made of words, inhibits the coherent or noncontradictory working of the other two dimensions of fiction. The result of this is that the critic can validate neither a wholly consistent thematic paraphrase of a given novel nor a wholly univocal phenomenological description of it as a system of assumptions about consciousnesses in their interrelation.

The primary motivation of the readings in this book is the one with which I began the study of literature: to devise a way to remain aware of the strangeness of the language of literature and to try to account for it. I began by saying that this book is not a work of "theory" as such. It is an attempt to interpret as best I can the texts of my seven novels. This means that there is no attempt to develop a tightly woven technical terminology to deal with repetition in fiction. In each chapter I use such language of interpretation as seems necessary for that particular novel, as much as possible language emerging from the novel in question or especially appropriate for it. In recent controversies about criticism there has been, so it seems to me, too much attention paid to this theory or that, to its terminology, and to its presumed or "theoretical" consequences, and not enough to the readings made possible by the theories in question. A theory is all too easy to refute or deny, but a reading can be controverted only by going through the difficult task of rereading the work in question and proposing an alternative reading. A recent skirmisher in the rarified atmosphere of pure theory argues that criticism went wrong when it became close reading.[18] This, if I may say so, is a major treason against our profession. That profession is nothing if it is not philology, the love of words, the teaching of reading, and the attempt in written criticism to facilitate the act of reading. What counts for most in literary criticism is the citations made and what the critic says about those citations. If this book sends readers back to the seven novels with minds more open to their complexities of repetitive form, more prepared to be startled by what they find there, even startled by aspects my accounts have left out or unwittingly distorted, the chapters will have done all that I could hope for them.

2
LORD JIM
Repetition as Subversion of Organic Form

As a first larger-scale example of the intertwining of the two modes of repetition in narrative, I choose Conrad's *Lord Jim.* This falls roughly midway in the historical span from which my seven novels come: from the early Victorian period to the eve of the Second World War. *Lord Jim* provides a particularly overt case of the issues I am investigating; it invites the reader to believe that it may be comprehensible according to some mode of the first, centered form of repetition, while the actual uses of repetition in the text forbid that comprehension. And to begin after the middle of the ninety-year period from which my novels are drawn may help to forestall the assumption that I am tracing a historical development, turn, or evolution from Victorian to modern, or from simple to complex, or from realist to symbolic, or from naive acceptance of narrative conventions to sophisticated and self-conscious artistry. The telling of such a literary historical story is itself a narrative open to the same kind of challenges all seven of my novels pose to the notion of a plot with beginning, middle, and end. Each of my novels belongs to a particular moment in English literary history, and in English social and political history too, but my claim is that these contexts do not fully determine the way repetition functions in works written in this moment or that. In each case, rather, as I shall try to show, particular materials—the historical facts of British imperialism in *Lord Jim,* for example, or social conditions in Yorkshire in the early nineteenth century in *Wuthering Heights*—become subject, when they are made into a novel, to the impossibility of telling a story which is a pure example of either of the kinds of repetitive form I have identified in my first chapter. The seven novels interpreted here are variants of this situation. They do not make a historical "progression," or a "degradation" either. My chapters are attempts at readings, not attempts at the construction of a history, unless the demonstration of a movement in place or a series of nonprogressive variations is considered to be a form of history. It may be that the activity of reading, if it is carried out with rigor, tends to inhibit or even make impossible that sort of story we tell ourselves which is given the name "literary history."

Lord Jim, like most works of literature, contains self-interpretative elements. Much of it is an explication of words and signs by means of other words, as narrator follows narrator, or as narration is inserted within narration. The critic who attempts to understand *Lord Jim* becomes another in a series of interpreters. He enters into a process of interpretation in which words bring out the meaning of other words and those words refer to others in their turn. No literary text has a manifest pattern, like the design of a rug, which the eye of the critic can survey from the outside and describe as a spatial form, but the intricacies of multiple narrators and time shifts in *Lord Jim* make this particularly evident. The textuality of a text, a "yarn" spun by Conrad, is the meshing of its filaments as they are interwoven in ways hidden from an objectifying eye. The critic must enter into the text, follow its threads as they weave in and out, appearing and disappearing, crisscrossing with other threads. In doing this he adds his own thread of interpretation to the fabric, or he cuts it in one way or another, so becoming part of its texture or changing it. Only in this way can he hope to identify the evasive center or ground which is not visible as a fixed emblem around which the story is spun, but is paradoxically, as Wallace Stevens says in "A Primitive Like an Orb," a "center on the horizon,"[1] a center which is outside and around rather than within and punctual.

Samuel Taylor Coleridge, that brilliant manipulator of the metaphors of Occidental metaphysics, presents an image of the work of art in its rounded unity corresponding to the assumption that there is such an interior center. Aesthetic wholeness in a narrative, he says, must be copied from the wholeness of a universe which circles in time around the motionless center of a God to whose eternal insight all times are co-present:

> The common end of all *narrative,* nay, of *all,* Poems is to convert a *series* into a *Whole:* to make those events, which in real or imagined History move on in a *strait* line, assume to our Understandings a *circular* motion—the snake with it's Tail in its mouth. Hence indeed the almost flattering and yet appropriate Term, Poesy—i.e. poiesis-*making.* Doubtless, to his eye, which alone comprehends all Past and all Future in one eternal Present, what to our short sight appears strait is but part of the great Cycle—just as the calm Sea to us *appears* level, tho' it indeed [be] only a part of a *globe.* Now what the Globe is in Geography, *miniaturing* in order to *manifest* the Truth, such is a Poem to that Image of God, which we were created with, and which still seeks Unity or Revelation of the *One* in and by the *Many.*[2]

The concept of the organic unity of the work of art, as this passage shows, cannot be detached from its theological basis. Nor can it separate itself from mimetic theories of art. Far from asserting the autonomy of the artwork, its way of being self-sufficiently rounded in on itself, Coleridge here describes the poem as an image or a representation, even the representation of a representation. Its globular roundness miniatures not God in his relation to the creation, but the image of God created in our souls which drives us to seek the one in the many. The poem is the image of an image. Moreover, the oneness revealed in and by the many is not intrinsic but extrinsic. It is the center of a circle made up of a series of events which move in sequence but are curved back on themselves, like the fabled snake with its tail in its mouth, by the attraction of that center, just as the soul "in order to be an individual Being . . . must go forth *from* God, yet as the *receding* from *him* is to *proceed* towards Nothingness and Privation, it must still at every step turn back toward him in order to *be* at all—Now, a straight Line, continuously retracted forms of necessity a circular orbit."[3] The creation, the soul, the work of art—all three have the same shape, the same movement, and the same relation to a generative center. They are related in a descending series of analogical equivalences, each a copy of the one above and all able to be defined by the same geometrical or zoological metaphors.

In place of this kind of doubling, twice removed, of God's universe by the little world of the work of art, Conrad presents for both cosmos and work of literature a structure which has no beginning, no foundation outside itself, and exists only as a self-generated web:

> There is a—let us say—a machine. It evolved itself (I am severely scientific) out of a chaos of scraps of iron and behold!—it knits. I am horrified at the horrible work and stand appalled. I feel it ought to embroider—but it goes on knitting . . . And the most withering thought is that the infamous thing has made itself; made itself without thought, without conscience, without foresight, without eyes, without heart. It is a tragic accident—and it has happened . . . It knits us in and it knits us out. It has knitted time, space, pain, death, corruption, despair and all the illusions—and nothing matters. I'll admit however that to look at the remorseless process is sometimes amusing.[4]

One way of looking at the remorseless process is by way of a novel, but a novel is not for Conrad an *image* of the horrible knitting machine and its work. It is part of the knitting, woven into its web. The infamous machine has made human beings and all their works too, including language and its power of generating or of expressing all the illusions. Works of art, like man's other works, are what they are "in virtue of that truth one and immortal which lurks in the force that made [the machine] spring into existence."[5] Product of the same force which has knit the rest of the universe, a work of art has the same kind of structure. A novel by Conrad, though it invites the reader to hope that he can find a center of the sort Coleridge ascribes to the good work of art, has nothing certainly identifiable outside itself by which it might be measured or from which it might be seen. It has no visible thematic or structuring principle which will allow the reader to find out its secret, explicate it once and for all, untie all its knots and straighten all its threads. The knitting machine cannot be said to be the origin of the cloth it knits, since what the machine knits is itself, knitter and knitted forming one indistinguishable whole without start or finish, continuously self-creating. The cloth exists as the process of its knitting, the twisting of its yarns as they are looped and knotted by a pervasive "force." This force is the truth one and immortal everywhere present but nowhere visible in itself, an energy both of differentiation and of destruction. "It knits us in and it knits us out."

A familiar passage in Conrad's *Heart of Darkness* describes the indirection characteristic of works of literature like *Lord Jim.* The passage uses a variant of the image of the knitted fabric in the letter to Cunninghame Graham. "The yarns of seamen," says the narrator, "have a direct simplicity, the whole meaning of which lies within the shell of a cracked nut. But Marlow was not typical (if his propensity to spin yarns be excepted), and to him the meaning of an episode was not inside like a kernel but outside, enveloping the tale which brought it out only as a glow brings out a haze, in the likeness of one of those misty halos that sometimes are made visible by the spectral illumination of moonshine."[6] Though the meaning is outside, it may only be seen by way of the tale which brings it out. This bringing out takes place in the interaction of its different elements in their reference to one another. These the critic must track, circling from one word or image to another within the text. Only in this movement of interpretation does the meaning exist. It is not a central and originating node, like the kernel of a nut, a solid and pre-existing nub. It is a darkness, an absence, a haze invisible in itself and only made visible by the ghostlike indirection of a light which is already derived. It is not the direct light of the sun but the reflected light of the moon which brings out the haze. This visible but secondary light and the invisible haze create a halo of "moonshine" which depends for its existence on the reader's involvement in the play of light and dark which generates it. Does this invitation to believe that there is an explanatory center, without positive identification of that center or even certainty about whether or not it exists, in fact characterize *Lord Jim?* I shall investigate briefly here a series of ways the novel might be interpreted.

The theme of *Lord Jim* is stated most explicitly toward the end of chapter 5, in Marlow's attempt to explain why he concerns himself with Jim:

> Why I longed to go grubbing into the deplorable details of an occurrence which, after all, concerned me no more than as a member of an obscure body of men held together by a community of inglorious toil and by fidelity to a certain standard of conduct, I can't explain. You may call it an unhealthy curiosity if you like; but I have a distinct notion I wished to find something. Perhaps, unconsciously, I hoped I would find that something, some profound and redeeming cause, some merciful explanation, some convincing shadow of an excuse. I see well enough now that I hoped for the impossible—for the laying of what is the most obstinate ghost of man's creation, of the uneasy doubt uprising like a mist, secret and gnawing like a worm, and more chilling than the certitude of death—the doubt of the sovereign power enthroned in a fixed standard of conduct.[7]

Jim is "one of us," an Englishman, son of a country clergyman, a "gentleman," brought up in the British traditions of duty, obedience, quiet faithfulness, and unostentatious courage. Nevertheless, he has committed the shockingly dishonorable act of deserting his ship and the helpless pilgims it carried. Jim's desertion seems especially deplorable to Marlow because Jim looks so trustworthy, so perfect an example of the unassuming nobility of the tradition from which he has sprung. "He had no business to look so sound," says Marlow. "I thought to myself—well, if this sort can go wrong like that . . . and I felt as though I could fling down my hat and dance on it from sheer mortification"; "He looked as genuine as a new sovereign, but there was some infernal alloy in his metal" (ch. 5). The descrepancy between what Jim looks like and what he is puts in question for Marlow "the sovereign power enthroned in a fixed standard of conduct." He does not doubt the existence of the standard, the seaman's code of fidelity, obedience, and obscure courage on which the British empire was built. He comes to question the power installed behind this standard and within it. This power, as its defining adjective affirms, justifies the standard as its king—its principle, its source, its law.

If there is no sovereign power enthroned in the fixed standard of conduct then the standard is without validity. It is an all-too-human fiction, an arbitrary code of behavor—"this precious notion of a convention," as Marlow says, "only one of the rules of the game, nothing more" (ch. 7). Nothing matters, and anything is possible, as in that condition of spiritual anarchy which takes over on the ship's boat after Jim and the other officers have deserted the *Patna* and left her to sink with eight hundred men, women, and children. "After the ship's lights had gone," says Jim, "anything might have happened in that boat—anything in the world—and the world no wiser. I felt this, and I was pleased. It was just dark enough, too. We were like men walled up quick in a roomy grave. No concern with anything on earth. Nobody to pass an opinion. Nothing mattered . . . No fear, no law, no sounds, no eyes—not even our own, till—till sunrise at least" (ch. 10). Marlow interprets Jim's words in a way which gives them the widest application to the derelict condition of a man who has lost faith, conviction, his customary material surroundings—whatever has given his world stability and order by seeming to support it from outside. "When your ship fails you," says Marlow, "your whole world seems to fail you; the world that made you, restrained you, taken [*sic*] care of you. It is as if the souls of men floating on an abyss and in touch with immensity had been set free for any excess of heroism, absurdity, or abomination. Of course, as with belief, thought, love, hate, conviction, or even the visual aspect of material things, there are as many shipwrecks as there are men . . . Trust a boat on the high seas to bring out the Irrational that lurks at the bottom of every thought, sentiment, sensation, emotion" (ch. 10).

Marlow's aim (or Conrad's) seems clear: to find some explanation for Jim's action which will make it still possible to believe in the sovereign power. Many critics think that in the end Marlow (or Conrad) is satisfied, that even Jim is satisfied. The circumstances of Jim's death and his willingness to take responsibility for the death of Dain Waris ("He hath taken it upon his own head"; ch. 45) make up for all Jim has done before. Jim's end reenthrones the regal power justifying the fixed standard of conduct by which he condemns himself to death.

Matters are not so simple in this novel. For one thing, there is something suspect in Marlow's enterprise of interpretation. "Was it for my own sake," he asks, "that I wished to find some shadow of an excuse for that young fellow whom I had never seen before?" (ch. 5). If so much is at stake for himself, he is likely to find what he wants to find.

Marlow attempts to maintain his faith in the sovereign power in several contradictory ways. One is to discover that there are extenuating circumstances. Perhaps Jim is not all bad. Perhaps he can be excused. Perhaps he can ultimately redeem himself. At other times Marlow suggests that in spite of appearances Jim has a fatal soft spot. He cannot be safely trusted for an instant. If this is so, then he must be condemned in the name of the kingly law determining good and evil, praise and blame. At still other times Marlow's language implies that Jim is the victim of dark powers within himself, powers which also secretly govern the universe outside. If there is no benign sovereign power there may be a malign one, a principle not of light but of blackness, "a destructive fate ready for us all" (ch. 5). If this is the case, there are indeed extenuating circumstances, precisely the "shadow of an excuse." To act according to a fixed standard of conduct which is justified by no sovereign power, as perhaps Jim does in his death, is the truest heroism. It is defiance of the shadowy powers which would undermine everything man finds good. If this is so, Jim's death is nevertheless in one sense still a sham. It is a sham in the sense that it is valued by no extrahuman judge. It is only one way of acting among others.

Perhaps, to pursue this line a little further, the source of all Jim's trouble is his romanticism, that childish image of himself as a hero which has its source in fraudulent literature and sticks with him all his life: "He confronted savages on tropical shores, quelled mutinies on the high seas, and in a small boat upon the ocean kept up the hearts of despairing men—always an example of devotion to duty, and as unflinching as a hero in a book" (ch. 1). Perhaps it is Jim's confidence in this illusory image of himself which is the source of his inability to confront the truth about himself and about the universe. Perhaps this confidence even paradoxically explains his repeated acts of cowardice. It may be that Jim's death is no more than the last of such acts, his last failure to face the dark side of himself which is so rudely brought back before him in the person of Gentleman Brown. His death may be no more than his last attempt to act according to a fictional idea of heroic conduct. Certainly the final paragraphs of the novel show Marlow by no means "satisfied." The ending is a tissue of unanswered questions in which Marlow affirms once more not that Jim is a hero or that Jim is a coward, but that he remains an indecipherable mystery:

> And that's the end. He passes away under a cloud, inscrutable at heart, forgotten, unforgiven, and excessively romantic . . . He goes away from a living woman to celebrate his pitiless wedding with a shadowy ideal of conduct. Is he satisfied—quite, now, I wonder? We ought to know. He is one of us—and have I not stood up once, like an evoked ghost, to answer for his eternal constancy? Was I so very wrong after all? Now he is no more, there are days when the reality of his existence comes to me with an immense, with an overwhelming force; and yet upon my honour there are moments, too, when he passes from my eyes like a disembodied spirit astray amongst the passions of this earth, ready to surrender himself faithfully to the claim of his own world of shades.
>
> Who knows? (Ch. 45)

The ending seems to confirm Marlow's earlier statement that the heart of each man is a dark forest to all his fellows and "loneliness" a "hard and absolute condition of existence": "The envelope of flesh and blood on which our eyes are fixed melts before the out-stretched hand, and there remains only the capricious, unconsolable, and elusive spirit that no eye can follow, no hand can grasp" (ch. 16).

On the other hand, all that seems problematic and inconclusive about *Lord Jim* when it is approached from the point of view of explicit thematic statements and by way of Marlow's interpretation of Jim may be resolved if the reader stands back from Marlow's perspective and looks at the novel as a whole. The detached view may see the truth, according to that proverb Marlow recalls which affirms that "the onlookers see most of the game" (ch. 21). Seen from a distance, *Lord Jim* may turn out to be a pattern of recurrent motifs which reveals more about Jim than Marlow comes to understand. Jim's feeling at his trial that "only a meticulous precision of statement would bring out the true horror behind the face of things" (ch. 4) may be the clue to the aesthetic method of the book. The episodes Marlow and others relate, the language they use, may reveal to the readers of the novel a secret hidden from Marlow, from Jim, and from all the characters, a secret known only to Conrad. He may have chosen this way to show forth the truth because only as a participant in its revelation can the reader understand it.

When *Lord Jim* is approached from the perspective of its narrative structure and its design of recurrent images it reveals itself to be not less but more problematic, more inscrutable, like Jim himself. I have elsewhere argued that temporal form, interpersonal relations, and relations of fiction and reality are three structuring principles fundamental to fiction.[8] *Lord Jim* is an admirable example of the tendency of these in their interaction to weave a fabric of words which is incapable of being interpreted unambiguously, as a fixed pattern of meaning, even though the various possibilities of meaning are rigorously delimited by the text.

To begin with the structure of interpersonal relations: Victorian novels were often apparently stabilized by the presence of an omniscient narrator, spokesman for the collective wisdom of the community, though, as my Victorian examples here demonstrate, such a narrator never turns out to be unequivocally the basis of the storytelling when a given Victorian novel is interpreted in detail. Such a narrator, if he were ever to exist, would represent a trustworthy point of view and also a safe vantage point from which to watch the hearts and minds of the characters in their relations to one another. Conrad, as many critics have noted, does not employ a "reliable" narrator. In *Lord Jim* no point of view is entirely trustworthy. The novel is a complex design of interrelated minds, no one of which can be taken as a secure point of reference from which the others may be judged.

The first part of the story is told by an "omniscient" narrator who seems like the narrator of a novel by Trollope or by George Eliot. This first narrator of *Lord Jim* has the same superhuman powers of insight, including direct access to the hero's mind, that is possessed by those earlier Victorian narrators. He relinquishes that access early in the story, as though it could not provide a satisfactory avenue to the truth behind Jim's life. He then returns in chapter 36, after Marlow's narrative to his almost silent auditors is over. He returns to introduce the man who receives the letter which is Marlow's "last word" about Jim. The bulk of the novel is made up of Marlow's telling of Jim's story to the group of listeners in the darkness who are the reader's surrogates. Those listeners stand between the reader and Marlow's telling. "He existed for me," says Marlow, "and after all it is only through me that he exists for you. I've led him out by the hand; I have paraded him before you" (ch. 21).

Many sections of the story are told to Marlow by Jim. In these the reader can see Jim attempting to interpret his experience by putting it into words. This self-interpretation is interpreted once more by Marlow, then by implication interpreted again by Marlow's listeners. The latter appear occasionally as intervening minds, as when one of them says: "You are so subtle, Marlow" (ch. 8). This overlapping of interpretative minds within minds is put in question in its turn, at least implicitly, by the "omniscient" narrator. He surrounds all and perhaps understands all, though he does not give the reader the sort of interpretative help provided by the narrator of *Middlemarch* or of *The Last Chronicle of Barset.* Even so, this narrator may have been brought back briefly near the end of the novel to suggest that the reader might be wise to put in question Marlow's interpretation of Jim, even though the narrator cannot or will not provide the reader with any solid alternative ground on which to stand.

Within Marlow's narrative there are many minor characters—Captain Brierly, the French lieutenant, Chester, Stein—who have their say in the story. They are irreplaceable points of view on Jim within Marlow's point of view. They are sources of parts of his story and offer alternative ways of judging it. Their own stories, moreover, are analogous to Jim's story, though whether in a positive or in a negative way is often hard to tell. Just as the crucial episodes in Jim's life echo one another, the jump from the *Patna* repeating his failure to jump in the small boat when he was in training and being repeated again by his jump over the stockade in Patusan ("Patusan" recalling *Patna*), so Captain Brierly's suicide is a jump ambiguously duplicating Jim's jumps (was it cowardly or an act of heroism following logically from a shattering insight into the truth of things?), while the French lieutenant's courage shows what Jim might have done on the *Patna*, and Stein's strange history echoes Jim's either positively or negatively. Stein appears to be either an unreliable narrator or a trustworthy commentator, depending on one's judgment of his life and personality. Is he a man who has bravely immersed himself in the destructive element to win an ultimate wisdom, or has he withdrawn passively from life to collect his butterflies and to give Marlow and the readers of the novel only misleading clues to the meaning of Jim's life?

Lord Jim is made up of episodes similar in design. In each a man confronts a crisis testing his courage, the strength of his faith in the sovereign power enthroned in a fixed standard of conduct. In each case someone, the man himself or someone else, interprets that test, or rather he interprets the words which the man's reaction to the test has already generated. There is even a parody of this pattern early in the novel, as if to call attention to it as a structuring principle or as a universal way in which men are related to one another. Just as Marlow seeks out the chief engineer of the *Patna* in the hospital "in the eccentric hope of hearing something explanatory of the famous affair from his point of view," so the doctor who is tending the engineer after his brandy debauch says he "never remember[s] being so interested in a case of the jim-jams before." "The head, ah! the head, of course, gone, but the curious part is that there is some sort of method in his raving. I am trying to find out. Most unusual—that thread of logic in such a delirium" (ch. 5). The reader of *Lord Jim*, like the doctor, must seek the thread of logic within a bewildering complexity of words. With these words Conrad attempts to express a truth beyond direct expression in words, "for words also belong to the sheltering conception of light and order which is our refuge" (ch. 33), our refuge from the truth hidden in the darkness. In the sequence of discrete episodes which makes up the novel, no episode serves as the point of origin, the arch-example of the *mythos* of the novel, but each is, by reason of its analogy to other episodes, a repetition of them, each example being as enigmatic as all the others.

A similar complexity characterizes the temporal structure of the novel. Jim says of his memory of watching the other officers struggle to get the *Patna*'s boat in the water: "I ought to have a merry life of it, by God! for I shall see that funny sight a good many times yet before I die" (ch. 9). Of an earlier moment before the officers desert the ship he says: "It was as though I had heard it all, seen it all, gone through it all twenty times already" (ch. 8). Each enactment of a given episode echoes backward and forward indefinitely, creating a pattern of eddying repetition. If there are narrators within narrators there are also times within times—time-shifts, breaks in time, anticipations, retrogressions, retellings, and reminders that a given part of the story has often been told before. Marlow, for example, like the Ancient Mariner, has related Jim's story "many times, in distant parts of the world" (ch. 4). The novel is made up of recurrences in which each part of the story has already happened repeatedly when the reader first encounters it, either in someone's mind, or in someone's telling, or in the way it repeats other similar events in the same person's life or in the lives of others. The temporal structure of the novel is open. *Lord Jim* is a chain of repetitions, each event referring back to others which it both explains and is explained by, while at the same time it prefigures those which will occur in the future. Each exists as part of an infinite regression and progression within which the narrative moves back and forth discontinuously across time seeking unsuccessfully some motionless point in its flow.

It might be argued that the sequence of events as the reader is given them by Conrad, in a deliberately chosen order, is a linear series with a beginning, middle, and end which determines a straightforward development of gradually revealed meaning moving through time as the reader follows word after word and page after page, becoming more and more absorbed in the story and more and more emotionally involved in it. This sequence, it might be argued, generates a determinate meaning. It is true that this linear sequence is shared by any reader and that it establishes a large background of agreement about what happens and even about the meaning of what happens. That Jim jumps from the *Patna* and that this is a morally deplorable act no reader is likely to doubt. But it is also true that the linear sequence of episodes as it is presented to the reader by the various narrators is radically rearranged from the chronological order in which the events actually occurred. This could imply that Conrad, the "omniscient narrator," or Marlow has ordered the episodes in such a way that the best understanding by the reader of a total meaning possessed by one or another of these narrators will be revealed. Or it may imply, as I think it does, that the deeper explanatory meaning behind those facts open to the sunlight, about which anyone would agree, remains hidden, so that any conceivable narrator of these facts or interpreter of them is forced to move back and forth across the facts, putting them in one or another achronological order in the hope that this deeper meaning will reveal itself. The narration in many ways, not least by calling attention to the way one episode repeats another rather than being clearly a temporal advance on it, breaks down the chronological sequence and invites the reader to think of it as a simultaneous set of echoing episodes spread out spatially like villages or mountain peaks on a map. *Lord Jim* too, to borrow the splendid phrase Henry James uses in his review of Conrad's *Chance*, is "a prolonged hovering flight of the subjective over the outstretched ground of the case exposed."[9] Insofar as the novel is this and not the straightforward historical movement suggested by Aristotle's comments on beginning, middle, and end in the *Poetics*, then the sort of metaphysical certainty implicit in Aristotle, the confidence that some *logos* or underlying cause and ground supports the events, is suspended. It is replaced by the image of a consciousness attempting to grope its way to the hidden cause behind a set of enigmatic facts by moving back and forth over them. If the "facts" are determinate (more or less) the novel encourages the reader to seek the "why" behind the events, some "shadow of an excuse." It is here, I am arguing, that the text does not permit the reader to decide among alternative possibilities, even though those possibilities themselves are identified with precise determinate certainty.

The similarities between one episode and another or one character and another in *Lord Jim* no doubt appear to be deliberately designed (whether by Conrad or by Marlow), like most of the cases of repetition discussed in this book. Such repetitions differ from those which are accidental or merely contingent, perhaps even insignificant, although the reader would do well not to be too sure about the existence of insignificant similarities. Moreover, the fact that Conrad probably consciously intended most of the repetitions I discuss here (though certainty about that is of course impossible) may be trivial compared to the way the novel represents human life as happening to fall into repetitive patterns, whether in the life of a single person, as Jim repeats variants of the same actions over and over, or from person to person, as Brierly's jump repeats Jim's jump. The question the novel asks and cannot unequivocally answer is "Why is this?" To say it is because Conrad designed his novel in recurring patterns is to trivialize the question and to give a misplaced answer to it.

Nor can the meaning of the novel be identified by returning to its historical sources, however helpful or even essential these are in establishing a context for our reading. The "source" of *Lord Jim,* as Conrad tells the reader in the Author's Note, was a glimpse of the "real" Jim: "One sunny morning in the commonplace surroundings of an Eastern roadstead, I saw his form pass by—appealing—significant—under a cloud—perfectly silent . . . It was for me, with all the sympathy of which I was capable, to seek fit words for his meaning." Norman Sherry, in *Conrad's Eastern World,* and Ian Watt, in *Conrad in the Nineteenth Century,* have discussed in detail the historical events which lie behind the novel.[10] *Lord Jim* can be defined as an attempt on Conrad's part to understand the real by way of a long detour through the fictive. To think of *Lord Jim* as the interpretation of history is to recognize that the historical events "behind" the novel exist now as documents, and that these documents too are enigmatic. They are as interesting for the ways in which Conrad changed them as for the ways in which he repeated them exactly. The novel is related to its sources in a pattern of similarity and difference like that of the episodes inside the novel proper. The facts brought to light by Sherry and Watt, for example the "Report of a Court of

Inquiry held at Aden into the cause of the abandonment of the steamship 'Jeddah,' "[11] do not serve as a solid and unequivocal point of origin by means of which the novel may be viewed, measured, and understood. The documents are themselves mysterious, as mysterious as the Old Yellow Book on which Browning based *The Ring and the Book* or as the dry, factual account of historical events included at the end of Melville's *Benito Cereno.* In all these cases knowledge of the historical sources makes the story based on them not less but more inscrutable, more difficult to understand. If there are "fit words" for Jim's "meaning" they are to be found only within the novel, not in any texts outside it.

Perhaps, to turn to a last place where an unambiguous meaning may be found, the pattern of images in its recurrences somehow transcends the complexities I have discussed. It may constitute a design lying in the sunlight, ready to be seen and understood. It will be remembered that Conrad attempts above all, as he says in the preface to *The Nigger of the "Narcissus,"* to make us *see.* Matching this is the recurrent image in *Lord Jim* according to which Marlow gets glimpses of Jim through a rift in the clouds. "The views he let me have of himself," says Marlow, "were like those glimpses through the shifting rents in a thick fog—bits of vivid and vanishing detail, giving no connected idea of the general aspect of a country" (ch. 6). The metaphorical structure of the novel may reveal in such disconnected glimpses a secret which cannot be found out by exploring its narrative, temporal, or interpersonal patterns, or by extracting explicit thematic statements.

A network of light and dark imagery manifestly organizes the novel throughout. It is first established insistently near the beginning in the description of the *Patna* steaming across the calm sea: "The *Patna,* with a slight hiss, passed over that plain luminous and smooth, unrolled a black ribbon of smoke across the sky, left behind her on the water a white ribbon of foam that vanished at once, like the phantom of a track drawn upon a lifeless sea by the phantom of a steamer" (ch. 2). Black against white, light against dark—perhaps the meaning of *Lord Jim* is to be found in Conrad's manipulation of this binary pattern.

This metaphorical or "symbolic" pattern too is systematically ambiguous, as may be seen by looking at two examples, the description of Jim's visit to Marlow's room after his trial and the description of Marlow's last glimpse of Jim on the shore. The juxtaposition of light and dark offers no better standing ground from which what is equivocal about the rest of the novel may be surveyed and comprehended than any other aspect of the text. The "visual aspect of material things" and the clues it may offer to the meaning of man's life sink in the general shipwreck which puts in doubt the sovereign power enthroned in a fixed standard of conduct:

> He remained outside, faintly lighted on the background of night, as if standing on the shore of a sombre and hopeless sea.
>
> An abrupt heavy rumble made me lift my head. The noise seemed to roll away, and suddenly a searching and violent glare fell on the blind face of the night. The sustained and dazzling flickers seemed to last for an unconscionable time. The growl of the thunder increased steadily while I looked at him, distinct and black, planted solidly upon the shores of a sea of light. At the moment of greatest brilliance the darkness leaped back with a culminating crash, and he vanished before my dazzled eyes as utterly as though he had been blown to atoms. (Ch. 16)

> He was white from head to foot, and remained persistently visible with the stronghold of the night at his back, the sea at his feet, the opportunity by his side—still veiled. What do you say? Was it still veiled? I don't know. For me that white figure in the stillness of coast and sea seemed to stand at the heart of a vast enigma. The twilight was ebbing fast from the sky above his head, the strip of sand had sunk already under his feet, he himself appeared no bigger than a child—then only a speck, a tiny white speck, that seemed to catch all the light left in a darkened world . . . And, suddenly, I lost him. (Ch. 35)

In one of these passages Jim is the light that illuminates the darkness. In the other he is the blackness that stands out against a blinding light which suddenly reveals itself from its hiding place and then disappears. Light changes place with dark; the value placed on dark and light changes place, as light is sometimes the origin of dark, dark sometimes the origin of light. Each such passage, moreover, refers to the others by way of anticipation or recollection, as the first of the texts quoted prefigures the second, but when the reader turns to the other passage it is no easier to understand and itself refers to other such passages. No one of them is the original ground, the basis on which the others may be interpreted. *Lord Jim* is like a dictionary in which the entry under one word refers the reader to another word which refers him to another and then back to the first word again, in an endless circling. Marlow sitting in his hotel room ceaselessly writing letters by the light of a single candle while Jim struggles with his conscience and the thunderstorm prepares in the darkness outside may be taken as an emblem of literature as Conrad sees it. A work of literature is for him in a paradoxical relation to a nonverbal reality it seeks both to uncover and to evade in the creation of its own exclusively verbal realm.

I claim, then, that from whatever angle it is approached *Lord Jim* reveals itself to be a work which raises questions rather than answering them. The fact that it contains its own interpretations does not make it easier to understand. The overabundance of possible explanations only inveigles the reader to share in the self-sustaining motion of a process of interpretation which cannot reach an unequivocal conclusion. This weaving movement of advance and retreat constitutes and sustains the meaning of the text, that evasive center which is everywhere and nowhere in the play of its language.

Marlow several times calls explicit attention to the unendingness of the process by which he and the readers of the novel go over and over the details of Jim's life in an ever-renewed, never-successful attempt to understand it completely and so write "Finis" to his story. "And besides," affirms Marlow apropos of his "last" words about Jim, "the last word is not said,—probably shall never be said. Are not our lives too short for that full utterance which through all our stammerings is of course our only and abiding intention? . . . There is never time to say our last word—the last word of our love, or our desire, faith, remorse, submission, revolt" (ch. 21). The reader will remember here those "last words" of Kurtz ("The horror! The horror!") which Marlow in another story hears and ironically praises for their finality, their power to sum up. If this theme is repeated within *Lord Jim,* these repetitions echo in their turn passages in other novels by Conrad. If *Heart of Darkness* leads to Marlow's recognition that he cannot understand Kurtz as long as he has not followed Kurtz all the way into the abyss of death, the "ending" of *Lord Jim* is Marlow's realization that it is impossible to write "The End" to any story: "End! Finis! the potent word that exorcises from the house of life the haunting shadow of fate. This is what—notwithstanding the testimony of my eyes and his own earnest assurances—I miss when I look back upon Jim's success. While there's life there is hope, truly; but there is fear, too . . . he made so much of his disgrace while it is the guilt alone that matters. He was not—if I may say so—clear to me. He was not clear. And there is a suspicion he was not clear to himself either" (ch. 16). Nor can he, I am arguing, ever be clear to us, except with the paradoxical clarity generated by our recognition that the process of interpreting his story is a ceaseless movement toward a light which always remains hidden in the dark.

Let there be no misunderstanding here. The situation I have just described does not mean that the set of possible explanations for Jim's action is limitless, indeterminate in the sense of being indefinitely multiple and nebulous. The various meanings are not the free imposition of subjective interpretations by the reader, but are controlled by the text. In that sense they are determinate. The novel provides the textual material for identifying exactly what the possible explanations are. The reader is not permitted to go outside the text to make up other possible explanations of his own. The indeterminacy lies in the multiplicity of possible incompatible explanations given by the novel and in the lack of evidence justifying a choice of one over the others. The reader cannot logically have them all, and yet nothing he is given determines a choice among them. The possibilities, moreover, are not just given side by side as entirely separate hypotheses. They are related to one another in a system of mutual implication and mutual contradiction. Each calls up the others, but it does not make sense to have more than one of them.

Would novels from an earlier period be more open to identification of a single, unequivocal meaning? Is the ambiguity of *Lord*

Jim a historical phenomenon, a feature of the time in which it was written, or of the historical and social conditions of its author, or is its presentation of specific incompatible possibilities of meaning among which it is impossible to choose characteristic in one way or another of works of literature of any period in Western culture? Only an investigation of some examples can begin to suggest tentative answers to those questions. I turn back now to several salient examples of earlier Victorian fiction to explore the workings of repetition in each.

3
WUTHERING HEIGHTS
Repetition and the "Uncanny"

"I don't care—I will get in!"

Emily Brontë, *Wuthering Heights*

LOCKWOOD'S "EJACULATION," as Brontë calls it, when he tries to get back into the Heights a second time, might be taken as an emblem of the situation of the critic of *Wuthering Heights.* This novel has been a strong enticement for readers. It exerts great power over its readers in its own violence, and in its presentation of striking psychological, sociological, and natural detail. It absorbs the reader, making him enwrapped or enrapt by the story. In spite of its many peculiarities of narrative technique and theme, it is, in its extreme vividness of circumstantial detail, a masterwork of "realistic" fiction. It obeys most of the conventions of Victorian realism, though no reader can miss the fact that it gives these conventions a twist. The reader is persuaded that the novel is an accurate picture of the material and sociological conditions of life in Yorkshire in the early nineteenth century. The novel to an unusual degree gives that pleasure appropriate to realistic fiction, the pleasure of yielding to the illusion that one is entering into a real world by way of the words on the page.

Another way the novel entices the reader is by presenting abundant material inviting interpretation. Like *Lord Jim,* it overtly invites the reader to believe that there is some secret explanation which will allow him to understand the novel wholly. Such an interpretation would integrate all the details perspicuously. It is in this way chiefly that the first, grounded form of repetition is present in this novel. The details, the reader is led to believe, are the repetition of a hidden explanatory source. They are signs of it. By "materials inviting interpretation" I mean all those passages in the novel which present something evidently meaning more than what is simply present. The surface of "literal representation" is rippled throughout not only by overtly figurative language but also by things literally represented which at the same time are signs of something else or can be taken as such signs. Examples would be the three gravestones by which Lockwood stands at the end of the novel, or the "moths fluttering among the heath, and hare-bells" and the "soft wind breathing through the grass" as he stands there.[1] Such things are evidently emblematic, but of what? Passages of this sort lead the reader further and further into the novel in his attempt to get in, to reach the inside of the inside where a full retrospective explanation of all the enigmatic details will be possible. Nor is this feature of style intermittent. Once the reader catches sight of this wavering away from the literal in one detail, he becomes suspicious of every detail. He must reinterrogate the whole, like a detective of life or of literature on whom nothing is lost. The text itself, in its presentation of enigmas in the absence of patent totalizing explanation, turns him into such a detective.

The reader is also coaxed into taking the position of an interpreting spectator by the presentation in the novel of so many models of this activity. Lockwood, the timid and civilized outsider, who "shrunk icily into [himself], like a snail" (I, ch. 1) at the first sign of warm response demanding warmth from him, is the reader's delegate in the novel. He is that familiar feature of realistic fiction, the naive and unreliable narrator. Like the first readers of the novel, like modern readers, in spite of all the help they get from the critics, Lockwood is confronted with a mass of fascinating but confusing data which he must try to piece together to make a coherent pattern. I say "must" not only because this is what we as readers have been taught to do with a text, but also because there are so many examples in the novel, besides Lockwood, of texts with interpretation or commentary, or of the situation of someone who is attempting to make sense of events by narrating them.

Lockwood establishes the situation of many characters in the novel and of its readers as interpreting witnesses in a passage near the start of the novel. He first boasts of his ability to understand Heathcliff instinctively, and then withdraws this to say he may be merely projecting his own nature: "I know, by instinct, his reserve springs from an aversion to showy displays of feeling—to manifestations of mutual kindliness . . . —No, I'm running on too fast—I bestow my own attributes over liberally on him. Mr Heathcliff may have entirely dissimilar reasons for keeping his hand out of the way, when he meets a would be acquaintance, to those which actuate me" (I, ch. 1). The second chapter gives additional examples of Lockwood's ineptness as a reader of signs or as a gatherer of details into a pattern. He mistakes a heap of dead rabbits for cats, thinks Catherine Linton is Mrs. Heathcliff, and so on. His errors are a warning to the overconfident reader.

Lockwood is of course by no means the only interpreter or reader in the novel. Catherine's diary is described by Lockwood as "a pen and ink commentary—at least, the appearance of one—covering every morsel of blank that the printer had left" (I, ch. 3) in all the books of her "select" library. That library includes a Testament and the printed sermon of the Reverend Jabes Branderham. Catherine's diary is written in the margin of the latter. Branderham's sermon is an interpretation of a text in the New Testament. That text is itself an interpretation by Jesus of his injunction to forgiveness as well as a reading of certain Old Testament phrases which are echoed, just as Jesus's interpretation (or that of the Gospel-maker) comes accompanied, characteristically, by a parable. A parable is an interpretation by means of a story "thrown beside" that which is to be interpreted, as in fact all of *Wuthering Heights* might be said to be, since Lockwood's narration is adjacent to or at the margin of the enigmatic events he attempts to understand. Branderham's sermon is "interpreted" by Lockwood's dream of the battle in the chapel, in which "every man's hand [is] against his neighbor" (I, ch. 3). The sound of rapping in the dream, in turn, is rationally "read," when Lockwood wakes, as the fir-branch scratching against the window, like a pen scratching on paper. That scratching is reinterpreted once more, in Lockwood's next dream, as the sound of

Catherine's ghost trying to get through the window. Lockwood, when he wakens again, and Heathcliff, when he comes running in response to Lockwood's yell, of course interpret the dream differently. Lockwood sees Heathcliff's frantic calling out the window to Catherine (" 'Come in! come in!' he sobbed. 'Cathy, do come.' ") as "a piece of superstition" (I, ch. 3).

These few pages present a sequence of interpretations and of interpretations within interpretations. This chain establishes, at the beginning, the situation of the reader as one of gradual penetration from text to text, just as Lockwood moves from room to room of the house, each inside the other, until he reaches the paneled bed inside Catherine's old room. There he finds himself confronting the Chinese boxes of texts within texts I have just described. The reader of *Wuthering Heights* must thread his or her way from one interpretative narrative to another—from Lockwood's narrative to Nelly's long retelling (which is also a rationalizing and conventionally religious explanation), to Isabella's letter, or to Catherine's dream of being thrown out of heaven, to her interpretation of this in the "I am Heathcliff" speech, and so on.

The novel keeps before the reader emblems of his own situation by showing so many characters besides Lockwood reading or learning to read.[2] The mystery Lockwood tries to understand is the "same" mystery as that which confronts the reader of the novel: How have things got the way they are at Wuthering Heights when Lockwood first goes there? What is the original cause lying behind this sad disappearance of civility? Why is it that the novel so resists satisfactory reasonable explanation? Lockwood, at the point of his deepest penetration spatially into the house and temporally back near the "beginning," encounters not an event or a presence open to his gaze, but Catherine's diary, another text to read. Catherine and Heathcliff, in their turns, are shown, in the diary, condemned to read two religious pamphlets, "The Helmet of Salvation" and "The Broad Way to Destruction," on the "awful Sunday" when they escape for their "scamper on the moors" under the dairy-woman's cloak. Edgar Linton reads in his study while Catherine is willing her own death. He tries to keep her in life by enticing her to read: "A book lay spread on the sill before her, and the scarcely perceptible wind fluttered its leaves at intervals. I believe Linton had laid it there, for she never endeavoured to divert herself with reading, or occupation of any kind" (II, ch. 1). Much later, the taming of Hareton is signaled by his patiently learning to read under the second Catherine's tutelage. Reading seems to be opposed to the wind on the moors, to death, and to sexual experience. Yet all the readers, in the novel and of the novel, can have as a means of access to these is a book, or some other mediating emblem.

Brontë's problem, once she had agreed with her sisters to try her hand at a novel, was to bend the vision she had been expressing more directly and privately in the Gondal poems to the conventions of nineteenth-century fiction, or to bend those conventions to accommodate the vision. Each technical device contributing to the celebrated complexity of narration in *Wuthering Heights* has its precedents in modern fictional practice from Cervantes down to novelists contemporary with Brontë. The time shifts, the multiplication of narrators and narrators within narrators, the double plot, the effacement of the author, and the absence of any trustworthy and knowing narrator who clearly speaks for the author are used strategically in *Wuthering Heights* to frustrate the expectations of a reader such as Lockwood. They are used to invite the reader to move step by step, by way of a gradual unveiling, room by room, into the "penetralium" of Brontë's strange vision of life.

The first who accepted this invitation was Brontë's sister Charlotte, or rather one should say almost the first, since the first reviews of *Wuthering Heights* precede Charlotte's essay. Charlotte Brontë's two prefaces, the "Biographical Notice of Ellis and Acton Bell" and the "Editor's Preface to the New [1850] Edition of *Wuthering Heights,*" are often the first thing the modern reader of the novel encounters, with the exception of some twentieth-century critic's introductory essay. The novel comes to the reader wrapped in layers of prefatory material. It is difficult to be sure where the margin of the introductions ends and where the novel "proper" begins. Where does the reader step over the threshold into the novel itself? If the modern critical essay is definitely outside, a kind of alien presence within the covers of the book, Charlotte's prefaces would seem to have privileged access to the house. They seem to be the last layer before entrance, the inside outside, or perhaps the first region actually within, the outside inside, an entrance room. Perhaps they should be thought of as liminal, as the threshold itself. In any case, the language of Charlotte's prefaces is often continuous with Emily's language, for example in its use of figures of speech drawn from Yorkshire scenery, though whether or not Charlotte's language distorts Emily's language by misusing it is another question.

Charlotte's prefaces establish the rhetorical stance which has been characteristic of criticism of this novel. This stance involves dismissing most previous critics and claiming one has oneself solved the enigma, cracked the code. Charlotte's prefaces also establish the situation of a reader confronting an enigmatic text as the appropriate emblem for those both inside and outside the novel:

> Too often do reviewers remind us of the mob of Astrologers, Chaldeans, and Soothsayers gathered before the "writing on the wall," and unable to read the characters or make known the interpretation. We have a right to rejoice when a true seer comes at last, some man in whom is an excellent spirit, to whom have been given light, wisdom, and understanding; who can accurately read the "Mene, Mene, Tekel, Upharsin" of an original mind (however unripe, however inefficiently cultured and partially expanded that mind may be); and who can say, with confidence, "This is the interpretation thereof." (P. 438)

Charlotte is here ostensibly praising the one previous review of which she approves, that by Sydney Dobell in the *Palladium* for September 1850. Dobell was persuaded that Charlotte Brontë had written *Wuthering Heights.* His review is by no means unintelligent, for example in what he says of Catherine Earnshaw: "in the very arms of her lover we dare not doubt her purity." In the end, however, Dobell only restates the enigma rather than solving it: "one looks back at the whole story as to a world of brilliant figures in an atmosphere of mist; shapes that come out upon the eye, and burn their colours into the brain, and depart into the enveloping fog. It is the unformed writing of a giant's hand; the 'large utterance' of a baby god."[3] Charlotte, in spite of her praise of Dobell, means to present herself as the first genuine reader of this "unformed writing," the first true interpreter of the "Mene, Mene, Tekel, Upharsin."

Charlotte's preface of 1850 confidently tells the reader, before he has even read the novel, what the text is to mean. The difficulty is that she presents in fact at least four incompatible readings, citing chapter and verse for each interpretation she proposes, without apparent awareness that they differ from one another. Her readings, moreover, function to throw the reader off the track. They attempt to shift the blame for the novel away from Emily by reducing its meaning to something Charlotte imagines Victorian readers will accept.

Emily Brontë was in *Wuthering Heights,* says Charlotte in the first reading she proposes, simply following nature. She was warbling her native woodnotes wild. The novel is not Emily speaking, but nature speaking through her. The novel "is rustic all through. It is moorish, and wild, and knotty as a root of heath. Nor was it natural that it should be otherwise; the author being herself a native and nursling of the moors" (p. 442).

This reading is immediately qualified and replaced by a new one. The true source of the novel, says Charlotte now, is the actual wild way of life of the peasants of Yorkshire. The novel is sociologically accurate. Emily is merely the innocent transcriber of fact: "She knew them; knew their ways, their language, their family histories; she could hear of them with interest, and talk of them with detail, minute, graphic, and accurate . . . Her imagination, which was a spirit more sombre than sunny, more powerful than sportive, found in such traits material whence it wrought creations like Heathcliff, like Earnshaw, like Catherine. Having formed these beings, she did not know what she had done" (pp. 442–443).

No, after all, this is not it either, Charlotte in effect says in proposing yet another reading. In fact Emily Brontë was a Christian. The novel is a religious allegory, with Heathcliff, for example, an incarnation of the Devil: "Heathcliff, indeed, stands unredeemed; never once swerving in his arrow-straight course to perdition." His love for Catherine is "a passion such as might boil and glow in the bad essence of some evil genius; a fire that might form the tormented centre—the ever-suffering soul of a magnate of the infernal world: and by its quenchless and ceaseless ravage effect the execution of the decree which dooms him to carry Hell with him wherever he wanders" (pp. 443, 444).

No, says Charlotte finally, this is not the true explanation or excuse. In fact, whatever the nature of the work, Emily is not to be blamed for it because she was not responsible for it. She was the passive medium through which something or someone else spoke, just as, for Rimbaud, in "les lettres du voyant," the metal is not to blame if it finds itself a trumpet ("Je est un autre."); and just as the speaker in some of Brontë's poems is subject to a "God of visions" who speaks through her without her volition. "But this, I know," says Charlotte; "the writer who possesses the creative gift owns something of which he is not always master—something that at times strangely wills and works for itself . . . Be the work grim or glorious, dread or divine, you have little choice left but quiescent adoption. As for you—the nominal artist—your share in it has been to work passively under dictates you neither delivered nor could question—that would not be uttered at your prayer, nor suppressed nor changed at your caprice" (p. 444).

Charlotte's prefaces, with their multiple interpretations, each based on some aspect of the actual text of *Wuthering Heights*, establish a program for all the hundreds of essays and books on *Wuthering Heights* which were to follow. They do this both in the sense that most readings could be lined up under one or another of Charlotte's four readings. They do it also in the sense that all these books and essays are also empirically based on the text. Each tends to be plausible, but demonstrably partial, though each also, like Charlotte's prefaces, tends to be presented with confident certainty. Each critic presents himself as the Daniel who can at last decipher the writing on the wall. Though the many essays on the novel do not exist on a common axis of judgment, that is, though they do not even raise the same questions about the novel, much less give the same answers, each critic tends to claim that he has found something of importance which will indicate the right way to read the novel as a whole.

There have been explanations of *Wuthering Heights* in terms of its relation to the motif of the fair-haired girl and the dark-haired boy in the Gondal poems; or by way of the motifs of doors and windows in the novel (Dorothy Van Ghent); or in terms of the symmetry of the family relations in the novel or of Brontë's accurate knowledge of the laws of private property in Yorkshire (C. P. Sanger); or in more or less orthodox and schematic Freudian terms, as a thinly disguised sexual drama displaced and condensed (Thomas Moser); or as the dramatization of a conflict between two cosmological forces, storm and calm (Lord David Cecil); or as a moral story of the futility of grand passion (Mark Schorer); or as a fictional dramatization of Brontë's religious vision (J. H. Miller); or as a dramatization of the relation between sexuality and death, as "l'approbation de la vie jusqu'à la mort," the approbation of life all the way to death (Georges Bataille); or as the occult dramatization of Brontë's lesbian passion for her dead sister, Maria, with Brontë as Heathcliff (Camille Paglia); or as an overdetermined semiotic structure which is irreducibly ambiguous by reason of its excess of signs (Frank Kermode); or as Brontë's effacement of nature in order to make way for specifically female imaginative patterns (Margaret Homans); or as the expression of a multitude of incompatible "partial selves" dispersed among the various characters, thereby breaking down the concept of the unitary self (Leo Bersani), or in more or less sophisticated Marxist terms (David Wilson, Arnold Kettle, Terry Eagleton).[4]

This list could be extended. The literature on *Wuthering Heights* is abundant and its incoherence striking. Even more than some other great works of literature this novel seems to have an inexhaustible power to call forth commentary and more commentary. All literary criticism tends to be the presentation of what claims to be the definitive rational explanation of the text in question. The criticism of *Wuthering Heights* is characterized by the unusual degree of incoherence among the various explanations and by the way each takes some one element in the novel and extrapolates it toward a total explanation. The essays tend not to build on one another according to some ideal of progressive elucidation. Each is exclusive.

All these interpretations are, I believe, wrong. This is not because each does not illuminate something in *Wuthering Heights.* Each brings something to light, even though it covers something else up in the act of doing so. The essays by Bataille, Kermode, Bersani, and Homans seem to me especially to cast light, but each could nevertheless be shown to be partial. No doubt my essay too will be open to the charge that it attempts to close off the novel by explaining it, even though that explanation takes the form of an attempted reasonable formulation of its unreason.

My argument is not that criticism is a free-for-all in which one reading is as good as another. No doubt there would be large areas of agreement among competent readers even of this manifestly controversial novel. It is possible to present a reading of *Wuthering Heights* which is demonstrably wrong, not even partially right, though I believe all the readings listed above are in one way or another partially right. They are right because they arise from responses determined by the text. The error lies in the assumption that the meaning is going to be single, unified, and logically coherent. My argument is that the best readings will be the ones which best account for the heterogeneity of the text, its presentation of a definite group of possible meanings which are systematically interconnected, determined by the text, but logically incompatible. The clear and rational expression of such a system of meanings is difficult, perhaps impossible. The fault of premature closure is intrinsic to criticism. The essays on *Wuthering Heights* I have cited seem to me insufficient, not because what they say is demonstrably mistaken, but rather because there is an error in the assumption that there *is* a single secret truth about *Wuthering Heights.* This secret truth would be something formulable as a univocal principle of explanation which would account for everything in the novel. The secret truth about *Wuthering Heights,* rather, is that there is no secret truth which criticism might formulate in this way. No hidden identifiable ordering principle which will account for everything stands at the head of the chain or at the back of the back. Any formulation of such a principle is visibly reductive. It leaves something important still unaccounted for. This is a remnant of opacity which keeps the interpreter dissatisfied, the novel still open, the process of interpretation still able to continue. One form or another of this openness may characterize all works of literature, but, as I suggested in Chapter 1, this resistance to a single definitive reading takes different forms in different works. In *Wuthering Heights* this special form is the invitation to believe that there is a supernatural transcendent "cause" for all events, while certain identification of this cause, or even assurance of its existence, is impossible.

Wuthering Heights produces its effect on its reader through the way it is made up of repetitions of the same in the other which permanently resist rational reduction to some satisfying principle of explanation. The reader has the experience, in struggling to understand the novel, that a certain number of the elements which present themselves for explanation can be reduced to order. This act of interpretation always leaves something over, something just at the edge of the circle of theoretical vision which that vision does not encompass. This something left out is clearly a significant detail. There are always in fact a group of such significant details which have been left out of any reduction to order. The text is over-rich.

This resistance to theoretical domination, both in the sense of clear-seeing and in the sense of conceptual formulation, is not accidental, nor is it without significance. It is not a result of Brontë's inexperience or of the fact that she overloaded her novel with elements which can be taken as having meaning beyond their realistic references. The novel is not incoherent, confused, or flawed. It is a triumph of the novelist's art. It uses the full resources of that art against the normal assumptions about character and about human life which are built into the conventions of realistic fiction. The difficulties of interpreting *Wuthering Heights* and the superabundance of possible (and actual) interpretations do not mean that the reader is free to make the novel mean anything he wants to make it mean. The fact that no demonstrable single meaning or principle of meaningfulness can be identified does not mean that all meanings are equally good. Each good reader of *Wuthering Heights* is subject to the text, coerced by it. The best readings, it may be, are those, like Charlotte Brontë's, which repeat in their own alogic the text's failure to satisfy the mind's desire for logical order with a demonstrable base. *Wuthering Heights* incorporates the reader in the process of understanding which the text mimes in Lockwood's narration. It forces him to repeat in his own way an effort of understanding that the text expresses, and to repeat also the baffling of that effort.

Wuthering Heights presents an emblem for this experience of the reader in a passage describing Lockwood's reaction to Nelly's proposal to skip rapidly over three years in her narration: "No, no," says Lockwood. "I'll allow nothing of the sort! Are you acquainted with the mood of mind in which, if you were seated alone, and the cat licking its kitten on the rug before you, you would watch the operation so intently that puss's neglect of one ear would put you seriously out of temper?" (I, ch. 7). This, I take it, is an oblique warning to the reader. Unless he reads in the "mood of mind" here described he is likely to miss something of importance. Every detail counts in this novel. Only an interpretation which accounts for each item and puts it in relation to the whole will be at once specific enough and total enough. The reader must be like a cat who licks her kitten all over, not missing a single spot of fur, or rather he must be like the watcher of such an operation, following every detail of the multiple narration, assuming that every minute bit counts, constantly on the watch for anything left out. There is always, however, a neglected ear, or one ear too many.

Nelly describes Lockwood's anxiety about the neglected ear as "a terribly lazy mood," to which Lockwood replies: "On the contrary, a tiresomely active one. It is mine, at present, and, therefore, continue minutely. I perceive that people in these regions acquire over people in towns the value that a spider in a dungeon does over a spider in a cottage, to their various occupants" (I, ch. 7). The kitten's neglected ear, like the spider in the dungeon, is not a "frivolous external thing." It is a small thing on the surface which bears relation to hidden things in the depths. This opposition between surface and depth is suggested when Lockwood says people at Wuthering Heights "live more in earnest, more in themselves" (I, ch. 7). To live in oneself is to be self-contained. This is opposed to living in terms of surface change and frivolous external things. Where people live in themselves, external things are not superficial or frivolous. They are rather the only signs outsiders have of the secret depths.

Lockwood next provides a final figure for his situation and for that of the reader. This is a somewhat peculiar metaphor of eating. It defines the reader's situation in terms of a possible filling or the possible satisfaction of an appetite. It also puts before the reader the opposition between a single thing which stands for a whole, and therefore may be deeply satisfying, and a multitude of details which make a superficial, finally unsatisfying, whole. Rural life as against urban life, the spider in the dungeon as against the spider in the cottage, are compared in what might be called a gustatory parable: "one state resembles setting a hungry man down to a single dish on which he may concentrate his entire appetite, and do it justice—the other, introducing him to a table laid out by French cooks; he can perhaps extract as much enjoyment from the whole, but each part is a mere atom in his regard and remembrance" (I, ch. 7).

How can the reader interpret this parable? Is it a hunger for "experience," or for "knowledge," and if for one or the other, experience of what, knowledge of what? There is in any case a clear opposition between, on the one hand, a relatively sparse field of experience which allows an intense concentration on what is there to be assimilated, and, on the other hand, a diffuse multitude of things to taste which distracts attention and makes it superficial. The intense concentration leads to satisfaction, a filling of the mind now and in memory. It seems as if the single object intensely regarded leads beyond itself, stands for more than itself. It perhaps stands for the whole. The diffuse multitude reduces each item to something which is not attended to in itself. It therefore neither leads beyond itself nor sticks in the memory as a means of reaching a whole. Each part is a mere atom in the beholder's regard and remembrance.

This parable is a recipe for how to read *Wuthering Heights.* Each passage must be concentrated upon with the most intense effort of the interpreting mind, as though it were the only dish on the table. Each detail must be taken as a synecdoche, as a clue to the whole—as I have taken this detail.

Take, for example the following passages:

> The ledge, where I placed my candle, had a few mildewed books piled up in one corner; and it was covered with writing scratched on the paint. This writing, however, was nothing but a name repeated in all kinds of characters, large and small—*Catherine Earnshaw,* here and there varied to *Catherine Heathcliff,* and then again to *Catherine Linton.*
>
> In vapid listlessness I leant my head against the window, and continued spelling over Catherine Earnshaw—Heathcliff—Linton, till my eyes closed; but they had not rested five minutes when a glare of white letters started from the dark, as vivid as spectres—the air swarmed with Catherines. (I, ch. 3)

> I had remarked on one side of the road, at intervals of six or seven yards, a line of upright stones, continued through the whole length of the barren: these were erected, and daubed with lime on purpose to serve as guides in the dark, and also when a fall, like the present, confounded the deep swamps on either hand with the firmer path: but, excepting a dirty dot pointing up here and there, all traces of their existence had vanished; and my companion found it necessary to warn me frequently to steer to the right or left, when I imagined I was following, correctly, the windings of the road. (I, ch. 3)

> I sought, and soon discovered, the three head-stones on the slope next the moor—the middle one grey, and half buried in the heath—Edgar Linton's only harmonized by the turf, and moss creeping up its foot—Heathcliff's still bare.
>
> I lingered round them, under that benign sky; watched the moths fluttering among the heath, and hare-bells; listened to the soft wind breathing through the grass; and wondered how anyone could ever imagine unquiet slumbers for the sleepers in that quiet earth. (II, ch. 20)

These three texts are similar, but this similarity is, in part at least, the fact that each is unique in the structural model it presents the reader. This uniqueness makes each incommensurate with any of the others. Each is, in its surface texture as language, "realistic." It is a description of natural or manmade objects which is physically and sociologically plausible. Such things are likely to have existed in Yorkshire around 1800. All three passages are filtered through the mind and through the language of the narrator. In all three, as it happens, this is the mind of the primary narrator of the novel, Lockwood. As always in such cases, the reader must interrogate the passages for possible irony. This irony potentially arises from discrepancies between what Lockwood knows or what he makes out of what he sees, and what the author knew and made, or what the reader can make out of the passages as he interprets the handwriting on the wall. All of the passages possibly mean more than their referential or historical meaning. They may be signs or clues to something beyond themselves. This possibility is opened up in the fissure between what Lockwood apparently knows or intends to say, and what the author may have known or intended to say. None of these passages, nor any of the many other "similar" passages which punctuate the novel, is given the definitive closure of a final interpretation within the text of the novel. In fact they are not interpreted at all. They are just given. The handwriting on the wall is not read within the novel. The reader must read it for himself.

When he does so, he finds that each such passage seems to ask to be taken as an emblem of the whole novel. Each is implicitly an emblem of the structure of the novel as a whole and of the way that whole signifies something beyond itself which controls its meaning as a whole. Each such passage leads to a different formulation of the structure of the whole. Each is exclusive and incongruous with the others. It seems to have an imperialistic will to power over the others, as if it wished to bend them to its own shape. It expands to make its own special reading of the whole, just as each of Charlotte Brontë's four readings of the novel do, or just as each of the hundreds of readings which have followed hers have tended to do. Each such reading implicitly excludes other passages which do not fit, or distorts them, twisting them to its own pattern.

The first passage would lead to an interpretation of the novel in terms of the permutation of given names and family names. This reading would go by way of the network of kinship relations in symmetrical pedigree and by way of the theme of reading. The critic might note that there do not seem to be enough names to go around in this novel. Relations of similarity and difference among the characters are indicated by the way several hold the names also held by others or a combination of names held by others. An example is "Linton Heathcliff," the name of the son of Heathcliff and Isabella. His name is an oxymoron, combining names from the two incompatible families. How can a name be "proper" to a character and indicate his individuality if it is also held by others? Each character in *Wuthering Heights* seems to be an element in a system, defined by his or her place in the system, rather than a separate, unique person. The whole novel, such a critic might say, not only the destiny of the first Catherine but also that of the second Catherine, as well as the relation of the second story to the first, is given in emblem in Lockwood's encounter with the names scratched on the windowsill and in his dream of an air swarming with Catherines. The passage is a momentary emblem for the whole. That whole, as it unfolds, is the narrative of the meaning of the emblem.

The second passage offers a model for a somewhat different form of totalization. The passage is a "realistic" description of a country road in Yorkshire after a heavy snow. If the reader follows Lockwood's example and considers every detail as possibly a clue to the whole and to what stands behind or beneath the whole, then the passage suggests that the novel is made of discrete units which follow one another in a series with spaces between. The reader's business is to draw lines between the units. He must make a pattern, like the child's game in which a duck or a rabbit is magically drawn by tracing lines between numbered dots. In this case, the line makes a road which leads the reader from here to there, taking him deeper and deeper across country to a destination, away from danger and into safety. The only difficulty is that some of the dots are missing or invisible. The reader must, like Lockwood, extrapolate. He must make the road to safety by putting in correctly the missing elements.

This operation is a dangerous one. If the reader makes a mistake, guesses wrong, hypothesizes a guidepost where there is none, he will be led astray into the bog. This process of hypothetical interpretation, projecting a thesis or ground plan where there is none, where it is faint or missing, hypotrophied, is risky for the interpreter. He must engage in the activity Immanuel

Kant, following rhetorical tradition, calls "hypotyposis," the sketching out of a ground plan where there is no secure indication of which line to follow.[5] Such an operation gives figurative names to what has no literal or proper name. The reader's safety somehow depends on getting it right. There is a good chance of getting it wrong, or perhaps there is no secure foundation for deciding between right and wrong.

Exactly how the activity of reading *Wuthering Heights* concerns the reader remains to be seen. It is clear that Lockwood, the reader's vicarious representative in the novel, often gets it wrong. If he is the reader's representative in the novel, he is an example of how not to do it, of how not to do things with signs. His relation to Heathcliff in the second passage cited above, as he is guided toward a goal he could not reach himself, may be taken to figure the relation between Lockwood and Heathcliff in the novel as a whole. That relation, in turn, inscribes within the text a figure of the reader's relation to the violent and inscrutable events he must try to interpret. If Lockwood is the outsider, seeing events from a distance, Heathcliff is the male character who is most involved and who ultimately dies into the heart of violence and mystery. He returns whence he has come, leaving Lockwood behind as survivor to tell the tale. Heathcliff may be a trustworthy guide, but he is also a dangerous one to follow all the way where he is going.

The third passage quoted makes explicit the situation of the survivor. This too may be taken as emblematic of the whole text in relation to what lies behind the events it narrates, or as emblematic of the narrator's relation to the story he tells, or as a figure of the reader's relation to the story told. Just as many of Wordsworth's poems, "The Boy of Winander," for example, or the Matthew poems, or "The Ruined Cottage," are epitaphs spoken by a survivor who stands by a tombstone musing on the life and death of the one who is gone, so all of *Wuthering Heights* may be thought of as a memorial narration pieced together by Lockwood from what he can learn. The first Catherine is already dead when Lockwood arrives at the Heights. Heathcliff is still alive as the anguished survivor whose "life is in the grave." By the end of the novel Heathcliff has followed Catherine into death. At the end, Lockwood stands by three graves. These, like the three versions of Catherine's name in my first emblematic text, can stand in their configuration for the story of the first Catherine: Catherine Earnshaw in the middle torn by her love for Edgar Linton, in one direction, and for Heathcliff, in the other, destroying their lives in this double love and being destroyed by it.

A gravestone is the sign of an absence. Throughout the whole novel Lockwood confronts nothing but such signs. His narration is a retrospective reconstruction by means of them. This would be true of all novels told in the past tense about characters who are dead when the narration begins, but the various churchyard scenes in *Wuthering Heights,* for example the scene in which Heathcliff opens Catherine's grave and coffin, keep before the reader the question of whether the dead still somewhere live on beyond the grave. The naiveté of Lockwood, even at the end of the novel, is imaged in his inability to imagine unquiet slumbers for the sleepers in the quiet earth. The evidence for the fact that this earth is unquiet, the place of some unnamable tumultuous hidden life, is there before his eyes in the moths fluttering among the heath and hare-bells. It is there in the soft wind breathing through the grass, like some obscurely vital creature. These are figures for what can only manifest itself indirectly. If Lockwood survives the death of the protagonists and tells their story, it may be this survival which cuts him off from any understanding of death. The end of the novel reiterates the ironic discrepancy between what Lockwood knows and what he unwittingly gives the reader evidence for knowing.

Each of these three passages can be taken in one way or another as an emblem of the structure of the whole narration and of the relation of that whole to the enigmatic ground on which it rests, the origin from which it comes and the goal to which it returns. Beginning with any one as starting place the reader or critic can move out to interpret the whole novel in the terms it provides. Each appropriates other details and bends them around itself. Each leads to a different total design. Each such design is incompatible with the others. Each implicitly claims to be a center around which all the other details can be organized.

Different as are the several schematic paradigms for the whole, they share certain features. Each is a figure without a visible referent. Whatever emblem is chosen as center turns out to be not at the center but at the periphery. It is in fact an emblem for the impossibility of reaching the center. Each leads to a multitude of other similar details in the novel. Each such sequence is a repetitive structure, like the echoes from one to another of the lives of the two Catherines, or like the narrators within narrators in Lockwood's telling, or like the rooms inside rooms he encounters at the Heights. Each appearance is the sign of something absent, something earlier, or later, or further in. Each detail is in one way or another a track to be followed. It is a trace which asks to be retraced so that the something missing may be recovered.

The celebrated circumstantiality of *Wuthering Heights* is the circumstantiality of this constant encounter with new signs. The reader of *Wuthering Heights,* like the narrator, is led deeper and deeper into the text by the expectation that sooner or later the last veil will be removed. He will then find himself face to face not with the emblem of something missing but with the right real thing at last. This will be truly original, the bona fide starting place. It will therefore be possessed of full explanatory power over the whole network of signs which it has generated and which it controls, giving each sign its deferred meaning. Through this labyrinth of linkages the reader has to thread his way. He is led from one to another in the expectation of reaching a goal, as Heathcliff leads Lockwood from marker to marker down that snowcovered road.

A further feature of this web of signs behind signs is that they tend to be presented in paired oppositions. Each element of these pairs is not so much the opposite of its mate as another form of it. It is a differentiated form, born of some division within the same, as the different Catherines in the passage discussed above are forms of the same Catherine; or as Heathcliff and Lockwood are similar in their exclusion from the place where Catherine is, as well as opposite in temperament, sexual power, and power of volition; or as Cathy says of Heathcliff not that he is her opposite, other than she is, but that "He's more myself than I am"; or as, in the passage describing the three graves, Edgar on one side of Catherine or Heathcliff on the other each represents one aspect of her double nature. The novel everywhere organizes itself according to such patterns of sameness and difference, as in the opposition between stormy weather and calm weather; or between the roughness of the Heights and the civilized restraint of Thrushcross Grange, or between inside and outside, domestic interior and wild nature outside, beyond the window or over the wall; or between the stories of the two Catherines, or between those who read and those who scorn books as weak intermediaries, or between people of strong will like Heathcliff, who is "a fierce, pitiless, wolfish man" (I, ch. 10) and people of weak will like Lockwood.

These apparently clear oppositions have two further properties. The reader is nowhere given access to the generative unity from which the pairs are derived. The reader never sees directly, for example, the moment in childhood when Cathy and Heathcliff slept in the same bed and were joined in a union which was prior to sexual differentiation. This union was prior to any sense of separate selfhood, prior even to language, figurative or conceptual, which might express that union. As soon as Cathy can say, "I *am* Heathcliff," or "My love for Heathcliff resembles the eternal rocks beneath" (I, ch. 9), they are already divided. This division has always already occurred as soon as there is consciousness and the possibility of retrospective storytelling. Storytelling is always after the fact, and it is always constructed over a loss. What is lost in the case of *Wuthering Heights* is the "origin" which would explain everything.

Another characteristic of the oppositions follows from this loss of the explanatory source. The separated pairs, differentiations of the same rather than true opposites, have a tendency to divide further, and then subdivide again, endlessly proliferating into various nuances and subsets. Once the "primal" division has occurred, and for Brontë as soon as there is a story to tell it has already occurred, there seems to be no stopping a further division. Once this primitive cell is self-divided it divides and subdivides perpetually in an effort to achieve reunification which only multiplies it in new further-divided life cells.

The sequence of generations in *Wuthering Heights,* for example, began long before the three presented in the novel. The name

Hareton Earnshaw and the date 1500 carved in stone above the front door of the Heights testify to that. The marriage of the second Cathy and the new Hareton at the end of the novel will initiate a new generation. The deaths of Heathcliff, Edgar Linton, and the first Catherine have by no means put a stop to the reproductive power of the two families. This force finds its analogue in the power of the story to reproduce itself. It is told over and over by the sequence of narrators, and it is reproduced again in each critical essay, or each time it is followed through by a new reader. The words on the page act like a genetic pattern able to program the minds of those who encounter it. It induces them to take, for a time at least, the pattern of the experience of those long-dead imaginary protagonists. The emblem for this might be that concluding scene in which Lockwood stands by the triple grave prolonging the lives of Edgar, Catherine, and Heathcliff by his meditation on the names inscribed on their tombstones. In this act and in the narration generated by it he prevents them from dying wholly. Many Victorian novels stress this double form of repetitive extension beyond the deaths of the protagonists, for example *Tess of the d'Urbervilles,* the topic of Chapter 5. *Wuthering Heights* gives this familiar pattern a special form by relating it to the question of whether Cathy and Heathcliff are to be thought of as surviving their deaths or whether they survive only in the narrations of those who have survived them.

Any of the oppositions which may be taken as a means of interpreting *Wuthering Heights* has this property of reproducing itself in proliferating divisions and subdivisions. Just as, for example, the name of the maiden Catherine caught between her two possible married names becomes an air "swarming" with Catherines, so the neat opposition within Christianity between good and evil, salvation and damnation, "The Helmet of Salvation" and "The Broad Way to Destruction," becomes the separation of sins into seven distinctions, and this in turn, in the Reverend Jabes Branderham's sermon, becomes a monstrous division and subdivision of sins, a dividing of the text, as Protestantism has multiplied sects and set each man's hand against his neighbor. Two becomes seven becomes seventy times seven, in a grotesque parody of a sermon: "he preached—good God! what a sermon: divided into *four hundred and ninety* parts—each fully equal to an ordinary address from the pulpit—and each discussing a separate sin!" (I, ch. 3).

Wuthering Heights is perhaps best read by taking one or more of its emblematic oppositions as an interpretative hypothesis and pushing it to the point where the initial distinction no longer clearly holds. Only by this following of a track as far as possible, until it peters out into the trackless snow, can the reader get inside this strange text and begin to understand why he cannot ever lucidly understand it or ever have rational mastery over it. The limitation of many critical essays on the novel lies not in any error in the initial interpretative hypothesis (that storm and calm are opposed in the novel, or that windows, walls, and doors are used emblematically, for example). The limitation lies rather in the failure to push the given schematic hypothesis far enough. It must be pushed to the point where it fails to hypothecate the full accounting for the novel which is demanded in the critical contract. At that point the mortgage on *Wuthering Heights* is foreclosed and the reader, it may be, confronts his mortality as reader, that vanishing of lucid understanding which his critical reason, the reason that divides and discriminates in order to master, has done everything to evade.

Why is it that, with this novel, the logical mind so conspicuously fails? What does this have to do with the gage or promissory note that both holds off death and risks death, puts one's death on the line, as a kind of mortgage insurance? Why is it that an interpretative origin, *logos* in the sense of ground, measure, chief word, or accounting reason, cannot be identified for *Wuthering Heights?* If such an origin could be found, all obscurity could be cleared up. Everything could be brought out in the open where it might be clearly seen, added up, paid off, and evened out. What forbids this accounting?

An economic metaphor of course pervades *Wuthering Heights.* Heathcliff uses his mysteriously acquired wealth to take possession of the Heights and the Grange. He takes possession of them because each thing and person in each household reminds him of Catherine. By appropriating all and then destroying them, he can take revenge on the enemies who have stood between him and Catherine. At the same time he can reach Catherine through them, in their demolition. This is a violently incarnated way to experience a paradoxical logic of signs:

> "What is not connected with her to me? and what does not recall her? I cannot look down to this floor, but her features are shaped on the flags! In every cloud, in every tree—filling the air at night, and caught by glimpses in every object by day, I am surrounded with her image! The most ordinary faces of men and women—my own features mock me with a resemblance. The entire world is a dreadful collection of memoranda that she did exist, and that I have lost her!" (II, ch. 19)

In this strange numismatics, each thing is stamped with the same image, the face of the person who is Queen to Heathcliff's Jack. In this novel no man is King or Ace. The Queen's countenance makes everything have value and pass current. There are problems with this coinage, however. For one thing, no one of these stamped images has a distinct number which indicates its worth in relation to other images or its exchange value in relation to goods or services. No orderly economic system of substitution and circulation is set up by this mint. Neither Heathcliff, nor Lockwood, nor the reader can buy anything with this money. There is, in fact, nothing left to buy, since there is nothing which is not coin stamped with the same image, of infinite value and so of no value.

The entire world is a dreadful collection of memoranda. Memoranda of what? Here is the second problem with this coinage. Each thing stands not for the presence of Catherine as the substance behind the coin, the standard guaranteeing its value, the thing both outside the money system and dispersed everywhere in delegated form within it. In this case, each thing stands rather for the absence of Catherine. All things are memoranda, written or inscribed memorials, like a note I write myself to remind me of something. They are memoranda that she did exist and that Heathcliff has lost her, that she is dead, vanished from the face of the earth. Everything in the world is a sign indicating Catherine, but also indicating, by its existence, his failure to possess her and the fact that she is dead. Each sign is both an avenue to the desired unity with her and also the barrier standing in the way of it.

From this follows the double bind of Heathcliff's relation to Hareton and to the second Cathy, both of whom he detests and loves because they look so much like the first Catherine. From this also follows the double bind of his relation to the Heights and to the Grange. He has taken much trouble to obtain them, manipulating the property laws of Yorkshire to do this, as C. P. Sanger has shown. If he possesses the two households, he can take possession of Catherine through them, since they are her property, stamped with her image, proper to her, as much hers as her proper name. But to possess her image, like appropriating her by uttering her name ("Cathy, do come. Oh do—*once* more! Oh! my heart's darling! hear me *this* time—Catherine, at last!"; (I, ch. 3), is to possess only a sign for her, not Catherine herself. He must therefore destroy the things he has made his own in order to reach what they signify. He must destroy Hareton and the second Cathy, as well as the two houses. If he destroys them, however, he will of course reach not Catherine but her absence, the vacancy which stands behind every sign that she once existed and that he has lost her. In the same way, his goal of "dissolving with her, and being more happy still!" (II, ch. 15) is blocked, in the coffin-opening scene, by the vision of Catherine's spirit not in the grave, "not under me, but on the earth" (II, ch. 15). To merge with her body, like merging with his new possessions by destroying them, is to join only a sign and to destroy its function as sign. When Heathcliff recognizes this, he abandons his goal of destroying the Heights and the Grange. This leaves him as far from his goal as ever. He will be an infinite distance from it as long as he is alive:

> "It is a poor conclusion, is it not," he observed, having brooded a while on the scene he had just witnessed [the second Catherine and Hareton reading a book together, a sign of their growing intimacy]. "An absurd termination to my violent exertions? I get levers and mattocks to demolish the two houses, and train myself to be capable of working like Hercules, and when everything is ready, and in my power, I find the will to lift a slate off either roof

> has vanished! My old enemies have not beaten me—now would be the precise time to revenge myself on their representatives—I could do it; and none could hinder me—But where is the use? I don't care for striking, I can't take the trouble to raise my hand! . . . I have lost the faculty of enjoying their destruction, and I am too idle to destroy for nothing. (II, ch. 19)

"But where is the use?" This extraordinary passage defines a complex economy of substitution and exchange which has broken down in an infinite inflation which has made the money worthless. The manipulation of the system is therefore of no use. Each element in this system is now without value either in relation to other elements it "represents" or in relation to what it stands for outside the system, since the standard behind the system has vanished, leaving it supported by nothing. It is like a paper currency which has no gold or silver, or no more credit, behind it, and so becomes again mere paper. The two houses and their land have represented Heathcliff's enemies. His enemies are those who stood between him and Catherine, forbidding their union. To destroy the houses is to destroy the enemies. His enemies, Hindley, Earnshaw, and Edgar Linton, are now dead. He must get at them through their living representatives, Hareton and the second Catherine, the scions of the two families, last of each stock. What these have always stood for is Catherine herself. To put this more exactly, they have stood for the infinite distance between Heathcliff and Catherine. This distance always exists as long as there are still signs for her. Everything resembles her, even Heathcliff's own features, but this resemblance is the sign that she is gone. To leave these signs in existence is to be tormented by the absence they all point to, but of which they also block the filling. To destroy them is to be left with nothing, not even with any signs of the fact that Cathy once existed and that he has lost her. There is no "use" in either destroying or not destroying. Within that situation Heathcliff remains poised, destroying himself in the tension of it, so that breathing or doing any slightest act is for him "like bending back a stiff spring" (II, ch. 19).

The critic's conceptual or figurative scheme of interpretation, including my own here, is up against the same blank wall as the totalizing emblems within the novel, or up against the same impasse that blocks Heathcliff's enterprise of reaching Cathy by taking possession of everything that carries her image and then destroying it. If "something" is incompatible with any sign, if it cannot be seen, signified, or theorized about, it is, in our tradition, no "thing." It is nothing. The trace of such an absence therefore retraces nothing. It can refer only to another trace, in that relation of incongruity which leads the reader of *Wuthering Heights* from one such emblematic design to another. Each passage stands for another passage, in the way Branderham's sermon, as I have said, is a commentary on Jesus's words, themselves a commentary on an Old Testament passage, and so on. Such a movement is a constant passage from one place to another without ever finding the original literal text of which the others are all figures. This missing center is the head referent which would still the wandering movement from emblem to emblem, from story to story, from generation to generation, from Catherine to Catherine, from Hareton to Hareton, from narrator to narrator. There is no way to see or name this head referent because it cannot exist as present event, as a past which once was present, or as a future which will be present. It is something which has always already occurred and been forgotten. It has become immemorial, remembered only veiled in figure, however far back one goes. In the other temporal direction, it is always about to occur, as an end which never quite comes, or when it comes comes to another, leaving only another dead sign, like the corpse of Heathcliff at the end of the novel, with its "frightful, life-like gaze of exultation" (II, ch. 20). "It" leaps suddenly from the always not yet of the future to the always already of the unremembered past. This loss leaves the theorizing spectator once more standing in meditation by a grave reading an epitaph, impelled again to tell another story, which will once more fail to bring the explanatory cause into the open. Each emblematic passage in the novel is both a seeming avenue to the desired unity and also a barrier forbidding access to it. Each means the death of experience, of consciousness, of seeing, and of theory by naming the "state" or "place" that lies always outside the words of the novel and therefore can never be experienced as such, and at the same time, in itself and in its intrinsic tendency to repeat itself, each emblematic passage holds off that death.

This "death" may be called an "it" in order not to prejudge the question of whether it is a thing, a place, a person, a state, a relationship, or a supernatural being. The various narrations and emblematic schemas of the novel presuppose an original state of unity. This ghostly glimpse is a projection outward of a oneness from a state of twoness within. This duality is within the self, within the relation of the self to another, within nature, within society, and within language. The sense that there must at some time have been an original state of unity is generated by the state of division as a haunting insight, always at the corner or at the blind center of vision, where sight fails. This insight can never be adequately expressed in language or in other signs, nor can it be "experienced directly," since experience, language, and signs exist only in one thing set against another, one thing divided from another. The insight nevertheless exists for us only in language. The sense of "something missing" is an effect of the text itself, and of the critical texts which add themselves to the primary text. This means it may be a performative effect of language, not a referential object of language. The language of narration in *Wuthering Heights* is this originating performative enacted by Lockwood, Nelly, and the rest. This narrative creates both the intuition of unitary origin and the clues, in the unresolvable heterogeneity of the narration, to the fact that the origin may be an effect of language, not some preexisting state or some "place" in or out of the world. The illusion is created by figures of one sort or another—substitutions, equivalences, representative displacements, synecdoches, emblematic invitations to totalization. The narrative sequence, in its failure ever to become transparent, in the incongruities of its not-quite-matching repetitions, demonstrates the inadequacy of any one of those figures.

Wuthering Heights, as I have said, is an example of a special form of repetition in realistic fiction. This form is controlled by the invitation to believe that some invisible or transcendent cause, some origin, end, or underlying ground, would explain all the enigmatic incongruities of what is visible. Conrad's *Heart of*

Darkness is another example of such a repetitive form, as is *Lord Jim*, discussed in Chapter 2. It is by no means the case that all realistic fiction takes this form, as my other examples will show. The special form of "undecidability" in *Wuthering Heights* or in other narratives in which repetition takes this form lies in the impossibility, in principle, of determining whether there is some extralinguistic explanatory cause or whether the sense that there is one is generated by the linguistic structure itself. Nor is this a trivial issue. It is the most important question the novel raises, the one thing about which we ought to be able to make a decision, and yet a thing about which the novel forbids the reader to make a decision. In this *Wuthering Heights* justifies being called an "uncanny" text. To alter Freud's formulas a little, the uncanny in *Wuthering Heights* is the constant bringing into the open of something which seems familiar and which one feels ought to have been kept secret, not least because it is impossible to tell whether there is any secret at all hidden in the depths, or whether the sense of familiarity and of the unveiling of a secret may not be an effect of the repetition in difference of one part of the text by another, on the surface.[6] In the oscillation between the invitation to expect the novel to be an example of the first, grounded form of repetition and the constant frustration of that expectation, *Wuthering Heights* is a special case of the intertwining of two forms of repetition described in Chapter 1.

I have suggested that the narration in *Wuthering Heights* somehow involves the reader's innocence or guilt. It may now be seen how this is the case. Any repetitive structure of the "uncanny" sort, whether in real life or in words, tends to generate an irrational sense of guilt in the one who experiences it. I have not done anything (or have I?), and yet what I witness makes demands on me which I cannot fulfill. The mere fact of passive looking or of reading may make one guilty of the crime of seeing what ought not to have been seen. What I see or what I read repeats or seems to repeat something earlier, something deeper in. That something hidden is brought back out into the open in a disguised repetition by what I see. It should be brought out now into full clarity. At the same time perhaps it should be kept secret, since it may possibly be one of those things which, to paraphrase Winnie Verloc in Conrad's *The Secret Agent,* does not stand much looking into. One way or the other I am forced to do something for which I will feel guilty. I am guilty if I reveal what ought to have been kept secret. I am guilty if I refuse the demand it makes on me to "get in," to penetrate all the way to the bottom of the mystery. The situation of the reader of *Wuthering Heights* is inscribed within the novel in the situations of all those characters who are readers, tellers of tales, most elaborately in Lockwood. The lesson for the reader is to make him aware that he has by reading the novel incurred a responsibility like that of the other spectator-interpreters.

"Thou art the man!"—this applies as much to the reader as to Lockwood or to the other narrators. The double guilt of Lockwood's narration as of any critic's discourse is the following. If he does not penetrate all the way to the innermost core of the story he tells, he keeps the story going, repeating itself interminably in its incompletion. This is like the guilt of the one who keeps a grave open, or like the guilt of a sexual failure. On the other hand, to pierce all the way in is to be guilty of the desecration of a grave, to be guilty, like Heathcliff when he opens Cathy's grave, of necrophilia. The punishment for that is to be condemned to go where the vanished protagonists are. Really to penetrate, to get inside the events, rather than seeing them safely from the outside, would be to join Cathy and Heathcliff wherever they now are. The reader's sense of guilt is systematically connected to the swarm of other emotions aroused in any good reader of *Wuthering Heights* as he makes his way through the book: affection for the two Catherines, though in a different way for each, and mixed with some fear of her intransigence in the case of the first Catherine; scorn for Lockwood, but some pity for his limitations; awe of Heathcliff's suffering; and so on.

The line of witnesses who feel one or another form of this complex of emotions goes from the reader-critic to Charlotte Brontë to Emily Brontë to that pseudonymous author "Ellis Bell" to Lockwood to Nelly to Heathcliff to Cathy, the inside of the inside, or it moves the other way around, from Cathy out to the reader. The reader is the last surviving consciousness enveloping all these other consciousnesses, one inside the other. The reader is condemned, like all the others, to be caught by a double contradictory demand: to bring it all out in the open and at the same time to give it decent burial, to keep the book open and at the same time to close its covers once and for all, so it may be forgotten, or so it may be read once more, this time definitively. The guilt of the reader is the impossibility of doing either of these things, once he has opened the book and begun to read: "1801—I have just returned from a visit to my landlord" (I, ch. 1).

The reading of the first present-tense words of the novel performs a multiple act of resurrection, an opening of graves or a raising of ghosts. In reading those first words and then all the ones that follow to the end, the reader brings back from the grave first the fictive "I" who is supposed to have written them or spoken them, that Lockwood who has and had no existence outside the covers of the book. With that "I" the reader brings back also the moment in the fall of 1801 when his "I have just returned" is supposed to have been written or spoken. By way of that first "I" and first present moment the reader then resurrects from the dead, with Lockwood's help, in one direction Hindley, Nelly, Joseph, Hareton, the two Catherines, Heathcliff, and the rest, so that they walk the moors once again and live once again at the Heights and the Grange. In the other direction are also evoked first Ellis Bell, the pseudonymous author, who functions as a ghostly name on the title page. Ellis Bell is a male name veiling the female author, but it is also the name of a character in the book: someone who has survived Lockwood, an "editor" into whose hands Lockwood's diary has fallen and who presents it to the public, or, more likely, the consciousness surrounding Lockwood's consciousness, overhearing what he says to himself, what he thinks, feels, sees, and presenting it again to the reader as though it were entirely the words of Lockwood. In doing this Ellis Bell effaces himself, but he is present as a ghostly necessity of the narrative behind Lockwood's words. The name Ellis Bell functions to name a spectator outside Lockwood, who is the primary spectator. Ellis Bell is another representative of the reader, overhearing, overseeing, overthinking, and overfeeling what Lockwood says, sees, thinks, feels, and writing it down so we can in our turns evoke Lockwood again and raise also that thin and almost invisible ghost, effaced presupposition of the words of the novel, Ellis Bell himself. Behind Ellis Bell, finally, is Brontë, who, the reader knows, actually wrote down those words, "1801—I have just returned . . ." at Haworth on some day probably in 1846. Brontë too, in however indirect fashion, is brought back to life in the act of reading.

If in Lockwood's dream the air swarms with Catherines, so does this book swarm with ghosts who walk the Yorkshire moors inside the covers of any copy of *Wuthering Heights,* waiting to be brought back from the grave by anyone who chances to open the book and read. The most powerful form of repetition in fiction, it may be, is not the echoes of one part of the book by another, but the way even the simplest, most representational words in a novel ("1801—I have just returned . . .") present themselves as already a murmuring repetition, something which has been repeating itself incessantly there in the words on the page waiting for me to bring it back to life as the meaning of the words forms itself in my mind. Fiction is possible only because of an intrinsic capacity possessed by ordinary words in grammatical order. Words no different from those we use in everyday life, "I have just returned," may detach themselves or be detached from any present moment, any living "I," any immediate perception of reality, and go on functioning as the creators of the fictive world repeated into existence, to use the verb transitively, whenever the act of reading those words is performed. The words themselves, there on the page, both presuppose the deaths of that long line of personages and at the same time keep them from dying wholly, as long as a single copy of *Wuthering Heights* survives to be reread.

4

HENRY ESMOND

Repetition and Irony

THACKERAY'S *HENRY ESMOND* is such an intricate tissue of repetitions and repetitions within repetitions that it can illustrate most of the modes of repetition in realistic fiction. It is also an admirable illustration of a certain self-unraveling intrinsic to the use of repetition in a novel as a means of affirming meaning and of affirming the author's authority. One tropological name for this unraveling of meaning is "irony," the trope without *logos. Henry Esmond* is a masterwork of Victorian irony, or of irony as such.

How can the reader thread his way among the different forms of repetition in this novel? What governs them or organizes them into a single web with a presiding figure? *Henry Esmond* repeats in displaced form certain configurations of person and event in Thackeray's own life, his relations to his family, to Mrs. Brookfield.[1] The novel is a way of working through that real life by a detour through a fiction which obscurely repeats it. Moreover, as Stephen Bann, in one of the best essays on *Henry Esmond,*[2] has said, the novel repeats with a difference the conventions of eighteenth- and nineteenth-century fiction: Fielding's *Tom Jones,* Scott's *Quentin Durward,* or Dickens's *Oliver Twist. Henry Esmond* plays ironically against those conventions, especially against the conventions of one familiar English form of the Bildungsroman, the story of the orphan or illegitimate child who learns about the world, discovers his parents, comes into his inheritance, and lives happily ever after.

Henry Esmond, in addition, is a "historical novel." It repeats in a fictional narration certain historical personages and events from the eighteenth century: Addison, Steele, Marlborough, the failure of the Pretender to take the throne, and so on. The novel in its first publication was a cunning replica of an eighteenth-century memoir, with an epigraph in Latin, an epistle dedicatory, and an elaborate title page. The style of Henry Esmond's "history . . . written by himself" imitates eighteenth-century syntax and vocabulary, as well as (in the first edition) spelling and typography, though not with entire consistency, as other critics have noted. Thackeray's own somewhat ugly face continually peeps through the mask.

One of the primary pleasures of reading Thackeray is purely stylistic. This pleasure is one of the effects of irony. It arises from the reader's sense of a constant slight discrepancy between "Thackeray himself" and the voice or tone he has momentarily adopted: Pendennis, Esmond, or the all-knowing narrator of *Vanity Fair.* One evidence for this, and one of the greatest "pleasures of the text" in *Henry Esmond,* is the subtle and unostentatious way in which motifs, once introduced—the color red, for example, or Diana, the moon—recur, cunningly woven into passages which remain, from Henry's point of view, seemingly no more than accurate descriptions of what was there to be seen. These repetitions reveal the presence of Thackeray himself, the artificer who has made it all. "Thackeray himself," in fact, insofar as the reader can know him in his writing, is this need to be himself by writing himself as someone else. This means a failure ever to be unequivocally "himself," since he remains always in expressions of himself in his writing an imaginary someone else.

Henry Esmond in itself, putting aside its relation to Thackeray, is one of the greatest of English novels of improvised or imaginary memory. Thackeray imagines a character and then imagines a complete memory for him. This memory has that structure of intensities and dimnesses, of inclusions and hiatuses, which is characteristic, it may be, of some "real memories." Within *Henry Esmond,* Henry, the first person "I" writing his memoirs in his old age in Virginia, repeats his youthful self, displacing it and bringing it close at the same time, by writing of that earlier self in the third person, as a "he." That writing contains a repertoire of the forms of repetition characteristic of realistic fiction, repetitions

within the fiction and repetitions by the fiction of things and texts outside. Of the former, the most striking is the repetition by Henry of his love for Rachel in his love of Rachel's daughter Beatrix. The novel joins Gérard de Nerval's *Sylvie,* Brontë's *Wuthering Heights,* Hardy's *The Well-Beloved,* and Proust's *A la recherche du temps perdu* in dramatizing a love which is passed from one generation to the next, or from one replica to the next, multiplying its strength in the repetitions. In all these novels, this dramatization is reinforced by a complex tissue of recurring motifs and scenes within the text. Images of portraits, of light, of sun and moon, of eyes, stars, jewels, and tapers, of red, the color of blood, recur throughout. Episode echoes episode. The meaning develops through these repetitions. In addition, *Henry Esmond,* like *The Well-Beloved* and like the other novels in this chain, is punctuated by allusions to previous texts—Biblical, classical, and vernacular. Henry's story repeats a long sequence of similar stories going back to antiquity and to the legendary prehistory of man. *The History of Henry Esmond, Esq.* incorporates or repeats the histories of Hamlet; of Oedipus and Aeneas; of Diana and Niobe; of Rachel, Jacob, and Esau.

All these elements are the given materials for interpreting *Henry Esmond.* Most readers would agree that these modes of repetition are there in the novel, would agree more or less on what they are, and would agree that they offer important data for any reading of the novel. The disagreements would come at a higher level, at the level of the attempt to make a definite interpretation. As I have said in the first chapter, the basic problem in understanding any repetitive series is to identify its basis, its ground, the law it exemplifies. What is the center which controls the tangle of repetitions? Just this search for authority governs *Henry Esmond* thematically, in its organization as a fabric of words, and in its relation to the various things outside the text it echoes. Whatever thread the critic chooses converges on the question of authority. On the stylistic level, this question becomes a search for the form of language which will give Henry Esmond, writing in his old age, authoritative command over the whole panorama of his life as it stands before that total memory he boasts of having.

What is the appropriate style in which to paint one's self-portrait accurately from the perspective of this total recall and so see oneself clearly? From the point of view not of the fictional Esmond but of the real Thackeray, the question is what form of fiction will give him authoritative indirect command over his own life. That life is obscurely represented in the novel. What mode of fiction will give an authentic purchase on reality? The critic of the novel faces a related question. What handle should the critic use to get hold of this novel, or, to vary the metaphor, what pathway should he follow to enter it so that he can reach its deepest recesses, find out the center of its labyrinth of echoing words? How can the critic speak authoritatively of it?

The system of thematic imagery, for example, which organizes in its recurrences this novel, is a traditional pattern of original light and reflected light, of golden sun and silver moon. The sun is the chief source of light. All other lights are secondary, pale reflections of that king and father light. The latter is an image of the transcendent and divine power. This system of imagery is introduced at the beginning of the novel, when Henry first encounters Rachel. She appears to him in the way Venus appeared to Aeneas, as a *Dea certe:* "Her golden hair was shining in the gold of the sun" (bk. I, ch. 1).[3] Later, the images are shifted to Beatrix, just as Henry's desire is displaced from mother to daughter: "Mrs. Beatrix could no more help using her eyes than the sun can help shining, and setting those it shines on a-burning" (bk. II, ch. 15); "There were times when this creature was so handsome, that she seemed, as it were, like Venus revealing herself a goddess in a flash of brightness. She appeared so now; radiant, and with eyes bright with wonderful lustre" (bk. III, ch. 9). On the other hand, Beatrix at another time is said to have been the moon, changeable and fickle, "crescent and brilliant," but shining with a borrowed light, and possessed of a "malicious joy" in causing harm (bk. I, ch. 12). She reminded Henry then "of the famous antique statue of the huntress Diana—at one time haughty, rapid, imperious, with eyes and arrows that dart and kill. Harry watched and wondered at this young creature, and likened her in his mind to Artemis with the ringing bow and shafts flashing death upon the children of Niobe; at another time she was coy and melting as Luna shining tenderly upon Endymion" (bk. I, ch. 12). Which is she, sun or moon, and what does it mean to say that she is either?

Throughout the novel Rachel, Beatrix, and other characters are measured by their relations to this solar-lunar polarity. This often occurs in unostentatious ways. Lord Mohun's name, for example, echoes in its pronunciation the word "moon" and indicates his role as a false pretender to power over the members of Esmond's family. "Esmond" also echoes "moon." It ends in the syllable that means "moon" in German. Is this a senseless accident or does it have meaning? The question, throughout, is the following: Which character may be legitimately described as genuine gold, true sun? Who is possessor of intrinsic worth allowing him or her to rule as sovereign over the others? Who is qualified by divine right to serve as the model for others, as the source of their reflected light or transfused value?

If the reader turns to the political theme of the novel, the issue is the same one in displaced form. Thackeray has placed the story of his alter ego, "a handsome likeness of an ugly son of yours," as he wrote to his mother,[4] in the period of political turmoil in England in the late seventeenth and early eighteenth centuries. During this period there was a multiple shift in dynasties, from the Stuarts to the House of Orange, then to the Hanoverian kings. The political question during all that time was a double one: What is the true source of kingship, and how, having established that, can one distinguish the true from the false pretenders to sovereignty? The clearest statement in *Henry Esmond* of the alternatives comes when Henry is about to lose his Stuart allegiance, his faith in the Pretender, and his belief in divine right at the same moment that he loses his infatuation with Beatrix. The political drama of the book is Henry's shift from the Stuarts to a "Whig" liberalism, "the manly creed . . . that scouts the old doctrine of right divine, that boldly declares that Parliament and people consecrate the Sovereign, not bishops, nor genealogies, nor oils, nor coronations" (bk. III, ch. 9). Thackeray, we know, had read carefully Macaulay's *History of England.* His novel reaffirms Macaulay's Whig interpretation of English history. For Macaulay the bloodless revolution of 1688 was the decisive event making modern "democratic" England possible.

If Henry's love for Beatrix parallels his belief in the Pretender, the family level of the novel parallels both the political level and the level of material motifs. On the family level too the search is for a true source of authority. It too is a question of legitimacy. Who is the genuine heir to the Castlewood title and by what right does he hold that title? How can Henry take his rightful place in the genealogical line? The novel traces the clear design of what Freud calls a "family romance," an Oedipal story in which the son replaces the father and takes the father's place in the mother's bed. The pattern is all the clearer for being repeated in different forms and in different generations. *Henry Esmond* expresses with great power a tangle of family feelings, for example the mixture of filial devotion, brotherly love, religious worship, and veiled sexual desire in Henry's love for Rachel: "No voice so sweet," as he says, when they are reconciled after the estrangement caused by his participation in the duel that kills Rachel's husband, "as that of his beloved mistress, who had been sister, mother, goddess to him during his youth—goddess now no more, for he knew of her weaknesses; and by thought, by suffering, and that experience it brings, was older now than she; but more fondly cherished as woman perhaps than ever she had been adored as divinity . . . And as a brother folds a sister to his heart; and as a mother cleaves to her son's breast—so for a few moments Esmond's beloved mistress came to him and blessed him" (bk. II, ch. 6).

By what right and by whose authority does Henry marry his "mother" and displace his "father"? Henry begins by seeking paternal or maternal authority in others. He ends by taking sovereignty upon himself, as the husband of Rachel and as the absolute ruler of his little kingdom of Castlewood in Virginia. The political and familial levels of the text converge when Frank Castlewood says of the Stuart Pretender, "He is not like a king: somehow, Harry, I fancy you are like a king" (bk. III, ch. 9). If the political drama of the novel is Henry's shift from royalist to Whig, the family drama is his shift from "worship" of Rachel or

Beatrix to allowing Rachel to worship him, after he has abdicated his rightful claim to be Viscount Castlewood in favor of Rachel's son Frank: " 'Don't raise me,' she said, in a wild way, to Esmond, who would have lifted her. 'Let me kneel—let me kneel, and—and—worship you' " (bk. III, ch. 2).

To mention Oedipus is to introduce the final stratum of repetition in this novel—all its references to earlier texts. These references keep before the reader's mind the fact that *Henry Esmond* is only the latest link in a chain going back to *Oedipus Rex* and to certain Old Testament versions of the "family romance," for example the story of Jacob and Esau. Which of these stories has authority over the others? Which is the archetype on which all are modeled? Is it the Oedipus story, as Freud was later to argue, and as the crucial function of references to Oedipus in *Henry Esmond* would seem to argue was the case for Thackeray too? What would it mean, for this particular novel, or indeed generally, to say that Oedipus is the type of mankind, that Henry Esmond, without knowing it or wishing it, repeats the life story of Oedipus? What authority does this story have for Thackeray, and what does it have to say about the search for genuine authority?

To enter *Henry Esmond* by any of these routes is to confront ultimately the same question. What is the basis of legitimate sovereignty? To try to identify the answer the novel provides, it may be useful to take a somewhat circuitous route to the goal. This route goes by way of the identification of certain assumptions operative in all of Thackeray's work. Thackeray's starting place as a novelist is double: an assumption about styles of narration and an assumption about the human self whose vicissitudes are to be explored by way of imaginary replicas in those narrations. On this double presupposition all Thackeray's work as a novelist is superposed. These assumptions are exposed in two of his earliest works, published in *Punch: Novels by Eminent Hands* (originally *Punch's Prize Novelists*) (1844–45), and *The Book of Snobs* (1846–47).

Novels by Eminent Hands is a series of comic and maliciously accurate parodies of popular novelists of the day: Bulwer, Disraeli, G. P. R. James, Cooper, and so on. Along with Max Beerbohm's *A Christmas Garland* (1912) and Proust's *Pastiches et mélanges*

(1919), they are the best such parodies in existence. Parody is a form of homage. It is also a form of literary criticism. In a master's "hands" it is one of the sharpest tools of insight and discrimination. The mode of parody is irony. By a slightly or grossly hyperbolic accentuation of stylistic features in the original, the parodist calls attention to those features and at the same time dismantles them by revealing their artificiality. Though the parodist may ridicule the style he parodies in the name of some proper style which he knows or for which he searches, his success as a parodist, as the parodies multiply, tends to suggest that there is no natural or "true" style. Any style, it would seem, can be undermined by parody. The parodist knows that a given story might be told in this style or in that style, though the style would determine to some degree the meaning the story would have. "Novels by Eminent Hands"—the title itself is a joke. It suggests that the novels were not written with the minds of their authors but were in their stylistic features produced unconsciously by craftsmen so trained in certain modes of narration that they are no longer the result of choice or thought. The books were written by hands working detached from bodies and brains, as the distinctive features of a man's handwriting or signature are not in his control.

This arbitrariness of the styles and conventions of narration remained one of Thackeray's constant assumptions. In the first edition of *Vanity Fair,* for example, in a passage often discussed, the narrator pauses at one point to say that the episode he is about to relate could be told in any one of a number of styles. He then proceeds to tell it first in the style of the "Silver Fork" novels, then in the style of the "Newgate" novels. Though these parodies were removed from subsequent editions of *Vanity Fair,* their corrosive implications remain latent within it. Once an author has reached the point of seeing any style of narration as artificial, it is difficult to return from that insight to claim, "I am now going to tell my story in the true, natural, unaffected style, without the falsification of any conventions." The parodist undermines his own enterprise. Whatever style he adopts is hollowed out by irony. He becomes his own parody, possessed only, in whatever mode he talks or writes, of the ventriloquist's gift for talking or writing as someone else.

This acute consciousness of the artifice in any literary language is evident also in Thackeray's habit, particularly in his early comic work, of adopting one pseudonym or another. Like Stendhal, Thackeray was a great inventor of pseudonyms and of the person and style to go with each invented name. At various times he wrote under the names of Theophile Wagstaff, Major Goliah Gahagan, Michael Angelo Titmarsh, George Savage Fitz-Boodle, Mr. Snob, and Mr. Charles James Yellowplush. The latter is an illiterate footman who in his turn adopts a nom de plume, a pseudonym within a pseudonym: C. Jeames de la Pluche. *Pendennis* is a first-person novel written as if by an imagined character, and later works like *The Newcomes* and *Philip* are presented as if written by Pendennis. Thackeray, it seems, had an aversion to writing in his own name. The implications of this penchant for pseudonymy are somewhat similar for Thackeray as for Stendhal. The man who takes a pseudonym, it may be assumed, has some doubt about who he is. He does not feel that he coincides wholly with himself, or with the given name and the patronymic which he wears before the world. He may find who he is by pretending to be someone else, by taking another name, another style, and wearing them as one wears a new suit of clothes on the assumption that "clothes make the man." The man who lives under a pseudonym, like the parodist, at once makes fun of the role he plays and at the same time uses it, he hopes, to express obliquely some aspect of himself, or perhaps to take on a self where there was none before if the name and habit should happen to stick. *Henry Esmond,* like *Pendennis,* or even like *Vanity Fair* (where Thackeray plays the role of the sad clown at the fair as well as of various other narrating personae), is continuous with the pseudonymous comic works. To the list of Thackeray's pseudonyms may be added Henry Esmond. Henry Esmond is a role Thackeray plays, a mask he wears, a name he goes by momentarily in the search by its detour to return to himself.

The Book of Snobs gives the other face of the double presupposition which underlies all Thackeray's work, or rather undermines it, since it is the presupposition of a lack of underlying support. It is two-faced also in being deceptive, duplicitous, like a double mask with no face behind it. *The Book of Snobs* is a series of sketches of various sorts of "snobs": military snobs, clerical snobs, university snobs, literary snobs, and so on. The full title of the book is *The Book of Snobs, By One of Themselves.* It takes a snob to know a snob. Just as the narrator of *Vanity Fair* does not exclude himself from the foolish vanity of the characters whose stories he tells, but is shown by the illustrator (Thackeray himself) in cap and bells looking with melancholy admiration at his own image in the mirror he holds in his hand, so no one can understand the mechanism of snobbery unless he is himself a snob. The deconstructive analysis of the mechanism of snobbery, such as the one performed by "Mr. Snob" in *The Book of Snobs,* does not liberate the analyzer from snobbery. It keeps him still implicated, since the analysis of snobbery in others, however clear-sighted and disillusioned, involves by that very fact the claim of superiority which is precisely one of the symptoms of snobbery. This double bind may not be by any means untied. To unknot it in one place makes a new knot somewhere else. On a large scale and in a more complex way, *Henry Esmond* is structured as just such another double bind, as I shall try to show. "You must not judge hastily or vulgarly of Snobs," says their anatomist: "to do so shows that you are yourself a Snob. I myself have been taken for one."[5] In fact the first of the two papers on "Literary Snobs" has a picture to match the one in *Vanity Fair.* It is illustrated with a sketch by Thackeray showing the author as Mr. Punch, with a big nose and a Napoleon hat, carefully copying on a tablet on his lap his own reflection in a mirror.

The Book of Snobs shows Thackeray's extreme sensitivity to what in our day has been called "mediated desire,"[6] the psychological mechanism whereby desire is never direct but always routed through the desire of someone else whose authority authenticates my desire. If he or she finds something desirable it must be worth having, but without the help of another I cannot tell what I should want to have or to do. I desire only what is desirable to others, or, in Thackeray's definition, "He who meanly admires mean things is a Snob" (p. 11).

The universal domination of snobbery, in the society Thackeray describes, follows from the absence of a true authority which can measure things according to an absolute standard of desirability. Thackeray's characters, as he says of those in *Vanity Fair*, are "a set of people living without God in the world."[7] That other person whose mean admirations I meanly copy is put by me in the place of God in a world without God, or in a world which has put itself outside God's help. It is impossible to know from Thackeray's phrasing or indeed from his work in general which of these quite different propositions he meant to affirm. Perhaps he meant to affirm both at once in an oscillating indecision. This indecision is focused on the word "without," which can mean either "outside of" or "entirely lacking." Since no other person has the right or the substance to play god in a world without God, mediated desire is always "mean," base and hypocritical, deceptive and self-deceptive. Its hollowness is proved, unhappily, more in possession than in unassuaged coveting. What I do not have and what others have or find desirable I want, but when I finally get it, it instantly loses the golden glow which had been reflected on it by the admiration of others. It or he or she becomes revealed in all its meanness and drabness, its lack of intrinsic value. This is Thackeray's melancholy or even "nihilistic" final wisdom. It is nihilistic in the precise sense in which the word is defined, for example, by Friedrich Nietzsche, as the devaluation of all values and their reduction to nought, *nihil*, nothing.[8]

The end of *Vanity Fair* provides the best and best-known formulation of this sad insight. It is an insight which, characteristically, calls on the Bible for its authority, according to that law whereby it is much easier to say something really dark if I can blame it on someone else, particularly on someone of acknowledged authority: "Ah! *Vanitas Vanitatum!* which of us is happy in this world? Which of us has his desire? or, having it, is satisfied?"[9] *Henry Esmond* also exemplifies this melancholy wisdom, not only in the large-scale story of Henry's disillusionment but in such episodes as the description of the way Beatrix is admired by each court buck just because she is admired by the others. In *Henry Esmond*, too, "There's some particular prize we all of us value, and that every man of spirit will venture his life for" (bk. III, ch. 2), but this prize is, precisely, an *idol*, a thing of no intrinsic value into which value has been projected: " 'tis I that have fixed the value of the thing I would have, and know the price I would pay for it" (bk. III, ch. 2), for, "Who, in the course of his life, hath not been so bewitched, and worshipped some idol or another?" (bk. III, ch. 6). *Henry Esmond* too is based on a mournful insight into the brevity and nullity of human life: "So night and day pass away, and to-morrow comes, and our place knows us not" (bk. III, ch. 6).

Parody, pseudonymy, and snobbery are names of starting places for Thackeray's work. He never abandons these or goes beyond them. They cannot in fact be gone beyond, since it is their nature to inhibit movement, except in place. Neither Thackeray nor his critic goes beyond the beginning; they execute a circular trajectory returning to the starting point, perhaps with better understanding of it, perhaps not. That remains to be seen.

I now turn to a description of the exact form that trajectory takes in *Henry Esmond.* What makes the line the reader knows already. They are the connections which can be made, the lines which can be drawn, intrinsic and extrinsic, among the various repeating elements I have identified: material motifs of sun, moon, blood, stars; the political theme of legitimacy; familial patterns; literary allusions. Those lines differ, however, depending on who draws them: Henry himself; "Thackeray," who stands as an ironic shadow behind Henry; the critic who traces the line once more in one way or another in his interpretation.

My image of the line is justified by Henry's use of it in his own language about himself. Speaking, in anticipation, of Beatrix's thoughtless words to her father about Lord Mohun, words which precipitate the duel in which the father, Castlewood, is killed ("I think my Lord [Mohun] would rather marry Mamma than marry me; and is waiting till you die to ask her"; bk. I, ch. 13) Henry says: "There is scarce any thoughtful man or woman, I suppose, but can look back upon his course of past life, and remember some point, trifling as it may have seemed at the time of occurrence, which has nevertheless turned and altered his whole career" (bk. I, ch. 12). Henry's life is a course or career. It is a line which is marked by various crucial points where the line turned. It also contains some gaps, sudden leaps which change that life. These were breaks which made a hiatus in his life. Over these his life jumped, and over them the retrospective narration must jump too in order to trace out the whole line. Henry uses this figure of the gap to speak of his year in prison for his participation in the duel in which Francis Castlewood is killed:

> At certain periods of life we live years of emotion in a few weeks—and look back on those times, as on great gaps between the old life and the new. You do not know how much you suffer in those critical maladies of the heart, until the disease is over and you look back on it afterwards. During the time, the suffering is at least sufferable. The day passes in more or less of pain, and the night wears away somehow. 'Tis only in after days that we see what the danger has been—as a man out a-hunting or riding for his life looks at a leap, and wonders how he should have survived the taking of it. (Bk. II, ch. 1)

This drawing of a line between point and point to make a pattern may be thought of, according to terms provided by the novel, either as the construction of a discursive memory or as the drawing of a true portrait. My emblematic use of the portrait is justified by the many references to portraits in the novel and by the symbolic value they are clearly meant to have.[10] There are, for example, several references to a portrait by Lely of the Dowager Lady Isabella Castlewood as Diana, "in yellow satin, with a bow in her hand and a crescent in her forehead; and dogs frisking about her" (bk. II, ch. 3). If Isabella, the wife of Henry's father, is Diana, so also is Beatrix repeatedly called Diana. Beatrix repeats her aunt, in nature and in role. Each becomes, or in Beatrix's case, almost becomes, a royal mistress, Isabella of Charles the Second, Beatrix of that poor king, no king, James the Third, the luckless Stuart Pretender.

The first appearance of the motif of the portrait applies to Henry himself. In the "Preface" by Henry's daughter Rachel Esmond Warrington, she writes: "I wish I possessed the art of drawing (which my papa had in perfection), so that I could leave to our descendants a portrait of one who was so good and so respected." The first pages of Henry's narration turn on the distinction between the idealized Louis the Fourteenth or Queen Anne as portrayed masked in grandeur by "the Muse of History" and the real king, "a little wrinkled old man, pock-marked, and with a great periwig and red heels to make him look tall," or the real Queen, "a hot, red-faced woman, not in the least resembling that statue of her which turns its stone back upon St. Paul's, and faces the coaches struggling up Ludgate Hill" (bk. I, Preface). Henry's implicit claim is that he has portrayed others accurately. Putting his art of picturing under the aegis of the "familiar" history of "Mr. Hogarth and Mr. Fielding" (bk. I, Preface), he also claims that he has drawn that accurate portrait of himself for which his daughter calls. He has "the art of drawing . . . in perfection" with words as well as with the sketching pencil.

The reference to Hogarth and Fielding alerts the knowing reader to what Thackeray's prototypes are for the technique of emblematic allusion he uses throughout *Henry Esmond.* Thackeray, like Dickens, begins with the eighteenth-century tradition of graphic and literary art as chief model for a technique of ironic analogy, achieving complex resonance through uninterpreted juxtaposition. An example is the scene in which Henry sees tiles of Jacob cheating Esau of his birthright in the bagnio where Castlewood dies from the wound he has received in the duel. A parallel is clearly intended, but Henry presents those tiles merely as vividly remembered fact. Such juxtapositions are a basic resource of Hogarth's art.

The means of Henry's supposedly accurate self-portrait is the putting together of such remembered images. Their validity lies in the fact that he remembers them. It is a basic presupposition of Henry's narrative of his life that he not only remembers it all but remembers it accurately. The novel is punctuated by the description of scenes, always involving images of light, which Henry claims are imprinted on his memory with extraordinary vividness and accuracy. These moments are the burning points of the narrative. They are its turning points too, bright spots of time between which the narrative is run, like the dots in the child's game which, connected by lines, reveal a pattern, a duck, a rabbit, or a face. To cite these passages seriatim once more (as they have often been cited in other essays discussing the theme of memory in *Henry Esmond*) is to indicate the key moments through which the narration is articulated as Henry "at the close of his life . . . sits and recalls in tranquillity the happy and busy scenes of it" (bk. I, ch. 7).

The phrasing in the last quotation indicates the Wordsworthian nature of Henry's enterprise. The emotions of the past are not felt at the time the narration is composed but are recollected in tranquillity. They are created again in another form by the words of the narration. They are recreated in a way they never existed at the time, since they are given in recollection. They are also given in the light of Henry's mature demystified vision and in the light of his insight into the system of repetitions which makes his life a pattern, a portrait.

Each of these remembered images is double, even triple or quadruple. It is given as it was at the time or as Henry thinks it was at the time, bathed in the emotions of the time, according to that Wordsworthian definition of the poetic imagination as the creation, on the basis of a state of tranquillity, of emotions appropriate to the images remembered. But how can one be sure that is in fact the way one felt at the time? Each image is also given in the secondary light of Henry's disillusioned interpretation of it, in his old age. The law of this double remembering is formulated in one place as follows: " 'Tis not to be imagined that Harry Esmond had all this experience at this early stage of his life, whereof he is now writing the history—many things here noted were but known to him in later days. Almost everything Beatrix did or undid seemed good, or at least pardonable, to him then, and years afterwards" (bk. I, ch. 12). The mark on the text of the discrepancy between the old Esmond and the young is the way he speaks of his young self in the third person, while he often uses "I" to speak of his old self in the present time of the writing down. The doubleness of all the remembered images lies in the gap between "he" and "I." Occasionally he uses "I" to speak of his young self, just as he occasionally drops into the present tense, the "historical present," for his narrative of past events, obliterating, for the moment, the distinction between past and present, "he" and "I." The effect of the historical present is hardly that of unmediated presentness. Its artifice calls attention to itself. It presents everything as image or phantasm, as an artifice of presentness brought back from the past by the words on the page, as a cinematic image is always present, though it is not to be mistaken for reality. The affirmed immediacy only increases the distance, the fictionalized effect:

> "How stupid your friend Mr. Steele becomes!" cries Miss Beatrix. "Epsom and Tunbridge! Will he never have done with Epsom and Tunbridge, and with beaux at church, and Jocastas and Lindamiras? Why does he not call women Nelly and Betty, as their godfathers and godmothers did for them in their baptism?"
>
> "Beatrix, Beatrix!" says her mother, "speak gravely of grave things." (Bk. III, ch. 3)

For the most part, Henry uses the past tense and the third person to tell his story. The effect of talking of one's past self in the third person, past tense, as a "he," is odd. It brings to the surface the fact that remembering is a kind of role-playing which hollows out the role that is played by repeating it with more or less irony. The present "I" plays the role of the past self who no longer exists. "He" is seen from the outside as another, but he can nevertheless, such is the power of memory, be played again, from the inside, with complete intimacy. We have in real life the kind of relation to our past selves, it may be, that a novelist writing as a third-person omniscient narrator has to his protagonist. By conflating the two modes here, the first-person autobiographical novel and third-person narration, Thackeray brings this similarity into the open. The "he" his "I" uses for young Henry is a sign for the difference and distance between the old Henry and the young. At the same time, it is an emblem of the way the novel is generated through Thackeray's performative act of playing the roles of both the young Henry and the old, both the "he" and the "I," in a phantasmal further doubling of that doubling.

If the phantom presence of Thackeray himself in each of the memory passages gives them a third level of significance, the fourth presence within them is the superimposition on each, as a kind of ghostly many-layered veil, of all the other similar passages. This occurs through the repetition in each of the same motifs. As each of these passages follows the last, they gradually accumulate into a resonating line of similar configurations, each echoing all the others and drawing its meaning from that echoing as much as from the intrinsic doubling of the combined perspectives of old Henry and young Henry which structures each taken separately. The meaning of this echoing is its affirmation that Henry's life hangs together. His life has meaning because the same elements recur in it and give it a total design justifying the drawing of a line connecting each part to all the others.

Here are the main members of the series, each with its quadruple perspective built into it. To cite them is to cite in miniature the whole book, since each concentrates in synecdochic focus one episode of Henry's life as he remembers it:

> To the very last hour of his life, Esmond remembered the lady as she then spoke and looked, the rings on her fair hands, the very scent of her robe, the beam of her eyes lighting up with surprise and kindness, her lips blooming in a smile, the sun making a golden halo round her hair. (Bk. I, ch. 1)

> How those trivial incidents and words, the landscape and sunshine, and the group of people smiling and talking, remained fixed on the memory! (Bk. I, ch. 1)

> Esmond long remembered how she looked and spoke, kneeling reverently before the sacred book, the sun shining upon her golden hair until it made a halo round about her. (Bk. I, ch. 7)

> Indeed, he scarce seemed to see until she was gone; and then her image was impressed upon him, and remained for ever fixed upon his memory. He saw her retreating, the taper lighting up her marble face, her scarlet lip quivering, and her shining golden hair. (Bk. I, ch. 8)

> And Harry remembered, all his life after, how he saw his mistress at the window looking out on him in a white robe, the little Beatrix's chestnut curls resting at her mother's side. (Bk. I, ch. 9)

He saw Lady Castlewood looking through the curtains of the great window of the drawing-room overhead, at my Lord as he stood regarding the fountain. There was in the court a peculiar silence somehow; and the scene remained long in Esmond's memory:—the sky bright overhead; the buttresses of the building and the sun-dial casting shadow over the gilt *memento mori* inscribed underneath; the two dogs, a black greyhound and a spaniel nearly white, the one with his face up to the sun, and the other snuffing amongst the grass and stones, and my Lord leaning over the fountain, which was bubbling audibly. 'Tis strange how that scene, and the sound of that fountain, remain fixed on the memory of a man who has beheld a hundred sights of splendour, and danger too, of which he has kept no account. (Bk. I, ch. 14)

Esmond went to the fire, and threw the paper into it. 'Twas a great chimney with glazed Dutch tiles. How we remember such trifles in such awful moments! . . . On the Dutch tiles at the bagnio was a rude picture representing Jacob in hairy gloves, cheating Isaac of Esau's birthright. The burning paper lighted it up. (Bk. I, ch. 14)

Her words as she spoke struck the chords of all his memory, and the whole of his boyhood and youth passed within him. (Bk. II, ch. 1)

'Tis forty years since Mr. Esmond witnessed those scenes, but they remain as fresh in his memory as on the day when first he saw them as a young man. (Bk. II, ch. 5)

They walked out, hand-in-hand, through the old court, and to the terrace-walk, where the grass was glistening with dew, and the birds in the green woods above were singing their delicious choruses under the blushing morning sky. How well all things were remembered! The ancient towers and gables of the Hall darkling against the east, the purple shadows on the green slopes, the quaint devices and carvings of the dial, the forest-crowned heights, the fair yellow plain cheerful with crops and corn, the shining river rolling through it towards the pearly hills beyond; all these were before us, along with a thousand beautiful memories of our youth, beautiful and sad, but as real and vivid in our minds as that fair and always-remembered scene our eyes beheld once more. We forget nothing. The memory sleeps, but wakens again; I often

> think how it shall be when, after the last sleep of death, the *reveillée* shall arouse us for ever, and the past in one flash of self-consciousness rush back, like the soul revivified. (Bk. III, ch. 7)

Esmond's narration presupposes and affirms a set of interrelated assumptions about memory. These assumptions form a system. Esmond's memory is strongly affective. He remembers not only the scenes but the emotions he believes he felt at that moment and which he feels again in reimagining the scene as he writes it down. His memory is primarily visual, but it mingles the other senses too in reinforcement of sight. He remembers the scent of a robe, the sound of a fountain bubbling, though there are, in the passages I have cited, no references to touch or to taste. In fact Esmond's memory (perhaps Thackeray's also) is not, like Proust's for example, strongly gustatory, nor is it tactile. Esmond remembers seemingly "trivial" details with extraordinary vividness. He says they are trivial, and that his memory has "taken no account" of scenes far more important, but it is obvious that these "trivial" details are significant, emblematic. They stand for the crucial relationships of his life, those to Rachel, those to Rachel's husband. In spite of Henry's decade of infatuation with Beatrix and the elaborately circumstantial narration of his unhappy courtship of her, none of the passages I have cited has to do centrally with Beatrix. Henry's "Fate," to use a word and a concept which often recur in his self-interpretation, is ultimately to marry Rachel and to live happily ever after. This is the significance of all these trivial details and of the vividness with which they, out of all possible details, remain fixed in his memory. They were prophetic signs, prolepses of his ultimate destiny.

Though Henry seems to be affirming here something like the Proustian doctrine of the intermittences of the heart and of the heart's affective memory, so that some things are remembered, but most forgotten, and memory is a series of vivid bright spots with the darkness of irremediable forgetting between, in fact Thackeray's doctrine of memory here is quite different from Proust's. Each trivial detail stands for a crucial moment in Esmond's relation to Rachel. Each is a pause in the forward movement of time, a missed heartbeat, so to speak, which remains hovering, cut off from the flow of before and after. Each is a static image, fixed on his memory, space here standing for time. The trivial detail, by a species of synecdoche, stands for the whole scene and gives Henry access to it. The whole scene, in turn, by another synecdoche, spatial panorama standing for temporal sequence, gives him possession of all his life. Place is the repository of memory, of a total memory which omits nothing and regathers all, with complete accuracy, as the circumstantial narration of what comes between each of these scenes and the next indicates. When Henry and Rachel walk out before Castlewood in the last of the passages I have quoted, they see not only all the details of the whole scene but, by means of them, all the details of the past: "all these were before us, along with a thousand beautiful memories of our youth, beautiful and sad, but as real and vivid in our minds as that fair and always-remembered scene our eyes beheld once more."

The latter passage indicates another important feature of Henry's memory and of these remembered scenes. Each stands by itself as a self-enclosed fixed image inscribed on the screen of Henry's total recall, each next to the others, like the pictures side by side in an Italian Renaissance fresco of scenes from a saint's life. At the same time, as the memories accumulate through time, each contains at the time it occurs echoes of the ones before. Henry's present memory is a memory of memories within a memory. It juxtaposes not only the present and a past time, but the past past times which were remembered when that past was present. Of each, except the first in the series, Henry could say what he says of the words of accusation Rachel speaks when she visits him in prison after the death of her husband. Each image is in resonance with all the others and calls them up, as "her words . . . struck all the chords of his memory, and the whole of his boyhood and youth passed within him." If Henry's memory is a spatial panorama of fixed pictures side by side, it is also a musical instrument with strings in tune at different pitches. To pluck one is to make them all vibrate.

Even the first encounter with Rachel is in more than one way a repetition. It is already a memory, jangling the strings of previous entities it echoes. Henry first sees Rachel (whose name is already a Biblical reference) in the portrait gallery at Castlewood, where hangs the portrait of Rachel's predecessor, Isabella, as Diana the huntress. Henry sees Rachel as a duplication of another "Dea certe," Venus appearing to Aeneas, "remembering," as he says, even in the intensity of his immediate response to his first glimpse of Rachel, "the lines of the Aeneis which Mr. Holt had taught him" (bk. I, ch. 7). No doubt, beyond that, as the echo of the *Aeneid* suggests, Henry's reaction to Rachel is spontaneously to treat her as a replacement for his real mother, Thomas Esmond's first Flemish wife. That real mother he does not remember at all ("for even his memory had no recollection of her"; bk. II, ch. 13), and she is long dead when he visits her grave in Flanders. Rachel fills the void created by her loss. Moreover, the first encounter with Rachel already echoes Henry's first encounter with Isabella. The latter occurred earlier, but is given later, since Henry begins his narration with his first vision of Rachel, as though that were the true beginning of his life, the origin of the fateful line his life has followed. He then circles back to describe what had preceeded that first encounter, the period of his life when he lived with his actual father, Thomas Castlewood, and was page to that father's wife Isabella. The first meeting with Isabella contains many of the same elements as the first meeting with Rachel. It is a grotesque artificial parody of that meeting. It occurred before but is presented after. This reversal obscures the fact that Henry's first meeting with Rachel is already a repetition, not a solid origin at all. What Isabella tries to be by painting herself, Rachel genuinely is. Or is she? Henry does not always think so. When he finally marries Rachel she, like everyone else except himself, has long since been bereft of divinity for him. The sun, the scent, the rings, eyes, the color gold, and the color red (lips in one case, petticoat, heels, and rouge in the other) occur in both first encounters. Here is Henry's first vision of Isabella:

> Indeed, the chamber was richly ornamented in the manner of Queen Elizabeth's time, with great stained windows at either end, and hangings of tapestry, which the sun shining through the col-

oured glass painted of a thousand hues; and here in state, by the fire, sate a lady, to whom the priest took up Harry, who was indeed amazed by her appearance.

My Lady Viscountess's face was daubed with white and red up to the eyes, to which the paint gave an unearthly glare . . . She wore a dress of black velvet, and a petticoat of flame-coloured brocade. She had as many rings on her fingers as the old woman of Banbury Cross; and pretty small feet which she was fond of showing, with great gold clocks to her stockings, and white pantofles with red heels; and an odour of musk was shook out of her garments whenever she moved or quitted the room. (Bk. I, ch. 3)[11]

Each episode in Henry's memory, then, is always, strangely, a memory within a memory, never, in spite of its sensuous vividness and quality of immediate presence, only the recovery of an immediate presence. Even when it occurred the "first" time it was always already also a repetition. No originating first is recoverable, neither the first of fulfilled possession nor that of some traumatic loss which makes Henry, like his creator, like all men and women, it may be, creatures of unassuaged and unassuageable desire. That "first" moment of loss Henry can never give as such.

A final peculiarity of Henry's memory is the key element in the system, making the other features possible. This is the way Henry characteristically speaks of himself as if he were already dead. He views his past life from beyond the grave, from a point where the series is apparently complete, so that no more items may be added to change it. Until a man or woman is dead, something may happen to him or to her, he or she may do something which will change utterly the meaning of the long line of events which make up his or her life. The manner of a person's death, for example by suicide, has strikingly this power. Henry speaks repeatedly as if it were no longer possible for him to change the meaning of his life by adding a new episode to the series. The last element has been added, the line has been drawn, the portrait is complete, and Henry can look back at it from outside life entirely, seeing it as a perfected pattern. He claims to view it with complete objectivity, as if he were God or a resurrected soul joined to God: "To the very last hour of his life, Esmond remembered"; "her image was impressed upon him, and remained forever fixed upon his memory"; "And Harry remembered, all his life after." How can he know yet about the last hour of his life or about whether something is to last all his life, unless he is already dead?

The final image Henry gives of his memory in the series quoted above is the most important, the one that authenticates all its other qualities of accuracy, vividness, completeness, and totalizing meaning. His memory is the sort of total instantaneous recall, he says, we shall have after we have died and have been born again in heaven, when "the *reveillée* shall rouse us for ever, and the past in one flash of self-consciousness rush back, like the soul revivified." This is the function of the convention whereby Henry speaks of himself in the third person, as though he were the "omniscient narrator" of someone else's life. The old Henry, writing his memoirs or his "history" in Virginia, claims to be able to view his past self as though he saw it with godlike perfection of knowledge.

What that view is, the portrait that gradually emerges, as the line is drawn from one bright spot to the next, can be resketched here. Henry begins his life as a "nameless bastard" (bk. II, ch. 8), in the state of need, desire, and abandonment he shares with his great prototype Oedipus. He seeks to find a name, a self, and a place in the world by discovering a legitimate authority in the world justified in giving him these securities. He seeks someone he can worship, someone like a king (or a queen), someone ruling by divine right, like a deity. He makes this search both in the political world and in the social one. He shifts from Rachel to Beatrix and puts his political faith first in James the Second, then in the Pretender, the second of each pair doubling the first in parody, just as Rachel already doubles Isabella and both double Henry's lost mother. Henry seeks everywhere some idol worthy of worship. He seeks someone who will have power to endow him with substance, with value, as a coin passes current when the king's countenance is stamped on it, or as the sun gives life to that on which it shines.

Henry's gradual discovery is that nothing and nobody outside himself are worth his worship. No one has the right to play the role of God to him in a world without God. Whatever golden luster this or that person has seemed to him to have—Rachel, or Beatrix, or that shabby prince—has been projected on them by Henry himself. The activity of Henry's narration, in relation to other people, is a process of unveiling, as he shows the tawdriness and vanity, the lack of intrinsic worth, in one person after another. The emblem of this process of demystification is that opening example of the undressing of the royal protrait of Louis the Fourteenth as Sun King. Henry reveals the little wrinkled old man underneath, pock-marked, with a great periwig and red heels to make him look tall.

Having undressed everyone else, having divested them all, one by one, of the auras they have seemed to have in his infatuated young eyes, Henry does not take the next step and undress also himself. He refuses to see that he, the emperor, also has no clothes. "De te fabula." He fails to see the relevance to himself of the epigraph from Horace for the imitation *Spectator* paper he writes attacking Beatrix. Having found nothing outside himself worthy of his worship, in the end he complacently allows others to kneel down and worship him. He takes his place as the head of the Esmond family, replaces all those who have been father-figures to him, marries the woman who has been in the place of a mother to him, and ends his life as the "king" of the new Castlewood in Virginia, revered by wife, children, servants, and slaves, the omnipotent sovereign of his own little kingdom. This he contrives to do without any apparent sense of guilt and without any awareness that he has been other than magnanimous and self-sacrificing, that he has ever been in the wrong.

He even manages to have it both ways in relation to the social sanction of his name and place. He discovers that his father had indeed married his mother and that far from being a "nameless bastard" he is the rightful heir to the Castlewood title. He is truly "the Right Honourable the Lord Viscount Castlewood," and Frank Castlewood only holds the title on his sufferance. He generously renounces his claim to the title in favor of Rachel's son Frank, burning the paper proving his identity at the same moment that he repudiates both Beatrix, his last amorous infatuation, and the Pretender, his last political mystification. Now he stands free of any belief in others, believing only in himself. At first he keeps secret his generosity in giving up the title, but gradually he lets it out, making sure that everyone knows who he really is. At the same time, since he has renounced the title, he can make good his project of being a self-made man and owing his value and selfhood to no one outside himself. This he expresses repeatedly by saying he intends to "make a name for himself." "If I cannot make a name for myself, I can die without one" (bk. II, ch. 1), he says early in his career. Later he feels that he is no longer a "nameless bastard" but has "won myself a name" (bk. II, ch. 8). Henry has the best of both ways. He is legitimately a nobleman, and so he has not arrogated to himself something society does not grant him the right to have. At the same time he has won himself a name. He is beholden to no one, not even to the family whose blood flows in his veins. He has cut off that genealogical line of succession. He has named himself, so to speak, and stands free of all, above all. He is a self-made man, a symbol of the rising bourgeois. Such is the grand portrait of himself Henry paints, tracing the line from point to point to its happy end in Virginia where Henry is, one might say, already out of this world.

The phantasmal, ironic presence of "Thackeray himself" behind every line Henry writes suffices to erase that line, to obliterate the kinglike protrait, and to draw another portrait in which Henry is indeed, like Louis, divested of poetry and shown to be but a little wrinkled old man, pock-marked. Henry is in fact quite short, as his daughter says in her preface, and his face was of course marked by the small-pox he brought home to the Castlewood household. Thackeray's pervasive irony has filled the text with details which have a double meaning, one ostensibly for Henry, one for the knowing reader. By tracing a new line from one to another of those second meanings, the reader can, if he accepts the author's invitation to do so, not only obliterate Henry's picture of himself, but also trace out the lines of an alternative portrait. The second image ironically doubles the first and undoes it.

Beatrix gives the most explicit sketch of this alternative face when she finally speaks her mind to Henry. She explains her sense of solitude, her jealousy of her mother Rachel, who has never liked her, and the reasons why she can never return Henry's love. Henry can succeed in discounting her unflattering portrait of him only by persuading himself and trying to persuade the reader that she is bad, wayward, untrustworthy, and destructive. In fact she speaks for the darkest insights into the human condition that this "melancholy" book provides. "You are a hypocrite, too, Henry," she says, "with your grave airs and your glum face. We are all hypocrites. O dear me! We are all alone, alone, alone" (bk. III, ch. 3). Later, when she rejects his suit, she says:

> Of all the proud wretches in the world Mr. Esmond is the proudest, let me tell him that. You never fall into a passion, but you never forgive, I think. Had you been a great man, you might have been good-humoured; but being nobody, sir, you are too great a man for me; and I'm afraid of you cousin—there! and I won't worship you, and you'll never be happy except with a woman who will . . . Mamma would have been the wife for you, had you been a little older, though you look ten years older than she does—you do, you glum-faced, blue-bearded little old man! You might have sat, like Darby and Joan, and flattered each other; and billed and cooed like a pair of old pigeons on a perch. (Bk. III, ch. 4)

Every word of this is true. Moreover, it seems to agree with Thackeray's judgment of his hero as we have it on external evidence. Henry is indeed a hypocrite. He has assumed the privilege of judging others, while refusing to judge himself. He pretends self-righteously to be better than he secretly knows he is. Like all the other characters he is alone and cannot, as he tries to do, depend on others to build a complacent and solid image of himself for himself. His self-righteousness does have something to do with the fact that he begins life as nobody. Being nobody, he cannot afford any insouciance. For him it is all or nothing. He therefore is a solemn man, a man without irony. He is indeed a glum-faced, blue-bearded little old man, and he is, as Beatrix says, finally happy only when Rachel worships him, when they flatter each other, like Darby and Joan. Thackeray at various times called Henry Esmond a "bore" and a "prig," "as stately as Sir Charles Grandison."[12] The novel as a whole he called "a book of cutthroat melancholy suitable to my state."[13]

The further outlines of the alternative portrait of Henry which emerge from following ironic double meanings in his self-portrait may be quickly traced. One form of this irony has already been identified. In analyzing the lack of worth of all other people Henry unwittingly provides the reader with the tools by means of which to identify Henry's own lack of worth. What applies universally must apply to him too. This reversal of meaning can be performed with any of the four systems of thematic recurrence which organize the novel.

Henry, for example, discovers that no one outside himself has the radiance of the true sun. He learns that the apparent location of golden solar worth shifts according to his projections of desire. Rachel, once seemingly the true sun, becomes in her turn the moon when Henry's infatuation shifts to Beatrix: "And as, before the blazing sun of morning, the moon fades away in the sky almost invisible, Esmond thought, with a blush perhaps, of another sweet pale face [Rachel's], sad and faint, and fading out of sight, with its sweet fond gaze of affection; such a last look it seemed to cast as Eurydice might have given, yearning after her lover, when Fate and Pluto summoned her, and she passed away into the shades" (bk. II, ch. 9). Applied to Henry, this suggests that any appearance of sovereign worth he has is only projected into him by the admiration of others, for example by Rachel's "worship" of him when they are married and live like Darby and Joan. All light is reflected. There is nowhere any true sun, or genuine gold, or the ontological substance these stand for according to a system of figures going back, in the West, to Plato and the Bible and their precursors. Esmond's name does not contain "moon" (*Mond*) inscribed within it for nothing. He is, like everyone and everything else in this novel, as fickle, as changeable, as secondary, as lacking in intrinsic light as the moon. He shines, like the moon, only with such reflected light as happens to come his way. In Thackeray's implicit deconstruction of the ancient system even the real sun, that light which illuminates the moon, is in its origin secondary. There is no sun in the sense of an independent sovereign head source of light, warmth, and value. There are only mock suns.

The same reversal may be performed with the other recurrent motifs. If there is no king who is not a "pretender," ruling without divine right only on the sufferance of those who have chosen him, then Henry has no right to claim to be the sovereign ruler of his little kingdom in Virginia. If Henry shows that in the social and family realms no man is intrinsically or by birth a nobleman, and no father lords it legitimately over his family, then he has no right to take the place of the father and head of his family, claiming that place both by inheritance of the bloodline and at the same time through his intrinsic merit.

The most elaborate redrawing of Henry's portrait of himself occurs when a different line is charted through all the literary allusions which punctuate the book. These include, as I have said, references to the Bible, to *Oedipus Rex*, to the *Aeneid*, and to *Hamlet.* All these stories are versions of that family romance of which the story of Oedipus is the "archetype," though the story of Rachel, Isaac, Jacob, and Esau is another version of it, as is of course *Hamlet,* and, in another way, the *Aeneid.* In its complete versions, this story involves father, mother, daughter, and son, or two jealous rival sons, like Henry's grandsons, children of that Rachel Esmond Warrington who writes the preface to *Henry Esmond* and so gives the reader the only perspective outside Henry's own as to what Henry was like. The story of those grandchildren is told in a later novel by Thackeray, *The Virginians* (1857–59). Like Eteocles and Polynices in the Oedipus cycle, they took opposite sides in a war, in this case the war for American independence. *The Virginians* demonstrates Thackeray's awareness that the Oedipal cycle was by no means closed by the "happy" ending of *Henry Esmond.*

The role of the Oedipus story as the key to a correct portrayal of Henry is indicated by the imitation *Spectator* paper Henry writes. This placement of the Oedipal story as archetype is already prepared for, near the beginning of the novel, along with an invitation to the reader to watch for puns and double meanings, in a curious interchange between Father Holt and Mrs. Tusher. This interchange occurs at the time of Henry's first meeting with Isabella:

> "Where I'm attached, I'm attached, Madame [says Mrs. Tusher to her mistress, Isabella]—and I'd die rather than not say so."
>
> "*Je meurs où je m'attache,*" Mr. Holt said with a polite grin. "The ivy says so in the picture, and it clings to the oak like a fond parasite as it is."
>
> "Parricide, Sir!" cries Mrs. Tusher. (Bk. I, ch. 3)

Henry is in fact both parasite and parricide. He here unintentionally gives the reader the labels which apply accurately to himself. Henry writes the *Spectator* paper as an attack on Beatrix, casting himself as author of the paper in the role of "Oedipus" and naming Beatrix as a "Jocasta" who is so wayward and inconstant that she has forgotten even the name of one of her suitors. "Can you help us, Mr. Spectator, who know everything, to read this riddle for her, and set at rest all our minds?" asks this "Oedipus" (bk. III, ch. 3). Though Henry puts the "de te fabula" of Horace as an epigraph to the paper, and though he boasts of having an elephant's memory for accuracy and completeness, he has forgotten the way the fable he borrows can be made to apply to himself, just as Lockwood, in *Wuthering Heights,* does not take seriously the imputation of guilt in Branderham's "Thou art the man." Henry, like Lockwood, gives the oracular saying but fails to read the riddle right. The text of the *Spectator* paper gives the reader the elements necessary to make that correct reading. It even indicates the principles on which the reading should be based. As the interchange between Father Holt and Mrs. Tusher depends on a pun whereby parasite and parricide are said implicitly to come to the same thing, since they sound alike, so the *Spectator* paper also turns on puns and double meanings. The paper has to do with a *lapsus,* a forgotten name which has been repressed, and of which Beatrix-Jocasta learns only that it may be spelled either with an "i" or with a "y."

The false *Spectator* paper has two parts. The first section tells the story of the forgotten name objectively and is signed "Oedipus." The second section tells the same story over again in the first person and is signed ostensibly by the man whose name Beatrix has forgotten, Cymon Wyldoats. The double "author" of Henry's *Spectator* paper invites the reader to take it in a double sense, to spell it out in one way according to Henry's intention and in another way according to its application to Henry himself. The *Spectator* paper is an emblem or parable of the way the whole of *Henry Esmond* should be read. When the *Spectator* paper and the novel as a whole are read in this second way, Henry is indeed an Oedipus, but an Oedipus manqué whose eyes remain blinded. He is an Oedipus who never reads the oracles right in their application to himself. He never understands his Oedipal guilt, though he gives the reader, in spite of himself, all the material for a correct reading. Henry means to be speaking of his faithful love for Beatrix when he says to her, "How long was it that Jacob served an apprenticeship for Rachel?" (bk. III, ch. 3). Beatrix and the reader understand that Henry's true Rachel is Rachel Castlewood: " 'For Mamma, ' says Beatrix. 'Is it Mamma your honour wants, and that I should have the happiness of calling you papa?' " (bk. III, ch. 3). In the same way, Henry means Beatrix by Jocasta, but the reader understands that his true Jocasta is Rachel. Like the Biblical Jacob, he has taken possession of a birthright which is not really his, even though it may be legally so, as Jacob has the inheritance legally after Esau has sold it. Like the Biblical Jacob, Henry is self-righteously unscrupulous in his dealings with women, shifting from one to another and hungry for their complete submission, in spite of his willingness to define himself as their humble servant and worshiper.

If Henry ironically repeats Jacob in ways he does not recognize, this is even more true of his relation to Oedipus. Like the Oedipus of the legend, Henry has been responsible for the death of the man who stands in place of a father to him. He ultimately takes that father's place in the bed of the woman who has been a mother to him. The scandalized Victorian reviewers were right to see incestuous implications in the familial and emotional configurations of the novel. Henry is the parasite and upstart who has sprung from a collateral line of his family, even though his father, thinking himself dying, had legally married his mother, whom he had seduced and got with child. This child enters into the domestic enclosure of the family and like a true parasite upsets its economy, causing the death of the father and taking the sexual and material goods of that family to himself. Parasite and parricide, he is the intruder, the upstart usurper, the breaker of the family line.

The secret identity between Henry and Lord Mohun is affirmed not only by their similar functions as intruders alienating the proper affections of the women of the Esmond family, but also in the similarity of their names. Mohun (pronounced "moon") echoes Es*mond*. Both have "Harry" as given names. The significance of this is indicated when things Mohun has done or had done to him are thought to have happened to Harry Esmond: "Yes. Papa says: 'Here's poor Harry killed, my dear;' on which Mamma gives a great scream; and oh, Harry! she drops down; and I thought she was dead too" (bk. I, ch. 13). Mohun is Henry's malign double. Acting as it were through Mohun, Henry is guilty in the two duels, the second repeating the first. First he kills his "father," Frank Castlewood, and then he kills Beatrix's fiancé, Lord Hamilton, putting an end to her hopes for worldly advancement. What Mohun unsuccessfully attempts, the seduction of Rachel—Henry Esmond triumphantly accomplishes. Rachel's "guilt" has been her long secret love for Henry, a love which even from the beginning is far from maternal. Ultimately, like Oedipus, Henry does marry his "mother," and he fathers a new Rachel, the Antigone figure in the story, in this superimposition of Biblical and Greek paradigms. Unlike Oedipus, however, Henry never comes to see his guilt and the havoc he has made in his family, though he has upset the generations and the line of succession, depriving each person of his or her rightful place.

This is the alternative portrait of Henry Esmond the reader is invited to draw by tracing another line through the data, the line indicated by all the ironic double meanings Thackeray has placed throughout the text. *Henry Esmond,* one might be tempted to say, is the indirect story or parable of this erasure of Henry's picture of himself and its replacement by another truer picture. The outlines of this other picture gradually emerge for the intelligent interpreter, as the narrative proceeds. The first picture loses its validity and disappears, like Eurydice fading back into the underworld, as Rachel does for Henry when she loses her divine glow. A good interpreter can read the signs right and make the right connections, threading his way correctly through all the clues. Though the method of *Henry Esmond* is irony, it would seem that irony in this case is used as the indirect expression of a wholly determinate and univocal meaning, a meaning which any good reader of the novel ought to identify. Is this so clearly the case, however? A futher step into the novel will indicate that my triumphant replacement of a "mistaken" reading by the "correct" one can itself in turn be undermined or indeed undermines itself.

Parable is a way of saying one thing and meaning another. The usual German word for parable (in the sense, for example, of the parables of Jesus in the New Testament) is *Gleichnis,* "likeness."

Thackeray, in a letter to his mother I have already quoted, describes his portrait of Henry Esmond as "a handsome likeness of an ugly son of yours." A likeness too says one thing by means of another thing and draws its meaning from the correspondence, with more or less of difference, between the two things. "Parable," and "likeness" seem appropriate terms to describe the procedure by means of which Thackeray says two things at once, creates one picture by means of another picture, says one thing and means another thing.

There is a difference, however, between saying two things at once and saying one thing and meaning another, and this makes all the difference. I have said that the instrument with which Thackeray creates for the reader the second truer picture of Henry is the trope of irony. Irony differs fundamentally from parable or from likeness. The latter leave the two pictures or the two narrative lines side by side, the one the support of the other. The moral or religious meanings of the parables of Jesus, however enigmatic those meanings are in themselves, or however enigmatic their relation to the story that supports them, do not question the referential validity of the realistic stories about fishermen, farmers, or ordinary folk which are the vehicle of their parabolic meanings. The one level of meaning is said to be genuinely "like" the other. The second meaning, the metaphorical or transported one, rests on the similarity as it is carried over. The meaning depends on keeping the validity of the vehicle untouched. In the case of irony, the second meaning undoes the first. As I have said, the second picture of Henry erases the first. It makes the reader see it as a hypocritical lie or self-deception.

In the definition of irony by Friedrich Schlegel, the master theorist of irony among the German romantics, the negativity inherent in irony is said to make it a permanent parabasis. According to Sören Kierkegaard's later definition, irony is "infinite absolute negativity."[14] Parabasis is the rhetorical name for that suspension of dramatic illusion when one of the actors in a play steps forward on the stage and speaks "in his own voice" in commentary, as in the "Epilogue" to *The Tempest.* A parabasis momentarily suspends the line of the action. Irony is a permanent parabasis. This means it suspends the line all along the line. Irony is the one figure of speech which cannot be figured spatially or as any sort of geometrical line. Nor is it locally identifiable as a turn of language or "figure of speech." Irony may pervade a whole discourse, as it does in the case of *Henry Esmond,* exactly identifiable nowhere, but present everywhere as a persistent double meaning blurring the line of sense from one end to the other of the text.

In suspending the line, irony suspends also itself. In this lies its "infinite absolute negativity." According to two other traditional definitions, irony is a needle which with its eye sees two ways, or a knife that cuts in both directions. The ironist cuts up into little bits beyond hope of reassembling the coherence of the narrative or argument he ironizes. In doing so, he cuts also himself and the alternative narrative or line of argument he presents. Irony is a dangerous-edged tool. He who lives by this sword dies by it too.

This does not mean that there may not be local ironies which are more or less limited or determinate. Such ironies may be contained within the larger frame-work of surface certainties about this or that fact—the fact, for example, that Beatrix tends to have a destructive effect on those around her. Most, though by no means all, good readers of *Henry Esmond* would agree that if the old Henry ironically undercuts the naïveté of his young self, that "he" of whom the "I" writes, the old Henry's judgments are in turn ironically undercut by an implicit circumambient judgment which can only speak indirectly, a judgment which may be called that of "Thackeray." To say that he who lives by irony dies of it too does mean, however, that irony, insofar as it has a tendency to spread out, proliferate, and pervade an entire discourse, as is the case in *Henry Esmond*, suspends the possibility of identifying certainly the underlying *logos* (cause, reason, meaning, or end) of the whole fabric which is woven of these smaller ironies. It takes away the reader's sense that he has somewhere solid ground to stand on from which to read the whole as a whole. Irony does this by putting in doubt those tools of interpretation—for example, seeing one thing as like another thing—with which the coherence of any interpretation is constructed, both the "first" and that "second" which is built on the ruins of the first, as well as the "third," and so on.

The way this happens in *Henry Esmond* is an admirable example of the self-destructive power of irony. This novel is one of the best texts in English fiction by means of which to explore the working of irony in narrative. Thackeray, I have said, sought authority over his own life by way of a detour representing that life in ironically displaced form in a fiction. He did this by means of the ventriloquism of an assumed voice and role. Thackeray wanted to understand and control his life by taking ironic authority over that assumed role and by showing the imagined person to have made a false interpretation of himself. Thackeray will present by irony the true interpretation and so indirectly a true interpretation of himself. He will come by way of the detour back to himself and so join himself to himself, taking possession of himself in a sovereign exercise of power. The reader is invited to follow in his turn this double line and to take full possession of the text of *Henry Esmond* in an authoritative interpretation based on his mastery of its ironical mode. He must replace one portrait by the other.

If irony is truly a permanent parabasis, this project cannot be carried out, either by the author or by the reader. Irony is the mode of language which cannot be mastered. It cannot be used as an instrument of mastery. It always masters the one who tries to master it or to take power with it. The means by which Henry paints his flattering portrait of himself is the taking of similarities as genuine identities. He not only claims to have a total memory of his own life, he also sees it as forming a coherent story, a "destiny" or "fate." He does this by identifying the various repetitions which make it hang together and link one part of it to another, as I have demonstrated by following out what Henry says of himself. An example is the way he sees himself as repeating Aeneas or sees each of his visions of Rachel as repeating the others. The alternative portrait traced out by the ironic double meanings uses exactly the same method of identifying similarities in order to draw a second line which replaces and erases the first. My drawing of the second portrait has depended at every point on the use of metaphorical similarities between one passage and another, one word and another, one narrative pattern and another. I have said, for example, that the second duel echoes the first, or that Esmond and Mohun are secretly identical in part because their names are similar. I have interpreted Esmond's life in terms of his unwitting reenactment of the story of Oedipus. In all this I have responded to invitations in the text. If Henry makes the mistake of seeing similarities as identities, I have done the same thing in my "second" reading. The reader is coaxed by the irony into replacing one metaphorical construction by another metaphorical construction. Henry paints a picture of himself as though he were already dead, embalming himself, so to speak. The reader brings him back alive once more beyond this death, but only to kill him once again in following out the ironic condemnation of him as an Oedipus manqué.

If the deconstruction of the first portrait depends on putting in question, by means of irony, the metaphorical connections Henry has made in order to draw a picture of himself, and if it unties all those connections, there is no reason why the same procedures should not be applied to the second metaphorical construction as have been applied to the first. What applies to the first must apply to the second. The undoing of the first by the second undoes also the second. The second destroys itself in the act whereby it fragments the first. If irony is "infinite absolute negativity," it can be in no way an instrument of tying up. It is only a power of dissolution, of analysis, or even of paralysis. If it is infinite negativity, it is also "absolutely" negative. It unties every line. Far from gaining mastery of himself by means of a detour through the ironic playing of a role, Thackeray remains permanently astray, distant from himself, unable to get back on the track and join his fictional self to his real self.

The same thing may be said, in a somewhat different form,[15] of the way the fictional aspects of Thackeray's story seem to make themselves more solid and plausible, more real, by being woven with circumstantial accounts of battles, political events, and so on, events which the reader knows really took place in history. This relationship too works both ways. The effect is as much or more to make historical narrative seem phantasmal, fictional. It can never be more than a subjective interpretation telling the way things seem to have been to this or that person. History has the same kind of insubstantiality as Henry Esmond's false portrait of himself. A rejection of "official" history, for example of poetized history like Addison's "The Campaign," is one of the recurrent themes of *Henry Esmond.* Thackeray's argument against such history reflects back on his own procedure, which is to try to tell the truth about himself indirectly, through an imaginary story set in a real historical scene.

The same kind of disarming also dissolves the reader's power over the text. Far from mastering *Henry Esmond* by a recognition and interpretation of its irony, the reader remains lost in a work which is undecidable in meaning, except insofar as the negative workings of irony in it may be precisely defined. From Thackeray's own time to the present, criticism has vibrated between seeing his novels as "cynical" or faithless and seeing them as based on absolute standards by means of which English bourgeois society is judged as lacking, as a Vanity Fair. The disagreements among critics who have interpreted Thackeray are no accident. No reader can claim certain authority over *Henry Esmond,* or decide between the reading that sees Esmond as a hero and the reading that sees him as a prig. The line is interrupted, even the line the reader follows to reach the understanding of the undoing of the line. This might be formulated by saying that where there is irony there is no authority, not even the authority to know for sure that there is no authority. To put this another way, there is no way to be sure that Henry's flattering self-portrait is not meant to be taken "straight," as it has been taken by many readers and critics.[16] It is impossible to be sure it is not Thackeray's true sense of himself, without irony, just as it is impossible to be sure that the Oedipal reading of the novel is the true one. The meaning vibrates among various possible configurations, since there is no solid base on which to construct a definitive interpretation.

Henry Esmond contains within itself, distributed here and there in the text, various emblems for this lack of ground and for the consequent fragmenting of any coherent line, even the line which puts in question the line. The story of Oedipus, for example, if it is taken as the archetype on which *Henry Esmond* is modeled, is, in Freud's interpretation of it, in that of Sophocles, or in the displaced version of the story in *Hamlet,* the narrative of the discovery that there is no authority, no father, no head source of meaning. It is the story of the discovery that one is oneself in the place of the father, but guiltily so, without any right to be there. The Oedipus story is the archetype of the discovery that there is no archetype.

It should be remembered that the "Oedipus complex" is itself an effect of language, whether in the person who suffers it or in an interpretation of the Oedipus story such as Thackeray's or Freud's. This is figured in the role of the various oracles, riddles, and prophecies in the story. These are, after all, linguistic formulations having performative power when they are read in one way or another. It is also figured in the mixing of generations and in the confusion or displacement of kinship names in the Oedipus story, where one man is husband and son of the same woman, and brother of his children. Such mixing occurs also in *Henry Esmond.* Who says the woman I love repeats my mother? Who says my life is governed by my rivalry for my father? I do. Who said the experiences of Oedipus were the fulfillment of the oracles? Oedipus did. If he did not know it was his father he killed or his mother he married, how could he be guilty of incest and parricide? The crimes come afterward, when he puts two and two together, sets the oracles against the facts and condemns himself. His sufferings and his self-condemnation are a reading of his life in terms of those oracular texts. Oedipus sees his life as repeating the oracles, as Freud created the Oedipus complex by reading his own life in terms of his reading of Sophocles' play. The meaning of the Oedipus story lies neither in the first element, the oracle, nor in the second, its fulfillment, but in between. It lies in the gap between the two and in the filling of that gap which makes the first a prophetic sign fulfilled by the second. The Oedipus complex always goes by way of language. It is, like Henry's reading of himself or my second reading by irony, an error in interpretation. It falsely takes similars as equals. Such a reading leads to a recognition of a lack of authority, but even the line leading to that recognition is without authority.[17] Henry in writing his imitation *Spectator* paper reads his life in terms of the story of Oedipus, as Freud also was to do. He creates in the paper a new oracle and then reads it. In the same way, the reader of the novel in his deeper insight into the implications of the *Spectator* paper reads it anew. The reader sets *Oedipus Rex, Hamlet, Henry Esmond,* and *The Interpretation of Dreams* side by side to make a story out of the lineup.

If the references to Oedipus and to his Biblical and literary replicas in *Henry Esmond* function not to affirm a ground but to put the existence of any certain ground in question, three characters in the novel personify in different ways the interruption of the narrative line. They incarnate an energy of discontinuity which undoes the novel's coherence. One such character is Father Holt, the Jesuit master of disguise. Father Holt appears and reappears in many different costumes in his futile machinations for the Stuart cause. Holt, who had been Henry's mentor and a father figure to him in his boyhood, is proud of his omniscience. His knowledge, however, is a sham knowledge. He is always slightly wrong. He consistently makes a false story out of distorted facts. He is in this a parody of Henry's claims to a total memory and to an omniscient understanding, like God's, of his life. "A foible of Mr. Holt's," says Henry when he meets the priest again in Flanders, ". . . was omniscience; thus in every point he here professed to know, he was nearly right, but not quite . . . Esmond did not think fit to correct his old master in these trifling blunders, but they served to give him knowledge of the other's character, and he smiled to think that this was his oracle of early days; and now no longer infallible or divine" (bk. II, ch. 13). "Nearly right, but not quite," and making a false claim to divine omniscience—these are good formulas for Henry's portrait of himself. In that portrait he makes a point of emphasizing his own shortcomings, but misses the most important ones, and falsely claims now to know it all.

The farewell to Father Holt, at the end of the book, emphasizes again Holt's indefatigable penchant for intrigue and disguise. It emphasizes also his failure to have obtained his goal by these strategies: "Sure he was the most unlucky of men: he never played a game but he lost it; or engaged in a conspiracy but 'twas certain to end in defeat. I saw him in Flanders after this, whence he went to Rome to the headquarters of his Order; and actually reappeared among us in America, very old, and busy, and hopeful. I am not sure that he did not assume the hatchet and moccassins there; and, attired in a blanket and war-paint, skulk about a missionary amongst the Indians" (bk. III, ch. 13).

Another character who personifies the interruption of the narrative line is Henry's real father, Thomas Esmond. Thomas's gift for telling lies corresponds to another of Henry's habits, as well as to one of Thackeray's habits. Thomas Esmond could always talk himself out of a tight situation, for example the situation of having fathered Henry, by making up a circumstantial story. Father Holt tells Henry of this in the chapter where Holt recounts what he knows of Henry's origins:

> "I must tell you that Captain Thomas, or my Lord Viscount afterwards, was never at a loss for a story, and could cajole a woman or a dun with a volubility, and an air of simplicity at the same time, of which many a creditor of his has been the dupe. His tales used to gather verisimilitude as he went on with them. He strung together fact after fact with a wonderful rapidity and coherence. It required, saving your presence, a very long habit of acquaintance with your father to know when his lordship was l——, —telling the truth or no." (Bk. II, ch. 13)

Here is an emblem of Henry's own narration. Like his father, Henry has the gift for stringing together fact after fact with solemn verisimilitude until it makes a coherent story. If Henry does this, so does Thackeray. He does it in a way even more like Thomas Esmond's storytelling than Henry's is, since Henry's narration is at least based on episodes that are presented as having really happened, whereas Thackeray's novel-writing, like novel-writing in general, is the making up out of whole cloth of plausible circumstantial stories. This is what Thomas Esmond does when he invents a previous life for himself, a father who is a Cornish squire, a shrewish wife there, and so on. Thackeray here momentarily brings to the surface, if the reader happens to think of the parallel, the lying or fictional nature of the text the reader is at that moment reading, with all its "facts" about Henry's life. The noticing of this parallel may remind the reader of the way Thackeray means to use his detour into lie as a strategy for dealing with his own life, for retaining mastery over it and over other people, for duping his creditors. To reveal the strategy in this way is to disable it. It makes the detour a permanent deviation into fiction. The road is suspended by the indirect, ironic revelation of its way of working.

The final and most important personification of this suspension is Beatrix. Though her manifest function in the novel is as a displacement of Henry's love for Rachel and as a means of dramatizing his tendency to love someone because she is desired by others, she also functions, more covertly, as his secret alter ego and as the embodiment of what is most negative in Thackeray's view of life. Like Henry, she is a demystifier of the pretenses of others, but she shows where such a procedure may lead if it is carried all the way. Certainly she is not a model to admire and imitate. Rather she is a demonstration of how destructive full clairvoyance about oneself and about others is. It might be better to be fooled. The novel as a whole, however, makes it difficult to go on fooling oneself, though readers who take Henry as a positive characterization have succeeded in doing so. Beatrix, in any case, is the embodiment in *Henry Esmond* of a dangerous feminine principle of skepticism. She represents a power of radical irony and faithlessness. She disbelieves in any hierarchy or authority. She has a woman's cynicism, a woman's knowledge that there is no king or legitimate male ruler, though she is also an example of the need certain women have to possess the embodiments of this pretended power, if only to destroy them.

She also knows there is no legitimate queen or goddess. "All the time you are worshipping and singing hymns to me," she tells Henry, "I know very well I am no goddess, and grow weary of the incense" (bk, III, ch. 4). As Henry says, "She was imperious, she was light-minded, she was flighty, she was false, she had no reverence in her character" (bk. II, ch. 15). Beatrix is Henry's unrecognized alter ego, his mirror image in a changed sex. If Henry breaks the line of succession in his family, Beatrix is also destructive wherever she enters. An example is the way she entices the Pretender away from London at the moment he might have seized the throne. In doing so she destroys the possibility of a Stuart succession. The difference is that Henry does not understand his destructive effects on those around him, while she does. "Though we are here sitting in the same room," she tells Henry, "there is a great wall between us" (bk. III, ch. 4). The wall is also a mirror in which he might see his secret face, the face he does everything to hide from himself and from the reader.

Beatrix is in many ways the most complex and even attractive characterization in *Henry Esmond,* as Becky Sharp is in *Vanity Fair,* though it would be risky to have anything to do with such a person in real life. Beatrix and Becky are Thackeray's contributions to the long line of selfish and destructive women presented in English fiction. Such figures are among the most memorable invented by English novelists of both sexes, Rosamund Vincy in *Middlemarch,* for example, Lizzie Eustace in *The Eustace Diamonds,* or Estella in *Great Expectations.* Beatrix is as changeable and wayward as the moon, her emblem. She causes devastation wherever she goes. Neither Henry nor Beatrix's mother nor anyone else is able to master her. She is utterly selfish and faithless. She manipulates social codes for her own advancement without believing in them. She is therefore, beneath the surface of her beauty and her gaiety, deeply melancholy. She has the melancholy of her nihilism. She knows that we are all alone, alone, alone, and that no prize is worth winning. This is Thackeray's knowledge too. It lies behind that irony he wears like a cloak he cannot remove. Beatrix is the embodiment in the book of that principle of irony on which *Henry Esmond* is based. She puts before the reader the corrosive power of that irony, its ability to break every continuity and to reduce everything to naught. More than any other feature of *Henry Esmond* she exposes the pretenses of Henry's picture of himself. She reveals his priggishness.

Beatrix also casts an annihilating shadow on Thackeray's pretense of mastery, as well as on any pretensions of sovereignty in the understanding of the novel the reader may have. That chain of pretenses can only be sustained by repudiating Beatrix. She must be cast out of the novel like a scapegoat, with all the sins of society upon her. Henry in the end repudiates her as without value, as immoral, as not worth loving. Thackeray has her grow fat and marry Tom Tusher. He takes away all her lunar or solar glow. The reader in his turn must ignore the lesson she teaches if he tries with a clear conscience to present a coherent interpretation of *Henry Esmond.*

Henry's narrative is based on a claim of total memory, as Thackeray's must be, and as the reader's interpretation must be too. The New Criticism, for example, like the archetypal criticism of Northrop Frye, bases its claim for a complete reading on the possibility of a total simultaneous integrating recall of all the details of the text in question. Beatrix, on the other hand, is the personification of reading or narrating as forgetting. This is foregrounded not only in the story of how she forgets the name of one of her lovers, but also in the way she lives only in the present instant. She is ready at any moment to forget and to betray the last lover in order to be ready without memory and without past for the next. She gives herself without loyalty and, of course, without giving herself, either sexually, so it seems, or in any other way, to each lover in turn. She forgets in between. If Henry, Thackeray, and the reader are drawers of lines, weavers of webs, Beatrix is the unweaver. She is the undoer of all lines and of all figures made with lines. This is asserted in a passage which explicitly uses this figure. It may be taken as a final emblematic image of Beatrix's role as the embodiment of the disintegrative power of irony: "If [Henry] were like Ulysses in his folly, at least she was in so far like Penelope that she had a crowd of suitors, and undid day after day and night after night the handiwork of fascination and the web of coquetry with which she was wont to allure and entertain them" (bk. III, ch. 3). *Henry Esmond* as a whole, insofar as Beatrix is the personification of the effects of irony in it, is, in its constant dismantling of itself, like that description of Proust's night work of forgetting given by Walter Benjamin. Benjamin, the reader will remember, uses this reversed image of Penelope's weaving and unweaving in a passage cited and discussed in the introductory chapter of this book.

Applied to *Henry Esmond,* Benjamin's distinction between the Penelope work of recollection and the Penelope work of forgetting leads to the following formulation: Henry's memory of his life is that false rationalizing daytime memory, stringing things together by way of what Benjamin elsewhere in his essay calls "identical" resemblance. The activity of irony in Thackeray's narrative, on the other hand, present everywhere in the book, but personified especially in Beatrix's disintegrating power, is that Penelope web of forgetting which works not by identities but by what Benjamin calls "opaque similarities."[18] Such similarities depend on difference and distance. They negate themselves in the same moment that they affirm themselves. Thackeray's irony continuously undermines the interpretation by way of repetitions the text nevertheless continuously invites the reader to make. *Henry Esmond,* in its totality, is therefore a large-scale expression of the negative relation between irony and repetition. If repetition creates meaning in fiction by making the forward movement of the narrative line turn back on itself and become significant thereby, irony loosens those connections. It makes the narrative line blur and finally break up into detached fragments. These may be put together this way or they may be put together that way, but never on the basis of that legitimate authority which, as I began by saying, *Henry Esmond* seeks.

5

TESS OF THE D'URBERVILLES

Repetition as Immanent Design

THE NARRATIVE FABRIC of *Tess of the d'Urbervilles* is woven of manifold repetitions—verbal, thematic, and narrative. At the same time, it is a story about repetition. This might be expressed by saying that the story of Tess poses a question: Why is it that Tess is "destined" to live a life which both exists in itself as the repetition of the same event in different forms and at the same time repeats the previous experience of others in history and in legend? What compels her to repeat both her own earlier life and the lives of others? What compels her to become a model which will be repeated later by others? The question on the methodological level might be phrased by asking not why literary works tend to contain various forms of repetition, which goes without saying, but what concept of repetition, in this particular case, will allow the reader to understand the way the repetitions work here to generate meaning. Another way to put this question is to ask what, for *Tess of the d'Urbervilles,* is the appropriate concept of difference. Are the differences between one example of a motif and another in a given case accidental or essential?

I shall concentrate on the interpretation of a single important passage in the novel, the one describing Alec's violation of Tess. This passage is one in which many forms of repetition are both operative and overtly named. I have called what happens to Tess her "violation." To call it either a rape or a seduction would beg the fundamental questions which the book raises, the questions of the meaning of Tess's experience and of its causes. Here is the passage:

> D'Urberville stooped; and heard a gentle regular breathing. He knelt and bent lower, till her breath warmed his face, and in a moment his cheek was in contact with hers. She was sleeping soundly, and upon her eyelashes there lingered tears.
>
> Darkness and silence ruled everywhere around. Above them rose the primeval yews and oaks of The Chase, in which were poised gentle roosting birds in their last nap; and about them stole the hopping rabbits and hares. But, might some say, where was Tess's guardian angel? where was the providence of her simple faith? Perhaps, like that other god of whom the ironical Tishbite spoke, he was talking, or he was pursuing, or he was in journey, or he was sleeping and not to be awaked.
>
> Why it was that upon this beautiful feminine tissue, sensitive as gossamer, and practically blank as snow as yet, there should have been traced such a coarse pattern as it was doomed to receive; why so often the coarse appropriates the finer thus, the wrong man the woman, the wrong woman the man, many thousand years of analytical philosophy have failed to explain to our sense of order. One may, indeed, admit the possibility of a retribution lurking in the present catastrophe. Doubtless some of Tess d'Urberville's mailed ancestors rollicking home from a fray had dealt the same measure even more ruthlessly toward peasant girls of their time. But though to visit the sins of the fathers upon their children may be a morality good enough for divinities, it is scorned by average human nature; and it therefore does not mend the matter.
>
> As Tess's own people down in those retreats are never tired of saying among each other in their fatalistic way: "It was to be." There lay the pity of it. An immeasurable social chasm was to divide our heroine's personality there-after from that previous self of hers who stepped from her mother's door to try her fortune at Trantridge poultry-farm.[1]

I have said that this passage describes Tess's violation. Yet, as almost all commentators on the scene have noted, the event is in fact not described at all, or at any rate it is not described directly. It exists in the text only as a blank space, like Tess's "beautiful feminine tissue . . . practically blank as snow as yet." It exists in the gap between paragraphs in which the event has not yet occurred and those which see it as already part of the irrevocable past. It exists in the novel as a metaphor. Doubtless Hardy was not free to describe such a scene literally. The reader will remember in this connection the notorious fact that in the first periodical version of *Tess*, in *The Graphic*, Hardy had to have Angel Clare wheel Tess and the other girls across a puddle in a wheelbarrow rather than carry them across in his arms. The episode of Tess's violation by Alec does not occur in *The Graphic* version at all. Even so, the effacement of the actual moment of Tess's loss of virginity, its vanishing from the text of the finished novel, is significant and functional. It is matched by the similar failure to describe directly all the crucial acts of violence which echo Tess's violation before and after its occurrence: the killing of the horse, Prince, when Tess falls asleep at the reins, the murder of Alec, the execution of Tess. Death and sexuality are two fundamental human realities, events which it seems ought to be present or actual when they happen, if any events are present and actual. In *Tess* they happen only offstage, beyond the margin of the narration, as they do in Greek tragedy. They exist in the novel in displaced expressions, like that gigantic ace of hearts on the ceiling which is the sign that Alec has been murdered, or like the distant raising of the black flag which is the sign that Tess has been hanged.

The sign in the novel of Tess's violation, the metaphor which is its indirect presence in Hardy's language, has a deeper significance than those of the more straightforward ace of hearts or black flag. Tess's rape or seduction exists in the novel in a metaphor of drawing. It is the marking out of a pattern on Tess's flesh. "Analytical philosophy," says the narrator, cannot explain "why it was that upon this beautiful feminine tissue . . . there should have been traced such a coarse pattern as it was doomed to receive." This metaphor belongs to a chain of figures of speech in the novel, a chain that includes the tracing of a pattern, the making of a mark, the carving of a line or sign, and the act of writing.

Writing and the making of a trace are also associated in the poem, "Tess's Lament." The poem, like the prefaces and the subtitle, says the novel again in a different way. Tess says in the poem:

> I cannot bear my fate as writ,
> I'd have my life unbe;
> Would turn my memory to a blot,
> Make every relic of me rot,
> My doings be as they were not,
> And gone all trace of me![2]

All the elements in this chain of metaphors in one way or another involve a physical act which changes a material substance, marking it or inscribing something on it. It then becomes no longer simply itself but the sign of something absent, something which has already happened. It becomes a "relic" or a "trace."

Hardy's feelings about Tess were strong, perhaps stronger than for any other of his invented personages. He even obscurely identified himself with her. The reader here encounters an example of that strange phenomenon in which a male author invents a female protagonist and then falls in love with her, so to speak, pities her, suffers with her, takes her to his bosom, as Hardy's epigraph from *Two Gentlemen of Verona* affirms he did in the case of Tess: "Poor wounded name, my bosom as a bed/Shall lodge thee." Trollope's feelings about Lily Dale in *The Small House at Allington* and in *The Last Chronicle of Barset* are another example of this. No good reader of *Tess of the d'Urbervilles* can fail, in his or her turn, to be deeply moved by the novel or by the poem cited above. I for one find the description of Angel Clare's failure to consummate his marriage to Tess almost unbearably painful. The emotional experience of following through the novel no doubt forms that background of agreement about the novel which is shared by almost all readers and forms the basis for discussions of it and even for disagreements about what the novel means. This might be compared to Roman Jakobson's persuasive argument that though theorists of prosody may endlessly disagree about the metrical form of a given set of verses, nevertheless the lines "have" a rhythm which is experienced, at least in some form, by any competent reader. It is because all good readers of *Tess* would agree that Tess suffers and even tend to agree that she does not wholly deserve her suffering, and it is because all good readers of *Tess* share in the narrator's sympathy and pity for that suffering, that we care about the question of why Tess suffers so. At the same time, apparently casual, peripheral, or "abstract" elements, such as the use of the figure of writing to describe Tess's deflowering, are not foreign to her suffering or to the reader's re-experience of it. The figures are a major vehicle for the communication of the emotional rhythms the novel and its adjacent poem create in the reader. What could be more moving than to know that Tess's self-hatred or self-disparagement is so great that, thinking of her life as having made an ugly inscription on the world, like a shocking graffito on a wall, she wants every "trace" of herself obliterated. Because the reader is moved, he may want to understand just what is implied by Hardy's repeated use of this metaphor.

The metaphor of the tracing of a pattern has a multiple significance. It assimilates the real event to the act of writing about it. It defines both the novel and the events it presents as repetitions, as the outlining again of a pattern which already somewhere exists. Tess's violation exists, both when it "first" happens and in the narrator's telling, as the re-enactment of an event which has already occurred. The physical act itself is the making of a mark, the outlining of a sign. This deprives the event of any purely present existence and makes it a design referring backward and forward to a long chain of similar events throughout history. Tess's violation repeats the violence her mailed ancestors did to the peasant girls of their time. In another place in the novel, Tess tells Angel Clare she does not want to learn about history, and gives expression to a vision of time as a repetitive series. Tess does not want to know history because, as she says, "what's the use of learning that I am one of a long row only—finding out that there is set down in some old book somebody just like me, and to know that I shall only act her part; making me sad, that's all. The best is not to remember that your nature and your past doings have been like thousands' and thousands', and that your coming life and doings'll be like thousands' and thousands' " (ch. 19).

Sex, physical violence, and writing all involve a paradoxical act of cutting, piercing, or in some way altering some physical object. The paradox lies in the fact that the fissure at the same time establishes a continuity. It makes the thing marked a repetition and gives it in one way or another the power of reproducing itself in the future. The word "paradox," in fact, is not, strictly speaking, appropriate here, since it presupposes a prior logical coherence which the paradox violates, going against what is normally taught or said. The dividing fissure which at the same time joins, in this case, is prior to logic, in the sense, for example, of the logical coherence of a plot with beginning, middle, and end. Any example of the division which joins is already a repetition, however far back one goes to seek the first one. This chapter attempts to identify this alogic or this alternative logic of plot and to justify giving it the Hardyan name of repetition as *immanent* design. Such a plot will be without beginning and end in the Aristotelian sense, and the elements in the "middle" will not be organized according to determined causal sequence. The acts of sexual conjunction, of physical violence, and of writing create gaps or breaks, as, for example, "an immeasurable social chasm was to divide our heroine's personality thereafter from that previous self of hers."

All three of these acts in *Tess* converge in the multiple implications of the metaphor of grafting used to describe the relation of Tess and Alec. The metaphor is overt when the narrator says that though the spurious Stoke-d'Urbervilles were not "of the true tree," nevertheless, "this family formed a very good stock whereon to regraft a name which sadly wanted such renovation" (ch. 5), or when Tess's father says of Alec, "sure enough he mid have serious thoughts about improving his blood by linking on to the old line" (ch. 6), or when her mother says, "as one of the genuine stock, she ought to make her way with 'en, if she plays her trump card aright" (ch. 7). The metaphor of grafting may be present covertly, according to a characteristically complex conjunction of motifs, when the rapid ride Tess takes with Alec in the dog cart, the ride that leads to Alec giving her "the kiss of mastery" (ch. 8), is described in the metaphor of a splitting stick: "The aspect of the straight road enlarged with their advance, the two banks dividing like a splitting stick; one rushing past at each shoulder" (ch. 8). Here come together the association of rapid motion with the sexual attraction between Alec and Tess, and the use of Tess's progress along the roads of Wessex as an emblem of her journey through life. Those roads are inscribed in ancient lines on the once virgin countryside as an inscription is traced out on a blank page. Both Tess's journeys and the roads themselves are versions of a cutting which is also the establishment of a new continuity, as a stick must be split to be grafted or linked on to a new shoot. The "kiss of mastery" which anticipates Alex's sexual possession of Tess is "imprint[ed]" (ch. 8), as though it were a design stamped with a die, and Tess tries to undo the kiss by "wip[ing] the spot on her cheek that had been touched by his lips" (ch. 8), as though the kiss had left a mark on her cheek. The word "graft" comes from a word meaning carving, cutting, or inscribing. "Graph" has the same etymology. With "graft" may be associated another word meaning a traced or carved-out sign, "hieroglyph." This word is used in the novel to describe Tess's naive expectation that she will see in Alec d'Urberville "an aged and dignified face, the sublimation of all the d'Urberville lineaments, furrowed with incarnate memories representing in hieroglyphic the centuries of her family's and England's history" (ch. 5).[3]

One more version of this motif has already been cited in Chapter 1 in the passages about Alec as the "blood-red ray in the spectrum of [Tess's] young life," and about the sun's rays as "like red-hot pokers." The sun is in this novel, as in tradition generally, the fecundating male source, a principle of life, but also a dangerous energy able to pierce and destroy, as Tess, at the end of the novel, lying on the stone of sacrifice at Stonehenge, after her brief period of happiness with Angel, is wakened, just before her capture, by the first rays of the morning sun which penetrate under her eyelids: "Soon the light was strong, and a ray shone upon her unconscious form, peering under her eyelids and waking her" (ch. 58). This association of death and sexuality with a masculine sun had been prepared earlier in the novel not only by the description of Alec as the blood-red ray but also, most explicitly, by the full context of the passage describing the sun's rays:

> The sun, on account of the mist, had a curious sentient, personal look, demanding the masculine pronoun for its adequate expression. His present aspect, coupled with the lack of all human forms in the scene, explained the old time heliolatries in a moment. One could feel that a saner religion had never prevailed under the sky. The luminary was a golden-haired, beaming, mild-eyed, God-like creature, gazing down in the vigour and intentness of youth upon an earth that was brimming with interest for him.
>
> His light, a little later, broke through chinks of cottage shutters, throwing stripes like red-hot pokers upon cupboards, chests of drawers, and other furniture within; and awakening harvesters who were not already astir. (Ch. 14)

These passages indicate what meaning the reader should ascribe to all the chain of red things in the novel: the red ribbon in Tess's hair; her mouth ("[Angel] saw the red interior of her mouth as if it had been a snake's"; ch. 27); those red lips with which she says the characteristic "ur" sound of her dialect; the strawberry that Alec forces her to eat; the roses that Alec gives her, with which she pricks her chin; the red scratches on her wrist in the reaping scene ("as the day wears on its feminine smoothness becomes scarified by the stubble, and bleeds"; ch. 14); the red stains made on her arms when, in an extraordinary scene, she approaches closer and closer under Angel's window, fascinated by his harp playing, making her way through "tall blooming weeds emitting offensive smells" ("She went stealthily as a cat through this profusion of growth, gathering cuckoo-spittle on her skirts, cracking snails that were underfoot, staining her hands with thistle-milk and slug-slime, and rubbing off on her naked arms sticky blights which, though snow-white on the apple-tree trunks, made madder [bright red] stains on her skin"; ch. 19; BL MS., f. 136, reads "blood-red" instead of "madder"); the red painted signs that have already been cited in Chapter 1 ("THY, DAMNATION, SLUMBERETH, NOT"); the "unwavering blood-colored light" reflected from the fire on the underside of the mantelshelf (BL MS., f. 28), or the "red-coaled glow" on Tess's face (ch. 34), as she makes her confession to Angel after their marriage; the "piece of blood-stained paper, caught up from some meat-buyer's dust heap" which "beat[s] up and down the road," "too flimsy to rest, too heavy to fly away" (ch. 44), when Tess makes her abortive attempt to appeal to Angel's parents after he has abandoned her; the "scarlet oozing" from Alec's face after Tess has struck him with her threshing glove, "heavy and thick as a warrior's" (an ironic reminiscence of the gloves of her "armed progenitors"; ch. 47); the growing blot of blood on the ceiling, like "a gigantic ace of hearts" (ch. 56), when Alec has been murdered. All these red things are marks made by that creative and destructive energy underlying events to which Hardy gave the name "Immanent Will." This is incarnated in one form in the sun. It is also diffused in all those agents which fecundate, injure, or make signs in the triple chain of recurrent acts—copulation, physical violence, and writing—which organizes this novel. It is in accord with the deep logic of these recurrent configurations that the passage about the masculine sun is followed by a description of the reaping machine whose "two broad arms of painted wood" are "of all ruddy things that morning the brightest," as "the paint with which they were smeared, intensified in hue by the sunlight, imparted to them a look of having been dipped in liquid fire" (ch. 14). Another passage concentrates all these elements in a single sentence: "The sun was so low on that short last afternoon of the year that it shone in through a small opening and formed a golden staff which stretched across to [Tess's] skirt where it made a spot like a paint-mark set upon her" (ch. 34; BL MS., f. 271, has "permanent mark").

The novel itself is defined in the prefaces as a mark imprinted on Hardy's mind, as a die strikes a coin, and repeated or re-inscribed in the words of the text. The novel is, Hardy tells his readers in his preface to the fifth edition, "an impression, not an argument"; he has "writ[ten] down how the things of the world strike him." In his preface of 1912 he describes the subtitle as "the estimate left in a candid mind of the heroine's character," a re-enactment of the tracing of a coarse pattern on Tess's virgin flesh. Here "candid" matches "practically blank as snow," and "estimate" matches the "measure" dealt by Tess's ancestors to long-dead peasant girls and measured out again less ruthlessly to Tess by Alec. "Estimate" and "measure" suggest "ratio," "proportion," or "logic" making a design, as a throw of the dice makes a pattern or as reproduction is the dissemination of a genetic code.

The novel proper is repeated by its title, by its subtitle, by the epigraph, and by its sequence of four prefaces or explanatory notes. These prefaces discuss the way the novel and its subtitle are repetitions. *Tess of the d'Urbervilles,* says Hardy in the note to the first edition, is "an attempt to give artistic form to a true sequence of things." The sequence existed first. The novel repeats it in a different form. "To exclaim illogically against the gods, singular or plural," he says in the preface to the fifth edition, "is not such an original sin of mine as he [Andrew Lang, who had attacked the novel] seems to imagine." The novel is the repetition of an older sin, Shakespeare's sin in *King Lear,* or the historical Gloucester's sin before that. In the preface of 1912 Hardy says that the subtitle, "A Pure Woman/Faithfully Presented," "was appended at the last moment, after reading the final proof." It is a summary of the whole, another form of duplication.

Besides calling attention to the way the book is a repetition, the prefaces are also themselves reaffirmations of the novel. They are attempts to efface it or to apologize for it which in that apology reiterate it or admit that once it is written it cannot be erased, as, within the fiction, Tess's life, once it has happened, can never not have been. The novelist in his own way repeats the fate of his heroine. Neither can escape from the reiteration of an act performed in the past. "The pages," says Hardy of the preface of 1892, "are allowed to stand for what they are worth, as something once said; but probably they would not have been written now." In the act of saying "I would not write them now," in effect he writes them over again. In the prefatory note of 1912, speaking of the subtitle, he says "*Melius fuerat non scribere.* But there it stands." Once more, in saying "It would have been better not to have written it," he recognizes that it is ineffaceable. The proofreader's delete sign turns into a "stet." He lets it stand not so much because he wants to as because he cannot do otherwise, just as Tess cannnot by any means satisfy her wish to have her life "unbe." As Hardy says in one of his poems, "Nor God nor Demon can undo the done."[4]

The same cluster of motifs is repeated again in the epigraph for the novel from *Two Gentlemen of Verona* cited above. There sex and writing, with a reversal of the usual polarities of male and female, are joined again in the image of Hardy's "bosom" as both a bed and a writing tablet on which are written Tess's name and her story, giving her an inscribed permanence there, as things past and forgotten, in Hardy's poems, exist permanently in his memory and in the words of the poems as they are written down, printed, and reprinted. It is not Tess herself who will be lovingly protected in Hardy's bosom, but her "wounded name."

In *Tess of the d'Urbervilles* each passage is a node, a point of intersection or focus, on which converge lines leading from many other passages in the novel and ultimately including them all. Though the passage I have chosen would strike any reader as especially important, it is not the origin or end of the others. To give another example, the sun is not the chief representative of the Immanent Will in the novel. The Immanent Will exists only in its representatives, and each representative has its own irreplaceable specificity and validity. Any motif in *Tess of the d'Urbervilles* exists only in the examples of it. None of these has a sovereign explanatory function for the others. Moreover, the chains of connection or of repetition which converge on a given passage are numerous and complex. The reader can only thread his way from one element to another, interpreting each as best he can in terms of the others. It is possible to distinguish chains of connection which are material elements in the text, like the red things; or metaphors, like the figures of grafting or of writing; or covert, often etymological, associations, like the connection of grafting with writing or cutting; or thematic elements, like sexuality or murder; or conceptual elements, like the question of cause or the theory of history; or quasimythological elements, like the association of Tess with the harvest or the personification of the sun as a benign god. None of these chains has priority over the others as the true explanation of the meaning of the novel. Each is a permutation of the others rather than a distinct realm of discourse, as the myth of the paternal sun is a version of the dangerous power of the all-too-human Alec d'Urberville, not its explanatory archetype.

Taken together, the elements form a system of mutually defining motifs, each of which exists as its relation to the others. The reader must execute a lateral dance of interpretation to explicate any given passage, without ever reaching, in this sideways movement, a passage which is chief, original, or originating, a sovereign principle of explanation. The meaning, rather, is suspended within the interaction among the elements. It is immanent rather than transcendent. This does not mean that one interpretation is as good as another but that the meaning must be formulated not as a hierarchy, with some ur-explanation at the top, truest of the true, but as an interplay among a definable and limited set of possibilities, all of which have force, but all of which may not logically have force at once. This does not exempt the reader from seeking answers to the question of why Tess is compelled to repeat herself and others and to suffer through those repetitions. The answers, rather, must lie in the sequence itself. In its proposal and rejection of a whole set of explanations by a cause outside the sequence, and in its presentation of a repetitive chain which develops its own immanent meaning, *Tess of the d'Urbervilles* is a special version of that intertwining of the two forms of repetition which I have discussed in Chapter 1.

Hardy's "attempt to give artistic form to a true sequence of things" in *Tess* contains recurring images of a chain, row, or sequence. The powerful emblematic effect of topography in the novel calls attention to the linear pattern, leading the reader to think of Tess's life as her journey through the series of places where she lives. The novel, moreover, is organized as a sequence of seasons. Tess in one place sees her life as "numbers of tomorrows just all in a line," each saying, "I'm coming! Beware of me! beware of me!" (ch. 19.) The motif of the series is introduced in the opening description by Parson Tringham of the d'Urberville ancestors "at Kingsbere-sub-Greenhill: rows and rows of you in your vaults, with your effigies under Purbeck-marble canopies" (ch. 1). Along these various forms of rows the reader must move, making each series, and the intertwined rope of thematic and figurative threads they make together, in one way or another into a meaningful totality.

My interpretation so far has suggested that the chains of meaning which converge on the passage describing Tess's violation are made of elements congruent with one another, as all the red things seem to mean the same thing. In fact this is not the case. The passage brings to the surface in a number of ways the method of permutation which establishes the relation among the elements in a given chain in Hardy's novel. In each new appearance the components are rearranged. The new example does not match the first, though it clearly repeats it. The relation among the links in a chain of meanings in *Tess of the d'Urbervilles* is always repetition with a difference, and the difference is as important as the repetition.

The way in which Tess's violation repeats with a difference previous events is made clear by its relation to the various models of explanation which are incorporated into the fabric of the description. These interpretations are canceled almost as soon as they are put forward, partly by their incompatibility with one another. Hardy's novels are puzzling not because they contain no self-interpretative elements, but because they contain too many irreconcilable ones. Criticism of Hardy has often erred by seizing on one element in a given novel as the single explanation of the meaning of what happens, leaving aside other explanations for which just as much textual evidence can be given. The most obvious form in *Tess of the d'Urbervilles* of that heterogeneity I consider to be characteristic of literature is the presence of multiple incompatible explanations of what happens to Tess. They cannot all be true, and yet they are all there in the words of the novel.

Part of the importance of the passage I have chosen to discuss lies in the fact that it so explicitly raises the question put before the reader, as I have said, by the book as a whole: "Why does Tess suffer so?" Various aspects of Hardy's way of presenting Tess's story keep this question insistently before the reader: the emphasis on its linear sequentiality, which implies a causal relation among the elements; the incompatibility between what Tess wills and what happens, which suggests that something outside her intention must be patterning her life. Her life, against her wishes, forms a sequence of repetitions. These give the whole a design which is a repetition of earlier fictional, historical, or mythological prototypes. The emergence of an unwilled or undesired pattern raises the question of its source. What is the originating power which causes Tess's life to fall into a symmetrical design leading her step by step to her execution? "Why was it," as the novel poses the question, ". . . there should have been traced such a coarse pattern?"

The passage describing Tess's deflowering proposes and rejects five possible answers to this question. The reason for the rejection in each case lies in the fact that though the explanatory model is duplicated by what happens to Tess, it is duplicated in the form of an ironic reversal. This invalidates the model as a straightforward explanatory cause.

The first of these anterior models is suggested by the location of Tess's violation among "the primeval yews and oaks of The Chase" (ch. 11). The Chase has been described earlier as one of the few prehistoric forests left in England. This forest, in the association of its name with hunting and in the antiquity of its trees, recalls the ancient forest that figures earlier in the novel and of which it may be said to be the displacement, the Vale of Blackmoor. Tess's home village of Marlott is located in Blackmoor. The Vale of Blackmoor was "known in former times," says the narrator, "as the Forest of White Hart, from a curious legend of King Henry III's reign, in which the killing by a certain Thomas de la Lynd of a beautiful white hart which the king had run down and spared, was made the occasion of a heavy fine" (ch. 2). Tess's violation in the Chase echoes the death of her legendary precursor, the white hart, but for Tess there is no king to spare her and to take vengeance on her violator. Rather she is victimized by men in manifold ways until her death. She takes vengeance into her own hands when she murders Alec, and thereby seals her doom and repeats that other legend, "the family tradition of the coach and murder" (ch. 57). There is an "obscure strain in the d'Urberville blood," Angel thinks as he looks down at Tess weeping with happiness on his shoulder, which predisposes them to sudden acts of violence.

Tess's re-enactment of the family tradition reverses its elements, if we take the first of Alec's versions of it, the one in which the man is a murderer. "One of the family," he tells Tess, "is said to have abducted some beautiful woman, who tried to escape from the coach in which he was carrying her off, and in the struggle he killed her—or she killed him—I forget which. Such is one version of the tale" (ch. 51). Tess's story is another version of the tale. As in its relation to the legend of the white hart, so in its relation to the family legend, the elements in the precursor event are rearranged in a new pattern with a new significance. In Henry III's time justice was done. Society was an organic fabric in which retribution could occur. In Tess's experience no secure moral or social order exists. Every reader of the novel remembers the irony of the narrator's final judgement: " 'Justice' was done, and the President of the Immortals, in Aeschylean phrase, had ended his sport with Tess" (ch. 59). Not so well known is the note in Hardy's autobiography in which he says that the phrase "President of the Immortals" has no proper theological reference. It is a figurative personification of the impersonal forces that rule the universe. These forces Hardy called the Immanent Will. In that famous Aeschylean phrase, says Hardy, quoting Campbell's *Philosophy of Rhetoric,* "the forces opposed to the heroine were allegorized as a personality . . . by the use of a well-known trope, . . . 'one in which life, perception, activity, design, passion, or any property of sentient beings, is attributed to things inanimate.' "[5]

The second interpretative model is implicitly rejected in the same way. Once again Tess's life repeats an anterior pattern, but repeats it with such a difference as to make the pattern of no use as an explanatory principle. The question in this case is the analogy between Tess's experience and the general fecundity of nature. Tess's "gentle regular breathing," as she lies asleep before Alec returns, is echoed by the "gentle roosting birds in their last nap." Her power of reproduction echoes that of "the hopping rabbits and hares" in the forest around. Part of the pathos of Tess's suffering arises from the fact that her bearing of Alec's child follows from "doing what comes naturally." Her act joins her to the general life of nature. In the magnificent reaping scene she becomes almost a part of inanimate nature as she moves rhythmically down the rows of harvested grain, "holding the corn in an embrace like that of a lover" (ch. 14), and pausing to suckle her child: "a field-woman is a portion of the field; she has somehow lost her own margin, imbibed the essence of her surrounding, and assimilated herself with it" (ch. 14).

Tess is as much a victim of man's inhumanity to natural creatures as those pheasants dying in the wood, wounded by hunters, whose necks she mercifully wrings in an episode much later in the novel (ch. 41). She is wrong to see in nature a personified reproach to her impurity:

> Walking among the sleeping birds in the hedges, watching the skipping rabbits on a moonlit warren, or standing under a pheasant-laden bough, she looked upon herself as figure of Guilt intruding into the haunts of Innocence. But all the while she was making a distinction where there was no difference. Feeling herself in antagonism she was quite in accord. She had been made to break an accepted social law, but no law known to the environment in which she fancied herself such an anomaly. (Ch. 13)

One meaning of the subtitle, "a pure woman," is a claim that Tess's behavior has been in accord with nature. Tess, however, unlike the rabbits and pheasants, dwells within human culture as well as within nature. Natural behavior by human being is always more than purely natural. Tess has broken no natural law and has done nothing different from what the rabbits and the pheasants do, but she has been made to break an accepted social law. In this her repetition of natural behavior is a repetition with a difference. Part of the poignancy of Tess's story lies in its demonstration of man's distance from nature. The relation of her life to its models in nonhuman nature can neither explain nor justify what happens to her.

The third interpretative model proposed in the passage is rejected even more decisively and with an even more bitterly ironic chiasmus: "But, might some say, where was Tess's guardian angel? where was the providence of her simple faith? Perhaps, like that other god of whom the ironical Tishbite spoke, he was talking, or he was pursuing, or he was in a journey, or he was sleeping and not to be awaked" (ch. 11). This rejects any interpretation of what happens to Tess by way of orthodox theology, while laying the ground for the irony in Angel Clare's name. By way of the Biblical echo it presents Tess's situation once more as a repetition with a difference in which the anterior model provides no satisfactory explanation of what happens to her. Just as Angel's name might lead the reader to hope he might serve as a human embodiment of Tess's missing guardian angel, while in fact he offers her no protection, so Tess's world as a whole is bereft of any providential presence. Things happen to her as they happen. They are guided from behind the scenes by no divine designer.

Tess in her simple faith is ironically not in the position of a Bible-reading Christian nor in that of the Old Testament believer in Jehovah. She is, rather, like the prophets of Baal, whose impotent God could not answer their prayer for magic fire under the sacrificial bullock. Those prophets were savagely mocked by Elijah, "the ironical Tishbite":

> And they took the bullock which was given them, and they dressed it, and called upon the name of Baal from morning even until noon, saying, O Baal, hear us. But there was no voice, nor any that answered. And they leaped upon the altar which was made. And it came to pass at noon, that Elijah mocked them, and said, Cry aloud: for he is a god; either he is talking, or he is pursuing, or he is in a journey, or peradventure he sleepeth, and must be awaked. And they cried aloud, and cut themselves after their manner with knives and lancets, till the blood gushed out upon them. (I Kings 18:26–28)

In the Old Testament story Elijah's prayers are answered with a fire which consumes the sacrifice. In Tess's world Christianity has replaced the worship of Baal as a belief in a God absent or dead. A modern-day Elijah would be as powerless as those impotent priests of Baal. In a context repeating in a new way the elements of fire, sacrifice, and an act of violence in which blood flows, Tess's violation repeats its Biblical prototype. It repeats it with a reversal of all the Old Testament valences, offering the reader no hope of a Biblical interpretation of Tess's experience.

The ironic relation between what happens to Tess and any Biblical interpretation of it is reinforced by a second reference to a Biblical explanation of the recurrences in human experience. The divine lust for vengeance visits the sins of the fathers on the children even to the third generation. Two wrongs, for Hardy, do not make a right. There may be the "possibility of a retribution lurking in the present catastrophe." Tess may be suffering for the sins committed by her mailed ancestors. Their violence is balanced by her suffering. This evening of the score is scornfully rejected as "a morality good enough for divinities." It is good enough for beings who are by nature unjust, meting out the savage morality of an eye for an eye, a tooth for a tooth. Such a morality of retribution is "scorned by average human nature" because it "does not mend the matter." Rather than removing the coarse pattern, repairing the tear, it repeats and prolongs the rent in the fabric. The impure cannot be returned to its purity. It cannot be made once more a tissue blank as snow.

In this case too, the new exemplar repeats its model with an ironic reversal of its elements. The "measure" dealt by Alec to Tess is incommensurate with the measure dealt by Tess's ancestors to the peasant girls of their time. Tess is a true d'Urberville. Her aristocratic ancestors dealt a ruthless measure to peasant girls, as one deals a hand of cards, takes measures, or promulgates a measure in the sense of a law. The word "measure" indicates ratio or proportion. It suggests a pattern which might be numbered, accounted for mathematically, like a genetic code. The measure is here a euphemism for sexual generation. A measure is a pattern, even if only a coarse pattern. In the present repetition, however, Tess is the peasant girl who is having the same "measure" dealt to her by an imitation d'Urberville. Alec is the upstart scion of an ignoble family. He needs to graft his blood on the old, authentic line, and his act is no more than a base parody of the brutal noblesse of Tess's artistocratic ancestors. The false needs the true, but the true, it seems, also needs the false. The present event makes the ancient model into a "pattern" by duplicating it in a debased and reversed form.

The fourth interpretative model, that of "analytical philosophy," seems to be unequivocally rejected: "Why so often the coarse appropriates the finer thus, the wrong man the woman, the wrong woman the man, many thousand years of analytical philosophy have failed to explain to our sense of order" (ch. 11). "Analytical philosophy" presupposes some underlying order in the world, and some governing power determining a fitness of things. The mismatching of man and woman through the centuries can be justified according to no philosophical system. It challenges our assumption that the universe makes sense.

A more specific reference underlies the passage, as a parallel passage earlier in the novel confirms:

> We may wonder whether at the acme and summit of the human progress these anachronisms will be corrected by a finer intuition, a closer interaction of the social machinery than that which now jolts us round and along; but such completeness is not to be prophesied, or even conceived possible. Enough that in the present case, as in millions, it was not the two halves of a perfect whole that confronted each other at the perfect moment; a missing counterpart wandered independently about the earth waiting in crass obtuseness till the late time came. Out of which maladroit delay sprang anxieties, disappointments, shocks, catastrophes, and passing-strange destinies. (Ch. 5)

Hardy has in mind the great comic myth, proposed by Aristophanes in Plato's *Symposium.* There was once a race of hermaphrodities, says Aristophanes, each formed of a man and a woman joined together to make a spherical and androgynous whole. This whole the gods divided. Each of the resulting hemispheres has since then wandered the world seeking to rejoin his or her counterpart.[6] Hardy's version of the human predicament repeats this situation with a characteristic difference, a crisscrossing of the pattern like those already encountered. This crisscrossing is figured also, it happens, in the geographical movements of the heroine. The story traces Tess's series of progressions through life across the landscape of Wessex. She goes from Marlott north to Trantridge, back to Marlott, down to Talbothays in the Valley of the Great Dairies, up to Flintcomb Ash, south again home when her father dies, further south to

Sandbourne where she kills Alec, then north again to Stonehenge and Wintoncester, where she dies. Her trajectory makes a design. This design is traced out by her failure to attain union with her missing other half. For Hardy, as opposed to Plato, there is no original unity. Though there may somewhere be a matching self of the opposite sex for each person, the two can never come together at the right time and place. Life for Hardy is a wandering detour across a gap opened up in time and place by the distance between each person and his or her missing half.

Near the end of *Beyond the Pleasure Principle* Sigmund Freud also alludes to the myth from the *Symposium.*[7] Both Hardy and Freud, with help from Plato, speculate, one in a scientific treatise, the other in a novel, that each man or woman moves forward through life repeating an unsuccessful attempt to reach again a seemingly lost primal unity. That unity may exist, however, in the counterpossibility both writers propose, only as a shadow generated by each person's imaginary original separation from his counterpart. Erotic desire is a mask for the death wish. Life is a detour on the journey toward death. For Hardy, as for Freud, only in death—not in any happy conjunction with my other half—can I escape my unappeasable desire for something which is missing.

"Thus the thing began," says the narrator of Tess's first meeting with Alec. "Had she perceived this meeting's import she might have asked why she was doomed to be seen and coveted that day by the wrong man, and not by some other man, the right and desired one in all respects—as nearly as humanity can supply the right and desired; yet to him who amongst her acquaintance might have approximated to this kind, she was but a transient impression, half forgotten" (ch. 5). For Plato, my other half was mine by right originally. For Hardy, my counterpart is met, if at all, only through a chance conjunction of two persons making their separate paths through the world. Angel Clare is Tess's most nearly proper mate. He encounters Tess by accident in the opening scene of the novel, at the May-Day dance, but the encounter fails to make a permanent impression on his memory. "Impression," the reader will remember, is a key word in the prefaces to *Tess.* If a work of literature records the transient impressions things make on the "candid" mind of the author, Tess has made but a transient impression on Angel, the man best fitted for her. The conjunction has occurred, but it has not made a deep enough impression to enter into his conscious memory, though the narrator's recording of this failure gives it the permanence of the words printed on the page. In fact, Angel's singling out of Tess from the other milkmaids, much later in the novel, in the Talbothays section, is caused, the narrator says, by his unconscious recognition that he has seen her before:

> And then he seemed to discern in her something that was familiar, something which carried him back into a joyous and unforeseeing [BL MS., f. 132: thoughtless] past, before the necessity of taking thought had made the heavens gray. He concluded that he had beheld her before; where, he could not tell. A casual encounter during some country ramble it certainly had been, and he was not greatly curious about it. But the circumstance was sufficient to lead him to select Tess in preference to the other pretty milkmaids when he wished to contemplate contiguous [BL MS., f. 132: weak] womankind. (Ch. 18)

Angel's noticing of Tess at the dairy farm is experienced as a species of déjà vu. The first encounter was not even noticed, but the second makes the first into an origin. That original, since it cannot be remembered as such, even seems to belong to some fabulous or mythical past, as though it were a reminiscence from another more joyous world.

This curious mechanism of "memory" whereby the second creates the meaning of the first and makes it a first is parallel, as I have said, to Freud's interpretation of hysterical trauma. For Freud, the first episode is sexual but not understood as such at the time. The second event is innocuous, but is experienced as a repetition of the first, liberating its traumatic effect. The trauma is neither in the first nor in the second, but in the relation between them. In a similar way, Tess makes an "impression" on Angel only when he encounters her at Talbothays, but that impression is dependent for its effect on his first encounter with her, when she did not make an impression on him. In a way parallel to this, the impression made by *Tess of the d'Urbervilles* on the minds of its readers, it may be, is dependent on the chains of repetition which structure it as a text, even (or perhaps better) when the reader is not fully conscious of those chains.

If Angel's first noticing of Tess is not the first, but already a repetition, Tess's first meeting with Alec is heavy with future consequences, in spite of the fact that it is the conjunction of the coarse with the finer, the wrong man with the right woman. As the narrator affirms, "In the ill-judged execution of the well-judged plan of things the call seldom produces the comer, the man to love rarely coincides with the hour for loving. Nature does not often say 'See!' to her poor creature at a time when seeing can lead to happy doing; or reply 'Here!' to a body's cry of 'Where?' till the hide-and-seek has become an irksome, outworn game" (ch. 5). Time in this novel is this failure of fit. The narrative is generated by the division between Tess and her proper mate. This spacing opens up the field of desire through which Tess wanders, driven by her longing for her missing counterpart. This "anachronism," this bad timing, makes possible inharmonious conjunctions like that of Tess and Alec. These are displaced or deformed parodies of the true conjunction that would satisfy desire. These false encounters are the shocks and catastrophes making up Tess's destiny—the death of Prince, her violation, the murder of Alec, her union, too late, with Angel.

The novel's earlier title, "Too Late Beloved" or "Too Late, Beloved," names the maladroit delays which put off Angel's love for Tess until it is too late for it to lead to a happy union except for a brief time just before death. The proper encounter comes only when Tess is at the edge of that death for which she consciously longs. "I wish I had never been born," she tells Alec when they separate after their brief liaison (ch. 12). During her visit to the tombs of the d'Urbervilles in their long rows, Tess asks vehemently, "Why am I on the wrong side of this door!" (ch. 52). In the poem "Tess's Lament," spoken apparently at a time after Angel has deserted Tess but before she has murdered Alec, she asks once more for death, this time in the form of a complete blotting out of all memory by others that she ever existed.

Completeness is not to be prophesied, or even conceived possible, because life is incompleteness. Completeness is death. If the time and the place were right, Tess might join her counterpart. Her individual existence would then disappear. When she meets her other half, it is already "the late time." They meet across the obstacle of her loss of virginity and of her brief liaison with Alec. She is already marked with the inexpungible stigma of "impurity." That impurity expresses the generative source, the Immanent Will. It is the mark of the sun upon her. This stigma keeps Tess from reaching the unity she desires. It has an irresistible power of genetic replication. Tess can die, her child, Sorrow, can die, but the pattern her life makes tends to repeat itself in apparently compulsive recurrences that constitute her "Fate." This pattern is at once the proleptic mark of the deferred joy and at the same time evidence that the joy has not yet been reached.

A happy, innocent union, such as that between Tess and Angel after she has murdered Alec, can for Hardy, in this novel at least, take place only in the shadow of death. The unmentioned existence of the corpse of Alec stands between Tess and Angel at their moment of greatest happiness. When she and Angel are alone together during their brief idyll, she is "thrown into a vague intoxicating atmosphere at the consciousness of being together at last, with no living soul between them; ignoring that there was a corpse" (ch. 57). She accepts death as the price she must pay for that happiness. "It is as it should be," she murmurs when she is captured at Stonehenge. "Angel, I am almost glad—yes, glad! This happiness could not have lasted. It was too much. I have had enough; and now I shall not live for you to despise me!" (ch. 58). Though the "compulsion to repeat" may be, as Freud argued, a disguise of the desire for death, this desire, it seems, cannot be satisfied. It cannot be satisfied because its goal does not exist, at least not as the point of undifferentiated origin to which all living organisms seem to have a desire to return. It exists rather as a phantasm generated by the incompleteness which is the true "beginning."

The notion of fate introduces the last model according to which Tess's violation may be understood as repetition. This model at first seems to invite the reader to interpret Tess's experience according to a conventional concept of destiny. This may be the idea, expressed by Tess in "Tess's Lament," that a person's life is inscribed already in some book of fate, and only copied from a predetermined pattern in its actual living through. It may be the idea that there is a designing mind controlling Tess's actions and forcing her to follow a certain pattern in her life. Tess's virgin flesh is "doomed to receive" the traces of a "coarse pattern." The pity of her life lies in the fact that "it was to be," according to the reading of it by her neighbors.

By the time the reader has followed out the implications of the reversal of the other models, he understands that Hardy's concept of fate cannot be dissociated from the notion of chance. Each crucial event in Tess's life is like a throw of the dice that creates one of the decisive configurations of her life—the chance encounter of Tess and Angel at the beginning, or the unlucky accident of the killing of Prince which leads Tess to seek her family's fortune at Trantridge, or the meeting of Tess's father with Parson Tringham which "originates" the whole sad sequence, or the misfortune that makes Tess's confessional letter slide under the rug in Angel's room rather than reach its intended destination. Each of these events is at once fated and accidental, like the mating of genes which creates a given individual. It happens by chance, as a fortuitous conjunction, but as the sequence of such chances lengthens out to form a chain it can in retrospect be seen to make a pattern of neatly repetitive events constituting Tess's destiny.

The episodes of *Tess of the d'Urbervilles* take place in a line, each following the last. Ultimately they form a row traced out in time, just as Tess's course is traced across the roads of southern England. Each episode in Tess's life, as it occurs, adds itself to previous ones, and, as they accumulate, behold!, they make a pattern. They make a design traced through time and on the landscape of England, like the prehistoric horses carved out on the chalk downs. Suddenly, to the retrospective eye of the narrator, of the reader, and ultimately even of the protagonist herself, the pattern is there. Each event, as it happens, is alienated from itself and swept up into the design. It ceases to be enclosed in itself and through its resonances with other events becomes a sign referring to previous and to later episodes which are signs in their turn. When an event becomes a sign it ceases to be present. It becomes other than itself, a reference to something else. For this reason Tess's violation and the murder must not be described directly. They do not happen as present events because they occur as repetitions of a pattern of violence which exists only in its recurrences and has always already occurred, however far back one goes.

In one way or another most analyses of prose fiction, including most interpretations of *Tess of the d'Urbervilles,* are based on the presupposition that a novel is a centered structure which may be interpreted if that center can be identified. This center will be outside the play of elements in the work and will explain and organize them into a fixed pattern of meaning deriving from this center. Hardy's insistent asking of the question "Why does Tess suffer so?" has led critics to assume that their main task is to find the explanatory cause. The reader tends to assume that Hardy's world is in one way or another deterministic. Readers have, moreover, tended to assume that this cause will be single. It will be some one force, original and originating. The various causes proposed have been social, psychological, genetic, material, mythical, metaphysical, or coincidental. Each such interpretation describes the text as a process of totalization from the point of departure of some central principle that makes things happen as they happen. Tess has been described as the victim of social changes in nineteenth-century England, or of her own personality, or of her inherited nature, or of physical or biological forces, or of Alec and Angel as different embodiments of man's inhumanity to woman. She has been explained in terms of mythical prototypes, as a Victorian fertility goddess, or as the helpless embodiment of the Immanent Will, or as a victim of unhappy coincidence, sheer hazard, or happenstance, or as the puppet of Hardy's deliberate or unconscious manipulations.

The novel provides evidence to support any or all of these interpretations. *Tess of the d'Urbervilles,* like Hardy's work in general, is overdetermined. The reader is faced with an embarrassment of riches. The problem is not that there are no explanations proposed in the text, but that there are too many. A large group of incompatible causes or explanations are present in the novel. It would seem that they cannot all be correct. My following through of some threads in the intricate web of Hardy's text has converged toward the conclusion that it is wrong in principle to assume that there must be some single accounting cause. For Hardy, the design has no source. It happens. It does not come into existence in any one version of the design which serves as a model for the others. There is no "original version," only an endless sequence of them, rows and rows written down as it were "in some old book," always recorded from some previously existing exemplar.

An emblem in the novel for this generation of meaning from a repetitive sequence is that red sign Tess sees painted by the itinerant preacher: THY, DAMNATION, SLUMBERETH, NOT. Each episode of the novel, or each element in its chains of recurrent motifs, is like one of these words. Each is a configuration which draws its meaning from its spacing in relation to the others. In the strange notation of the sign-painter, this gap is designated by the comma. The comma is a mark of punctuation which signifies nothing in itself but punctuation, a pause. The comma indicates the spacing in the rhythm of articulation that makes meaning possible. Each episode of the novel is, like one of the words in the sign, separated from the others, but when all are there in a row the meaning emerges. This meaning is not outside the words but within them. Such is the coercive power of pre-established syntactic sequences, that a reader is able to complete an incomplete pattern of words. Tess completes in terror and shame the second sign the painter writes: THOU, SHALT, NOT, COMMIT ——, and the reader knows that the relation of 'Liza-Lu and Angel will repeat in some new way the universal pattern of suffering, betrayal, and unfulfilled desire which has been established through its previous versions in the book.

Tess wanders through her life like a sleepwalker, unaware of the meaning of what she is doing. She seeks a present satisfaction which always eludes her until her final happiness in the shadow of death. Her damnation, however, slumbereth not. This "damnation" lies in the fact that whatever she does becomes a sign, takes on a meaning alienated from her intention. Hardy affirms his sense of the meaning of Tess's story not by explaining its causes but by objectively tracing out her itinerary so that its pattern ultimately emerges for the reader to see.

Hardy's notion of fatality is the reflex of his notion of chance. Out of the "flux and reflux—the rhythm of change" which "alternate[s] and persist[s] in everything under the sky" (ch. 50) emerges as if by miracle the pattern of repetitions in difference forming the design of Tess's life. Such repetitions produce similarity out of difference and are controlled by no center, origin, or end outside the chain of recurrent elements. For *Tess of the d'Urbervilles* this alternative to the traditional metaphysical concept of repetition emerges as the way the text produces and affirms its meaning. If the heterogeneity of *Wuthering Heights* lies in the way it invites the reader to seek some transcendent origin which will explain the repetitive elements the text presents, while at the same time frustrating that search, and if *Henry Esmond* shows how pervasive irony makes it impossible to decide certainly the meaning of a repetitive series, *Tess of the d'Urbervilles,* like Hardy's other novels, brilliantly explores the implications for an understanding of human life of a form of repetition which is immanent. Such a sequence is without a source outside the series. Different as are the four novels I have read so far in this book, all four are versions of the invitation, generated by the words of the novel, to believe that there is some single explanatory principle or cause, outside the sequence of repetitive elements in the text, accompanied in one way or another by a frustration of the search that belief motivates.

On the basis of this definition of immanent repetition, it is possible to identify what Hardy means by the first half of his definition of *Tess of the d'Urbervilles* as "an attempt to give artistic form to a true sequence of things." The artistic form is the novelist's interpretation of the events. This interpretation does not falsify the events, but it imposes meaning on them by reading them in a certain way, as a sentence may have entirely different meanings depending on how it is articulated. The meaning is there and not there. It is a matter of position, of emphasis, of spacing, of punctuation. In the preface of 1892 Hardy recognizes the revolutionary effect such a new emphasis may have. It reverses the usual positions of value. To be led by a new "sentiment" of human worth or meaning to call the "impure" the "pure" may lead to an overturning of the usual relations of possession and dominance in society. The chain of family and social connections may be upset by something that begins in a passing impression. The adverse critics of Tess, said Hardy in this preface, that to the fifth edition,

> may have causes to advance, privileges to guard, traditions to keep going; some of which a mere tale-teller, who writes down how the things of the world strike him, without any ulterior intentions whatever, has overlooked, and may by pure inadvertence have run foul of when in the least aggressive mood. Perhaps some passing perception, the outcome of a dream hour, would, if generally acted on, cause such an assailant considerable inconvenience with respect to position, interests, family, servant, ox, ass, neighbour, or neighbour's wife . . . So densely is the world thronged that any shifting of positions, even the best warranted advance, galls somebody's kibe. Such shiftings often begin in sentiment, and such sentiment sometimes begins in a novel.

In his quietly ironic way, Hardy is claiming a powerfully subversive effect for his novel. When by "pure inadvertence" he wrote the novel and summarized its impression on his candid mind by giving it the subtitle "A Pure Woman/Faithfully Presented," he initiated a shifting of positions, like the altered emphasis on words in a sentence. This shifting would, if acted on, ultimately rearrange the chain of power relationships in society.[8]

Attention is insistently called to the act of reading, in the broad sense of deciphering, throughout *Tess.* One way is the many examples of false interpretation which are exposed by the narrator. These include the comic example of the bull who thought it was Christmas Eve because he heard the Nativity Hymn, or the more serious dramatization of Angel's infatuation with Tess and his interpretation of her as like Artemis or like Demeter (ch. 20), or the description of Tess's "idolatry" of Angel (ch. 34), or Tess's false reading of nature as reproaching her for her impurity. All interpretation is the imposition of a pattern by a certain way of making cross-connections between one sign and those which come before and after. Any interpretation is an artistic form given to the true sequence of things. Meaning in such a process emerges from a reciprocal act in which both the interpreter and what is interpreted contribute to the making or the finding of a pattern. The notion that interpretation is both invention and discovery is neatly expressed in a passage in *The Life of Thomas Hardy:* "As, in looking at a carpet, by following one colour a certain pattern is suggested, by following another colour, another; so in life the seer should watch that pattern among general things which his idiosyncrasy moves him to observe, and describe that alone. This is, quite accurately, a going to Nature; yet the result is no mere photograph, but purely the product of the writer's own mind."[9] To add a new interpretation to the interpretation already proposed by the author is to attach another link to the chain of interpretations. The reader takes an impression in his turn. He represents to himself what already exists purely as a representation. To one purity the reader adds a subsequent purity of his own. This is Hardy's version of the notion of multiple valid but incompatible interpretations I am proposing in this book. I would myself put greater stress, however, as Hardy himself does in the passage in *Tess* with which I shall end this chapter, on the coercive power of the sequence itself to determine the interpretation, though it may be a complex and dissonant reading which is imposed, a reading combining incompatibilities which all demand to be recognized as valid by the reader.

In *Tess of the d'Urbervilles,* in any case, the narrator always presents not only the event with its "objective" elements, but also his interpretation of the event. At the same time he shows his awareness that the interpretation is "purely" imposed not inherent, except as it is one possibility among a limited repertoire of others. An example would be the "objective" description of the sun casting its beams on Tess. This is first interpreted as like the act of a god, but that interpretation is then ironically undercut: "His present aspect . . . explained the old time heliolatries in a moment" (ch. 14). The narrator's act in not only describing the true sequence of things but also giving it artistic form is shown as what it is by its doubling within the text in the interpretative acts of the characters. The narrator always sees clearly what is "subjective" in Tess's reading of her life, but this insight casts back to undermine his own readings. These multiple acts of interpretation are not misinterpretations in relation to some "true" interpretation. Each telling, even the most clear-sighted one, is another reading in its turn. The bare "reality" Angel sees when he falls out of love with Tess is as much an interpretation as the transfiguration of the world he experiences when he sees her as a goddess and the world as irradiated by her presence.

The power of readings to go on multiplying means that Tess's wish to be "forgotten quite" cannot be fulfilled. The chain of interpretations will continue to add new links. Tess can die, but the traces of her life will remain, for example in the book which records the impression she has made on the narrator's imagination. Her life has a power of duplicating itself which cancels the ending her failure to have progeny might have brought. The life of her sister will be, beyond the end of the book, another repetition with a difference of the pattern of Tess's life. Beyond that, the reader comes to see, there will be another, and then another, ad infinitum. If the novel is the impression made on Hardy's candid mind by Tess's story, the candid reader is invited to receive the impression again in his turn, according to that power of a work of art to repeat itself indefinitely to which the novel calls attention in a curious passage concerning Tess's sensitivity to music. Here is a final bit of evidence that Hardy saw the principle of repetition, in life as in art, as impersonal, immanent, and self-proliferating rather than as controlled by any external power, at least once a given repeatable sequence gets recorded in some form of notation or "trace." The "simplest music" has "a power over" Tess which can "well-nigh drag her heart out of her bosom at times" (ch. 13). She reflects on the strange coercive effect church music has on her feelings: "She thought, without exactly wording the thought, how strange and godlike was a composer's power, who from the grave could lead through sequences of emotion, which he alone had felt at first, a girl like her who had never heard of his name, and never would have a clue to his personality" (ch. 13). In the same way, *Tess of the d'Urbervilles,* as long as a single copy exists, will have its strange and godlike power to lead its readers through some version of the sequences of emotion for which it provides the notation.

6

THE WELL-BELOVED

The Compulsion to Stop Repeating

He was subject to gigantic fantasies still. In spite of himself, the sight of the new moon, as representing one who, by her so-called inconstancy, acted up to his own idea of a migratory Well-Beloved, made him feel as if his wraith in a changed sex had suddenly looked over the horizon at him. In a crowd secretly, or in solitude boldly, he had often bowed the knee three times to this sisterly divinity on her first appearance monthly, and directed a kiss toward her shining shape.

Hardy, *The Well-Beloved*

I

Art thou pale for weariness
Of climbing heaven and gazing on the earth,
Wandering companionless
Among the stars that have a different birth,—
And ever changing, like a joyless eye
That finds no object worth its constancy?

II

Thou chosen sister of the Spirit,
That gazes on thee till in thee it pities . . .

Shelley, "To the Moon"

"Till in thee it pities . . ." Shelley's fragment breaks off here. Pities what? The answer may be that the unquiet human spirit in pitying the moon's inconstancy pities its own companionless wandering. It sees in the moon a sisterly image of itself. The moon's inconstancy is the reflex of the beholder's. His joyless eye too sees no permanent source of joy in any object outside itself and so constantly changes. That unwillingly skeptical look reveals, in spite of itself, the worthlessness of any object on which it gazes. In the same way, Jocelyn Pierston, the hero of Hardy's *The Well-Beloved,* in one of his deepest moments of self-understanding, recognizes that his elusive well-beloved, whom he has seen incarnated in woman after woman, only to have her vanish each time on a closer approach, is really his self-image, his "wraith" or double "in a changed sex." The passage is strikingly like Shelley's unfinished poem.

The similarity to Shelley is scarcely surprising in a novel which not only draws its epigraph from *The Revolt of Islam* but also contains citations of *Prometheus Unbound* and *Epipsychidion,* as well as another quotation from *The Revolt of Islam.* Hardy's work is steeped in echoes of Shelley. *The Well-Beloved* is so much under the aegis of Shelley that it might be defined as a parody of him, or as an interpretation of his work, or as a subterranean battle to combat his influence. As Harold Bloom wittily puts it, apropos of Hardy's admirable last book of poems, the posthumously published *Winter Words,* the strength of Hardy's writing is "that it makes us read much of Shelley as though Hardy were Shelley's ancestor, the dark father whom the revolutionary idealist failed to cast out."[1] I should agree with this, except for the characterization of Shelley as a "revolutionary idealist." Shelley was already as much a skeptic as Hardy, a fact which Hardy well understood. *The Well-Beloved* takes from Shelley the theme of a brother-sister love, or of a narcissistic loving of oneself in the beloved. Such a love searches for a perfecting of oneself by joining oneself to a double of the other sex. (In *Laon and Cythna,* the first version of *The Revolt of Islam,* the lovers are brother and sister.) Like Shelley, Hardy explores the relation of this theme to the problem of writing or of the creative imagination, and to the problem of transcendent origin. As with many great writers, a central theme of Hardy's writing is literature itself, its nature and powers. More or less hidden in the earlier novels, this theme surfaces in the last one, *The Well-Beloved.* It surfaces in the form of an interrogation of the relation between erotic fascination, creativity, and Platonic metaphysics which makes *The Well-Beloved* one of a group of important nineteenth-century novels about art.

I have said that *The Well-Beloved* is an important novel. Certainly it is an odd one. It tells the story of a sculptor who falls in love with a girl, his cousin Avice, then twenty years later with her daughter, the second Avice, and then, after another interval of twenty years, with the granddaughter of the first Avice, Avice the third. In no case, in the final version of the novel, is this love consummated. *The Well-Beloved* superficially obeys, as do Hardy's earlier novels, the conventions of nineteenth-century realism, with its commitment to social and psychological verisimilitude. The Anniversary Edition of Hardy's works even contains what purports to be a photograph of the "cottage of Avice Caro" on the Isle of Portland. Nevertheless, the basic plot of *The Well-Beloved* can scarcely be said to be "realistic" in the ordinary sense. Hardy took note of this in the preface, dated January 1897, when he remarked that as "the interest aimed at is of an ideal or subjective nature, and frankly imaginative, versimilitude in the sequence of events has been subordinated to the said aim." This clash of incompatible features, mimetic realism in the mode of representation and fantasy in the action, has led some readers to dismiss the book. In fact it is an irreplaceable part of Hardy's work. It takes its place with Nerval's *Sylvie* and *Aurélia,* with Thackeray's *Henry Esmond,* and with Proust's *A la recherche du temps perdu* as another exploration of the association of love, repetition, artistic creativity, and religious longing. In *The Well-Beloved,* as in these companion texts, love is intensified when the beloved is the repetition of an earlier beloved, and this fact is associated with the artist's powers of representation. Jocelyn's series of repetitive loves embodies in his emotional life what might be called the "theory of signs" which is presupposed in Hardy's writing.

The Well-Beloved (1897) brings to an end Hardy's cycle of novels which begins with *Under the Greenwood Tree* (1872), or even before that with the never-published "The Poor Man and the Lady," written in 1868, and with *Desperate Remedies* (1871). The cycle culminates with *Tess of the d'Urbervilles* (1891) and *Jude the Obscure* (1895). The relation of *The Well-Beloved* to *Tess* and *Jude* is so close that one may claim the two greater novels cannot be fully understood in separation from their less famous sister. After Hardy withdrew *Tess* from periodical publication by Tillotson & Son (when they raised moral objections to it after the novel was half set in type), *The Well-Beloved* was the "something light" which he wrote for Tillotson in its place. The two versions of *The Well-Beloved,* that of 1892 in *The Illustrated London News* and the radically revised book version of 1897, bracket *Jude the Obscure.* There are many parallels in theme, phrasing, characterization, and dramatic structure among the three novels. An example is the similarity between the relations of Jude, Sue, and Arabella in *Jude the Obscure,* and those of Jocelyn, Marcia, and the Avices in *The Well-Beloved.* Another example is the Shelleyan and Platonic theme of the perfect lovers, two halves of a single androgynous whole. This theme is central in *The Well-Beloved,* but is already present in *Tess,* as I showed in the previous chapter.

Not only do Hardy's novels and poems repeat one another in theme, having as their constant subject betrayal, grotesque incongruity in clashing desires, and perpetual dissatisfaction in love; the suffering love causes is also in each case associated with repetition. All Hardy's novels in one way or another pose the question, "Why is it that most human beings go through life somnambulistically, compelled to repeat the same mistakes in love, so inflicting on themselves and on others the same suffering, again and again?" *The Well-Beloved* brings to an end the series of novels exploring this question by providing something so close to a definitive answer that the tension of the question dissolves, and novel-writing becomes no longer possible. That tension had always consisted in the difference between what the narrator of a novel by Hardy knows and what the protagonist knows, even at the end, as in Henchard's "& that no man remember me" in *The Mayor of Casterbridge,* or in Tess's "I am ready," or in Jude's "Let the day perish wherein I was born." The hero of *The Well-Beloved* begins, when the reader first meets him, with an approximation of the narrator's insight. He knows, half ironically, that in his infatuation with his elusive well-beloved he is bewitched by a fantasy. By the end of the novel he is fully demystified. Against the final self-judgments of Hardy's other late protagonists one may set the deeper disillusionment of Jocelyn's hysterical laughter, bitterer than any tears, which ends the first version, or his "Thank heaven I am old at last. The curse is removed," in the final version.[2] Jocelyn's fuller knowledge, even when the reader first meets him, means that his story is not so much, like *Tess of the d'Urbervilles,* the demonstration of an unwilled compulsion to repeat, as it is a dramatization of the futility of a more or less deliberate attempt to stop repeating and so win what Hardy in "Wessex Heights" calls "*some* liberty."[3]

In *The Well-Beloved* the somewhat covert structure and meaning of Hardy's earlier novels are brought more fully into the open. *The Well-Beloved* functions as an interpretation of the earlier novels or even as their parody. By presenting a schematic and "unrealistic" version of the pattern they share, it brings out their latent meaning. It calls attention to the rigid artifice of Hardy's stories. This artifice is masked in the earlier novels by the greater psychological and social versimilitude, and by the inclusion of more of the apparent irrelevance of life as it is, or at any rate of life as it was represented by the great Victorian realists. The way Jocelyn is cured by his final illness both of his infatuation with his well-beloved and of his artistic creativity may be taken as an emblem of this final laying bare of the motivating energy of Hardy's fiction. This laying bare also reveals the hidden connection between the theme of love and the theme of art.

If *The Well-Beloved* ended the novels, the writing of Hardy's great lyric poetry was not disabled. The extraordinary sequence of volumes of poetry leading finally to the posthumous *Winter Words* followed his cessation of the writing of fiction. He wrote many new poems up to the end, though even the final volume contains some poems written as early as the 1860s. The poems speak from the vantage point of Hardy's deepest skepticism and sense of loss, and so the writing of poetry was possible even from the perspective of a "full look at the Worst."[4] The poetry did not depend on the presence, except in remembered retrospect, of someone beguiled by love and by its unassuageable desire. *The Well-Beloved* puts its protagonist, at the end, where the speaker of Hardy's poems characteristically stands from the beginning.

Marcel Proust, with his characteristic brilliance as a critic, recognized the importance of *The Well-Beloved.* He saw that it is exemplary of the repetitive symmetries of Hardy's work as a whole, and he saw also the way it can be seen as a clue to the meaning of those symmetries. Proust's reading of Hardy comes in the passage in "La Prisonnière" in which Marcel explains to Albertine his notion that a great writer or artist, a Vermeer, Stendhal, Dostoevsky, or Hardy, creates the same work over and over throughout his life: "the great writers have never written more than a single work, or rather have refracted across diverse milieux that unique beauty which they bring into the world." In Hardy's case, the characteristic artistic signature is the "stonemason's geometry" of his novels.

> You remember this well enough in *Jude the Obscure,* but have you seen in *The Well-Beloved* the blocks of stone which the father takes from the island coming by boat to be set up in the studio of the son where they become statues; in *A Pair of Blue Eyes,* the parallelism of the tombs, and also the parallel line of the boat, and the contiguous railroad cars in which are the two lovers and the corpse; the parallelism between *The Well-Beloved,* where the man loves three women, *A Pair of Blue Eyes* where the woman loves three men, etc., and finally all those novels which can be superimposed on top of one another, like the houses vertically set up one above the other on the rocky soil of the island?[5]

The juxtaposition of Proust, Stendhal, and Dostoevsky with Hardy will support the claim of another kind of importance for *The Well-Beloved.* If it closes the great sequence of Hardy's own novels, it may also be seen as bringing to an end a form of prose fiction characteristic of the Victorian novel. This happens more than chronologically. *The Well-Beloved* in various ways, like novels contemporary with it by James or by Conrad, challenges the assumptions which had apparently been taken for granted in most Victorian novels. One difference between Victorian and twentieth-century fiction in English, at least so it seems, is the relatively overt sophistication of the latter about the fictionality of fiction. A twentieth-century novelist is usually more openly aware of the dependence of his work on all sorts of conventions. These conventions, far from seeming a direct imitation of things as they are, are seen as artificial. The text indicates in one way or another an awareness that novels could be written according to more than one convention of storytelling.

It is easy to exaggerate this difference. Most Victorian novels are a good bit more explicitly self-conscious about their status as fiction than might at first appear. Many critics are now investigating such aspects of works by Dickens, George Eliot, Trollope, or Thackeray. Even so, most Victorian novels at least superficially maintain the illusion that they are imitated from some extralinguistic reality. They present themselves as a species of history. They are, moreover, committed, at least in their apparent form, to the notion that the stories they tell have definite contours, a beginning, a middle, and an end. The end is especially important. It is the *telos* of the whole, the goal toward which the life of the protagonist has been tending. The end of a Victorian novel retrospectively sums it up. The ending gives the story a definitive meaning in the death of the protagonist or in a marriage justifying the traditional conclusion: "They lived happily ever after." Twentieth-century fiction seems likely to be more ostentatious in putting these mimetic and teleological assumptions in question. *Tess of the d'Urbervilles,* for example, is "Victorian" by the definition I am suggesting. It moves fatefully forward toward its end in Tess's execution. Nevertheless, as I pointed out in Chapter 5, *Tess* is an example of the open-endedness which also tends to characterize Victorian novels in one way or another. "Every limit is a beginning as well as an ending," says George Eliot in the Finale of *Middlemarch.*[6] In *Tess of the d'Urbervilles* this countermovement to the desire to tell a single story with a definitive ending is present in the hints that the life of 'Liza-Lu, Tess's sister, will in one way or another repeat Tess's life. *The Well-Beloved,* if it anticipates the more overt open-endedness of many twentieth-century novels, also brings into the open some of the embarrassments and difficulties of making a firm ending which many Victorian novels manifest.

Hardy's difficulty in making *The Well-Beloved* conform to normal conventions of realistic fiction is easier to see in the New Wessex Edition, which prints for the first time in a single volume both the ending of the book version of 1897 and the radically different ending of the periodical version of 1892. The full meaning of the novel emerges only through the juxtaposition of the two versions. The final version is a sequence of three episodes each repeating a different form of the others. Jocelyn falls in love, one after the other, with the first, the second, and the third Avice—mother, daughter, and granddaughter. He sees each in turn as an avatar of his goddess, the well-beloved. For different contingent reasons in each case, he fails all three times to consummate his love, returning at last to Marcia, the woman he had joined briefly in a casual liaison. In the version of 1892 Jocelyn actually marries Marcia, and also ultimately marries the third Avice, though the marriage is annulled when Marcia returns.

The most striking difference between the two versions is the reuse in the later version of the same material—the same scenes, the same phrases—for a radically different episode at the end. In the first version Jocelyn resolves to commit suicide by drowning himself. He feels his way in the darkness down the stone passage to the beach and steals a boat without oars to float out to sea, where he knows he will be caught in "The Race." In the final version, the same scene, with the same details, is rewritten as a description of the elopement of the third Avice and her lover in order to avoid her promised marriage to Jocelyn. The superimposition of the two endings compels the reader to think of the three episodes of the novel not as leading in some necessary order from one to another but as alternative versions of the same story, piled one on top of the other like the stone houses of Jocelyn's native island. The presence of two quite different endings for the novel, either one of which makes a plausible conclusion, forbids the reader to interpret the novel in terms of a necessary momentum toward a single conclusion. Moreover, a reading of the two versions reinforces the reader's sense that the novel is contrived, fantastic, openly fictional, detached from any model in the real world. *The Well-Beloved* is clearly something that Hardy has written, not something copied directly from real life. It is something that he might have written otherwise. In fact he has written it otherwise, changing it radically from one version to the next. The changes affirm his sovereign power as creator over a fiction which no longer needs to validate itself by its presumed correspondence to some "reality" outside literature.

The Well-Beloved anticipates twentieth-century experimentation and recapitulates in its own way the experimentation of, say,

Cervantes or Sterne. If its self-conscious artifice reminds the reader of Sterne, it also anticipates, for example, John Fowles's *The French Lieutenant's Woman,* with its two alternative endings, between which the novelist will not choose: "The only way I can take no part in the fight is to show two versions of it."[7] Fowles is an acknowledged follower of Hardy. The fact that *The Well-Beloved* exists in two versions makes it foreshadow J. L. Borges's more elaborately theoretical "The Garden of the Forking Paths." That story proposes the monstrous notion of a labyrinthine work of fiction which would present exhaustive permutations of every possible alternative for each episode. *The Well-Beloved,* with its three sequential versions of the same story of frustrated love and its two endings, already has a structure something like that of Borges's imagined novel. In fact there are four possible endings suggested for *The Well-Beloved.* The ending in the first version is one, and in the second version Jocelyn might or might not succeed in committing suicide. A fourth ending is shadowed forth when he considers returning to America, ostensibly to seek Marcia but really to disappear so the third Avice will be free to marry the young man she loves.

Doubt of the power of a single ending to determine unequivocally the meaning of a narrative sequence was, after all, not foreign to the Victorians. Though they thought a novel should have a single definitive text, they were nevertheless master manipulators of multiple plots, as much so as Shakespeare and his contemporaries. A multiplotted novel often presents, more or less openly, alternative workings out of the same narrative materials. The meaning of such a novel lies not in the predominance of one story over the others but in the relations of similarity and difference established by their juxtaposition. *Wuthering Heights,* as I have tried to show in my chapter on it here and in an earlier essay,[8] is a Victorian novel which overtly presents two versions of the same story. One of Trollope's greatest novels, *He Knew He Was Right,* is a good example of the less ostentatious development, in the various plots, of several possible endings for the same story. Moreover, there are Victorian novels which present an ending so unexpected by most readers, so apparently out of tone with the rest of the novel, as to have been scandalous, at least to their original readers. The surprise of an unexpected ending may make the reader realize that it would have been possible to justify any one of a series of possible endings. Each ending would have been consistent with certain features of the book, while no ending could fulfill all the possible threads of expectation the text establishes. George Meredith's *The Ordeal of Richard Feverel* is such a novel. Certain Victorian novels, finally, do in fact have two different endings. Dicken's *Great Expectations* is the best known, though Hardy's own *The Return of the Native* has a ghostly footnote at the end of the penultimate chapter informing the reader that he had intended to have Diggory Venn disappear mysteriously from the heath, "nobody knowing whither," rather than marry Thomasin. "Readers," says Hardy, "can therefore choose between the endings, and those with an austere artistic code can assume the more consistent conclusion to be the true one."[9] If *The Well-Beloved* anticipates Fowles or Borges, it also brings into the open those subversions of the idea of a single ending which were already latent in one way or another in Victorian fiction.

The signal importance of *The Well-Beloved,* from this perspective, might be expressed by saying that the problem of endings is thematized in the story. The question of alternative endings is not a superficial formal problem, something which results from Hardy's difficulty in deciding how to finish the novel. Rather, it is one of the things Jocelyn's story is about. The reasons for Hardy's difficulty with the ending and the answers to the puzzles of Jocelyn's life are analogous. Proust's interpretation of Hardy is misleading insofar as it suggests that there is some single form, some unique "beauty," which each of Hardy's novels incarnates in a different way, just as Jocelyn is mistaken when he thinks he loves an immortal goddess who momentarily embodies herself in this or that mortal girl. *The Well-Beloved* is concerned to demystify this belief in a transcendent prototype. The traditional form of the novel, with its fixed beginning, causal sequence, and determined end, works powerfully to reinforce belief in some form of metaphysical ground, some reason or *logos,* behind the story. *The Well-Beloved* therefore either must have a form which corresponds to its antimetaphysical theme, or must reinforce, in spite of itself, the belief it aims to uncover as a delusion. The double ending of *The Well-Beloved* corresponds to its ambiguities of thematic meaning.

The reader might be tempted to believe that if *The Well-Beloved* does not have a single clear ending, at least it has an unequivocal beginning. Jocelyn's infatuation with the first Avice, the reader might think, establishes a fixed pattern of loving from which he is unable to free himself, so that he loves the first Avice in her doubles, the second and third Avices. An admirable episode at the beginning of the first version, cut from the final version, makes such an interpretation impossible, and even the final version makes it clear that Jocelyn's courtship of the first Avice has behind it a long string of loves as "the migratory, elusive idealization he call[s] his Love," has "flitted from human shell to human shell an indefinite number of times" (pt. I, ch. 1). If the novel has two endings it also has two beginnings. Those in both versions indicate that far from being the first of his loves, Avice is only one of a long line stretching back into the past, prior to anything the reader can learn from the text, but present, in the first version, in the old bundles of love letters which Jocelyn tries unsuccessfully, at first alone and then in Avice's presence, to burn: " 'I see—I see now!' she whispered, 'I am—only one—in a long, long row!' From the white sheets of paper round about her seemed to rise the ghosts of Isabella, Florence, Winifred, Lucy, Jane, and Evangeline—each writer from her own bundle respectively—and Maud and Dorothea from the flames. He hardly knew what to say to the new personality in the presence of the old" (p. 206).

"I am—only one—in a long, long row!"—this is just what Tess says at one of her moments of insight into her situation: "What's the use of learning that I am one of a long row only" (*Tess*, ch. 19). Far from being a beginning, Avice, like Tess, is only an intermediate digit somewhere in the midst of a long series stretching before and after into misty vagueness. Of this series neither the beginning nor the end is given nor can in principle be given. The antecedent items in the row do not disappear. They remain, both in *Tess* and in *The Well-Beloved*, as written records which inhibit the possibility of action initiatory or free. The difficulty Jocelyn has in burning his old love letters in the first version of the novel is an admirable emblem of this.

The questions raised by Jocelyn's strange story are similar to those raised by *Tess of the d'Urbervilles.* The difference is that *The Well-Beloved* more clearly asks why it is impossible to stop a chain of repetitions. What is it, the novel implicity asks, that compels Jocelyn, like the protagonists of Hardy's other novels, to repeat the pattern of a love doomed to cause suffering and dissatisfaction, even if he more or less deliberately attempts to avoid doing the same thing over and over? What is it that compels the narrator to tell the strange story over again? Why does Hardy (who differs from the imagined narrator and whose motivations are therefore different) write such an odd novel, one which so openly flies in the face of the "realistic" conventions he for the most part obeys? If explanations by way of origin, end, or governing prototype do not suffice to interpret it, and are forbidden by the text itself, what explanation, rational or irrational, will satisfy the mind's uneasiness concerning it?

A certain narrative design is repeated in a number of different strata of the text of *The Well-Beloved.* It is repeated also in the relation of this novel to texts before and after, texts by Hardy or by others. The fullest understanding of the novel is achieved by moving back and forth from one of those versions of the pattern to another, interpreting each by the others. The design in question exists on the level of the physical scene in which the story is for the most part enacted, namely the Isle of Slingers and its surrounding ocean. It exists on the level of traditional social relations on the island, as well as in its material culture of buildings, roads, gardens, and quarries. It exists as the design of Jocelyn's story, in his failure ever to possess any of the Avices, and also in the connection of this to the "bubbling spring" of artistic creativity which dries up at the same moment he is "cured" of his infatuation with his well-beloved. The structure is repeated again in the relation of *The Well-Beloved* to other works by Hardy. It is once more repeated, though not in quite the same way, in the novel's relation to works by other writers before and after, both those by authors whose works Hardy knew or who knew his work and those by authors to whom the relation was indirect.

The pattern exists again, finally, in the relations among four personages: Thomas Hardy the man, the fictive narrator of the novel, its hero, and the author of any critical essay on the novel. In all these cases the structure is that of repetition which attempts to put a definitive stop to a row but only succeeds in prolonging it, in keeping it open.

Why should one wish to make an end, and what is it that forbids fulfillment of this modest wish? The patterns in question in their interrelation, each as the emblem of the others, will give the answer, though the answer is alogical, "past surmise and reason's reach."[10] For this "reason" it can only be given in the patterns, never in a wholly perspicuous conceptual language. In Jocelyn's case the desire to escape from repetition expresses itself both in his work as a sculptor and in his love for the various Avices, as well as in his love for the other women with whom he has been infatuated. It expresses itself also in the strange bar which keeps him from union with any of the Avices. Jocelyn's love is vigorously heterosexual. Nevertheless, there is something missing in it, some inhibition which weakens it. The Avices are all closely related to him, since each native of the island is a near relation of all the others. Something like the prohibition against incest therefore operates to forbid his union with them. As his "sisters," they are also, in a manner of speaking, his female images in the mirror, his wraiths in a changed sex. All love, for Hardy, even the most mature heterosexual love, has this narcissistic component. It is the displacement of the self's love for itself.

Jocelyn's artistic creativity is a further displacement of his sexual desire. Each stands for the other. Jocelyn's work as a sculptor has only one subject. He makes statue after statue of the "well-beloved," the goddess of love, Venus or Astarte, those deities worshiped by the old Romans and Phoenicians on his native isle. This goddess is his female counterimage, whom he both desires and fears. The concentration in *The Well-Beloved* on a single genetic strain, product of immemorial intermarrying generations, reinforces the notion, present also in the passage about the moon, that the merging of lover with beloved is the mating of a man with his image in the mirror. This is reinforced by the reduction of the beloved in the three successive love stories to a series of persons with the same name, grandmother, mother, daughter, all cousins of the lover, representations of the single island face, which is Jocelyn's face too. In Hardy's other novels, even in *Jude the Obscure,* there is more exogamy. The drama of *The Well-Beloved* is throughout a more internal one. It is the story of the single consciousness divided against itself, striving to merge again with itself, seeing in others even of the other sex only its own double.

The topic of sexual desire is the vehicle of the theme of writing as repetition. Each theme, it might be better to say, is the vehicle of the other. The relation of the two themes of the novel—artistic creation and erotic fascination—is established in a way characteristic of Hardy in the preface he wrote in 1912 for the Wessex Edition of his work. This way is indirect and quietly ironic and yet defiant. In Chapter 5 I showed how the preface to *Tess of the d'Urbervilles* commits again a "crime" for which it seemingly apologizes. Something of the same sort happens in the preface to *The Well-Beloved.* In this case, the association of writing with crime becomes explicit.

It is surprising, Hardy says in the preface, apropos of the island's propensity to generate fantasies, "that the place has not been more frequently chosen as the retreat of artists and poets in search of inspiration," but then, he adds, "to be sure, one nook therein is the retreat, at their country's expense, of other geniuses from a distance." These other geniuses are the fifteen hundred criminals incarcerated in the prison on the Isle of Portland. Hardy himself and his surrogate spokesman, the narrator, are also geniuses from a distance. They are "kimberlins." They are natives neither in the way Jocelyn's laborer father is absorbed in the life of the island nor in the way Jocelyn himself is a native of natives made a fantast by the slight distance from that life his leisure gives him. Thomas Hardy, the outlander in search of inspiration, needs the native-born fantast in order to have something to write about, just as he needs his imaginary spectator counterpart, the narrator, to tell the story. Hardy's act of imagination prolongs and duplicates their acts of imagination, making a chain of repetitions which matches in a different register the chain of repetitions in Jocelyn's series of loves. The echoes in the novel of many earlier texts—the Bible, Virgil, Wyatt, Shakespeare, Crashaw, Milton, Shelley, and Tennyson—form another repetitive chain parallel to the other two.

The peninsular Isle of Slingers, "home of a curious and well-nigh distinct people, cherishing strange beliefs and singular customs," has, says Hardy in the preface, a power to generate odd acts of imagination, especially in those who have some leisure. The figure used to describe these fantasies emphasizes the way they seem to grow "naturally," like herbage, from the stone of the island, as have seemingly also grown the strange customs of the people living there: "Fancies, like certain soft-wooded plants which cannot bear the silent inland frosts, but thrive by the sea in the roughest of weather, seem to grow up naturally here, in particular amongst those natives who have no active concern in the labours of the 'Isle.' " To have an active concern in the labors of the Isle is to be part of the endless pattern of creation and death, cycle after cycle, each canceled cycle leaving its ruin behind. Jocelyn's father cuts the stone but has no understanding of the statues his son makes of it. The Avices live and die apparently without understanding the fantastic drama of repetitive love in which they participate. Such involvement forbids the detachment necessary for that fantasy form of these cycles imagination takes. These fantasies take two forms in the novel. Both are incarnated in Jocelyn, in a curious relation of mutual reinforcement and mutual inhibition.

One form of imagination is the love dream which determines the strange series of Jocelyn's infatuations. This, says Hardy in the preface, is both particular to the island peninsula, bred like a sea plant from its rock, and at the same time common to all men. Similarly, in the general preface to the Wessex Edition of his work Hardy says that in his novels the "apparently local" is "really universal": "Hence it [the peninsula] is a spot apt to generate a type of personage like the character imperfectly sketched in these pages—a native of natives—whom some may choose to call a fantast . . . , but whom others may see only as one that gave objective continuity and a name to a delicate dream which in vaguer form is more or less common to all men, and is by no means new to Platonic philosophers." The "delicate dream" is the erotic form of Platonism, the belief that an earthly woman incarnates a celestial archetype, the universal Woman, the goddess on whom all earthly women are modeled. The drama of this dream is the one all Hardy's work in one way or another explores.

The Well-Beloved brings into the open more clearly than any other work by Hardy the reasons why this drama is always a story of dissatisfaction. It also brings into the open the way it is a drama of projected meanings. The real women—each of the three Avices, but also Marcia, and all the other women from off the island whom Jocelyn at one time or another loves—are signs for the goddess, the well-beloved. The goddess is the spiritual woman who seems to enter into the body of each mortal woman, as a meaning enters into a word or some other sign. Jocelyn experiences repeatedly the vanishing of that spiritual presence as he moves closer and closer to its embodiment. Each time he is left with the "dead" body alone. That body is like a word which has been repeated so often it becomes an empty sound. "We are a strange, visionary race down where I come from," says Jocelyn as he tries to explain his experience to a friend, "and perhaps that accounts for it. The Beloved of this one man, then [he means himself], has had many incarnations—too many to describe in detail. Each shape, or embodiment, has been a temporary residence only, which she has entered, lived in awhile, and made her exit from, leaving the substance, so far as I have been concerned, a corpse, worse luck!" (pt. I, ch. 7).

In such an experience of disillusionment the once-beloved becomes no longer the sign of a spiritual plentitude, but the sign of an absence, of nothing at all. She becomes an empty emblem, a nest from which the bird has flown, "a language in living cipher no more" (pt. II, ch. 3). Jocelyn's erotic fantasies are an occasion for experiencing a linguistic problem, the incompatibility of meaning with the signs for it and the emptying out of belief in a transcendent referent when this incompatibility is recognized. The epigraph from Shelley's *The Revolt of Islam* which Hardy chose for the novel expresses this succinctly: "One shape of many names." This calling attention, in the word "names," to the specifically linguistic component of Jocelyn's mystified love echoes the epigraph from *Two Gentlement of Verona* for *Tess of the d'Urbervilles:* "Poor wounded name . . ." If the earthly women Jocelyn loves are like names, signs for the invisible goddess, Hardy the writer preserves Tess and her story, in spite of her wish to have her life "unbe," by writing it down, that is, by turning Tess into a name. The bodies of the women Jocelyn loves function as the "many names" for the "one shape" of the elusive well-beloved, just as the body of a word, its material substance as marks on a page or as acoustical vibrations, carries its meaning.

The same drama is enacted in a different way in the other mode of Jocelyn's island-bred tendency to fantasy. Like his series of erotic fascinations, Jocelyn's sculpture takes the form of a potentially endless sequence of statues of the goddess. Each statue, as it is completed, becomes mere stone once more, an empty sign, and so Jocelyn must begin another statue, just as his love for real women always "dies of contact."[11]

Jocelyn's art and his strange love life are inversely related. His power as a sculptor is strongest during the time after he has been abandoned by Marcia. It seems as if his loving and his carving must have a common source. What is used for one is not available for the other: "During the many uneventful seasons that followed Marcia's stroke of independence . . . , Jocelyn threw into plastic creations that ever bubbling spring of emotion which, without some conduit into space, will surge upwards and ruin all but the greatest of men" (pt. I, ch. 9). The spring of emotion is creative and affirmative. This is true both as it expresses itself in Jocelyn's loving and as it expresses itself in his sculpture. The same force, if it is capped, becomes explosively destructive, except in the greatest of men, which apparently means those who have a superhuman power of repression to match the power of the well of emotion. In Jocelyn's case the well finally exhausts itself in his last illness. He is cured simultaneously of his loving and of his artistic creativity: "The artistic sense had left him, and he could no longer attach a definite sentiment to images of beauty recalled from the past" (pt. III, ch. 8). The symbol for this removal picks up the image of the bubbling spring of creativity and completes the novel in a final version of this motif: "His business was, among kindred undertakings which followed the extinction of the Well-Beloved and other ideals, to advance a scheme for the closing of the old natural fountains in the Street of Wells, because of their possible contamination" (pt. III, ch. 8). This attempt to make an end short of death is, as I shall show, necessarily futile.

As Proust saw, it is not without significance that Jocelyn in his London studio, at the height of his artistic powers and artistic success, makes his statues of blocks of stone cut out by his quarryman father from the rock of his native isle. That island is in fact a peninsula, a presqu'île. It is a single phallus-shaped block of limestone jutting out into the sea, a male member of stone four miles long. The monumental stones the father cuts out of this living rock are erected by Jocelyn in his studio and then made into images of his goddess. The island is already ambiguous in its sexuality, like Jocelyn himself, or like his name. The stone, moreover, combines unity with the multiplicity of generation or of dissemination. The technical name Hardy uses for the stone of the island is "oolite," eggstone. It is a rough limestone with egg-shaped calcareous grains in it. The word "oolite" is a new Latin translation of the German *Rogenstein,* roe stone. The stone is not single but made of innumerable stratified layers. These layers are one above the other like the stone houses on the island, each the bones of a generation of tiny sea creatures, crossed out like a mistaken passage in a piece of writing. Hardy borrows the latter figure in his citation from Shelley's *Prometheus Unbound* at the opening of the novel (quoted below). The "eggs" are not the beginning of a new life cycle but the dead remnants of one passed through. Houses or statues may make these bones rise again. Throughout *The Well-Beloved,* what dies does not disappear but has the power, even in its cancellation, to initiate new cycles of the life-generating exchange of energy:

> The towering rock, the houses above houses, one man's doorstep rising behind his neighbour's chimney, the gardens hung up by one edge to the sky, the vegetables growing on apparently almost vertical planes, the unity of the whole island as a solid and single block of limestone four miles long, were no longer familiar and commonplace ideas. All now stood dazzlingly unique and white

> against the tinted sea, and the sun flashed on infinitely stratified walls of oolite,
>
> The melancholy ruins
> Of cancelled cycles, . . .
>
> with a distinctiveness that called the eyes to it as strongly as any spectacle he had beheld afar . . . He stretched out his hand to the rock beside him. It felt warm. (Pt. I, ch. 1)

If the whole island is a somewhat epicene male emblem, contradictory in import, single and multiple at once, seeds and eggs together, dead and yet life-giving, the ocean into which the peninsula juts is the female counterpart. The female implications focus on the tidal sway of the waves and on that dangerous maelstrom called the Race which whirls just beyond the tip of the Isle. As Jocelyn drifts alone into the Race in one ending, so in the other Henri drifts with his bride-to-be into the Race, in a scene which doubles and parodies the first ending. In the first ending the Race casts Jocelyn back to life, refusing his attempt to find oblivion by joining himself to the sea. In the second ending the couple who will initiate the new generation pass through the Race as they begin their life together. It was that same sea whose rhythmic moaning mingled with the cries of the second Avice when the third Avice was born:

> The sea moaned—more than moaned—among the boulders below the ruins, a throe of its tide being tuned to regular intervals. These sounds were accompanied by an equally periodic moan from the interior of the cottage chamber; so that the articulate heave of water and the articulate heave of life seemed but differing utterances of the self-same troubled terrestrial Being—which in one sense they were. (Pt. II, ch. 13)

The feminine matrix of the sea seems to have priority over "the peninsula carved by time out of a single stone," since the stone is made of shells and bones generated out of the sea. The two together, female sea and male peninsula, are the relics of an immemorial process of generation. Season after season makes one more ephemeral set of myriad shoals of little sea animals. In dying, they add one more layer of stone, in an endless rhythm of giving birth and dying which is a form of speech and of which human parturition is one more sentence or phrase. These utterances are articulate language in two ways. They are rhythmic signs as they are spoken. They leave the readable signs of themselves behind as remnants at the end of the life cycle. Both in nonhuman nature and in the human world, which grows from nature and is part of it, these endless life cycles are a product of the ever-repeated intermarriage of the same with the same. Like Jocelyn's love letters, they are traces of the long row stretching into that past, the "done" which Hardy says it is impossible to "undo."[12]

The proliferation of life-forms out of the ocean, in its production of a remnant which is a gigantic emblem of the sexual relation, is matched by the sociological structure of life on the peninsula. Only a single face and a handful of surnames exist on the Isle. Marriage with an outlander or kimberlin is discouraged. Marriage therefore is usually intermarriage, a mating of close relations within the same genetic line. Moreover, an immemorial custom of trial sexual relations before marriage is sometimes still practiced on the Isle. Such a sex act is doubly illicit: between consanguineous persons, it is a kind of incest, and it is initially unhallowed by a formal marriage tie. These matings leave ever-new generations, one Avice after another, like the stone houses above stone houses on the island, and like its infinitely stratified stone. All these patterns are emblems for the totality of biological life, including human life as Hardy sees it. Human life is not "symbolized" by the stone peninsula and the sea. It is part of their interaction. It arises from that interaction and returns to it, leaving its marks in layers on the island, just as the little sea beasts have done and are doing still on the seafloor:

> The three Avices, the second something like the first, the third a glorification of the first, at all events externally, were the outcome of the immemorial island customs of intermarriage and of prenuptial union, under which conditions the type of feature was almost uniform from parent to child through generations: so that, till quite

> latterly, to have seen one native man and woman was to have seen the whole population of that isolated rock, so nearly cut off from the mainland. (Pt. III, ch. 2)

If to mate with one's close cousin in a premarital union is to commit a kind of incest, such intermarriage might be defined as an attempt to get back the lost unity, to retrace the steps that have led to the differentiation of life. *The Well-Beloved* dramatizes, in its different versions of the same pattern, a contradictory desire. Like all desire, the one in question here is posited on the sense that something is missing. The goal of the desire is to find that something missing, to achieve completion, to fill the gap. Hardy focuses on the male's desire to fulfill himself. The male wishes to complete himself or to make up for a lack by joining himself to a beloved of the opposite sex. The beloved is goddess, mother, mistress, sister, mirroring counterpart, all in one, the lover's wraith in a changed sex. Jocelyn's desire is contradictory because its fulfillment would be his death and so not the fulfillment of desire. He would die in the death of the desire which defines him as lacking something. Incompletion and the impossibility of being completed is an intrinsic feature of the self in this case. Jocelyn needs to obtain what he lacks in order to be truly himself, truly a self. On the other hand, his selfhood, what he is, is that lack. If it were to be filled he would cease to be himself. The "he" in question would vanish. Between the two desires, the desire to maintain his separateness and so keep a self which is no self and the desire to complete himself and so die as himself, Jocelyn hovers. He is able neither to act nor not to act. His hesitation prolongs the row of recurrences, whether he acts or does not act. In either case the result is the same, the extension of the series. The series cannot by any operation be brought to an end. It has an intrinsic tendency to extend itself on and on.

The inhibition against concluding the pattern or bringing its meaning fully into the open is not the fear that the way back to the primordial unity may be blocked. It is rather the fear that this unity is an illusion, that it never existed. The haunting dread is that there is no undivided sense, source, and patron of meaning governing the chain. However far back one goes, there may be only an initial division, an initial lack. If this is the case, then the satisfaction of desire in the future may also be impossible. If there were an original signifier, a father force who would solidly guarantee meaning, then Jocelyn might acquire that paternal potency. Jocelyn could then become a substantial self by possessing the mother or some sister-surrogate for the mother. If there is no such patron, if the beloved is a projection or mirror image of Jocelyn himself, then the emptiness of the beloved, the revelation that she is a sign referring to nothing, is the revelation of his own emptiness or impotence.The discovery that the beloved is my twin, that I love myself in the beloved, shows the futility of the attempt to found the self by a displacement of its love for itself to the love of its own image in a changed sex.

Jocelyn experiences this futility both in the failure of his sculpture and in the failure of his loving. Only the Avices, because he does not possess them, retain their auras. Jocelyn's refusal to mate with any of the Avices holds off the final revelation of his lack and so keeps him going. His response to the beloved as the repetition of an earlier beloved, a sign for an earlier sign, both obscures this revelation and obscurely makes it. Jocelyn loves the second and third Avices as repetitions of the first. To merge with the Avice who is one's ghostly image, sister, or second self, or to marry the second or third Avice and find that she is not a repetition of the spiritual substance seemingly once incarnated in the first Avice, but rather a repetition of her lack of substance, would be for Jocelyn to discover that the source of his bubbling creativity is an absence, not a positive fecundating power. This recognition he instinctively postpones.

Jocelyn's deepest fear is that he may not be able to achieve the goal of death. The lack of paternal origin may mean the impossibility of reaching a satisfactory end. If Jocelyn were to survive in his offspring, the "thing in man that heeds no call to die" would continue its proliferations, making more and more layers of stone. The quoted phrase comes from "Heredity" (CP, p 434), a poem based on a journal entry for February 19, 1889: "The story of a face which goes through three generations or more, would make a fine novel or poem of the passage of Time. The differences in personality to be ignored." Hardy's comment on this in the *Life* connects it not only with the poem but also with *The Well-Beloved*: "This idea was to some extent carried out in the novel *The Well-Beloved*, the poem entitled 'Heredity,' etc."[13] Two poems, "Heredity" and "The Pedigree," and three novels, *The Well-Beloved*, *Tess of the d'Urbervilles*, and *Jude the Obscure*, are in part responses to Hardy's reading, in the latter part of 1890, of the English translation by Edward B. Poulton of August Weismann's *Essays on Heredity* (Oxford, 1899).[14] Weismann's book propounds a theory of the immortality of the germ plasm. It is also referred to at crucial places in Freud's *Beyond the Pleasure Principle*, his most elaborate development of the notion of a death wish which is inhibited by the compulsion to repeat. For Hardy, as for Freud (and rather unexpectedly under the influence of the same prior writer), the self both wants to die and wants to postpone death, partly through a fear that death as total quiescence may be impossible to obtain. Even to join oneself to one's sister or second self would not be to die wholly. It would only be a way of ensuring survival, not the survival of an "I" but the survival of an "it." The ultimate grimness of the human condition in *The Well-Beloved*, as in Hardy's work generally, is not the universality of death but the fact that it may be impossible to die. Whatever Jocelyn does, whether he acts or does not act, whether he speaks or keeps silent, he only prolongs the detour to death. In Jocelyn act all his ancestors. Whatever he does echoes something those forebears have already done. Even his most idiosyncratic action becomes a repetition, since all variations of lovemaking and the refusal of love have already been performed innumerable times. What Jocelyn does in both endings of the novel, however different from one another they are, comes in this to the same thing. As repetitions, his actions add themselves to the series and keep it open, however hard he tries to bring an end to the sequence of recurrences which has made up his life. Whatever he does contains in itself the necessity of still more repetitions.

The relations of the narrator, the author, and the reader to Jocelyn's story exemplify this tendency in Hardy's work for repetitive patterns to go on repeating. They exemplify also the way this tendency both reveals the lack of an original support of meaning and postpones full recognition of this lack.

The narrator of *The Well-Beloved* is not the author, since the narrator has powers of mobility and clairvoyance no real human being could possess. The narrator is a detached witness, like all Hardy's narrators. He is for the most part ironic, withdrawn, coolly demystifying in his analyses. He looks back dispassionately from some indeterminate later time toward the past of the story. He also possesses a superhuman power of insight into the secrets behind the merely visible exteriors of the people and scenes he describes. This power is expressed intermittently, mostly in relation to Jocelyn. The narrator usually sees from a distance, like a recording camera eye.

If the narrator of *The Well-Beloved* exists chiefly as an onlooker and as a dry, ironic voice offering a minimum of disillusioning explanation, the preface suggests a more intimate and paradoxical relation. The narrator fulfills Hardy's claim that the island is not only a place where fantasies are native but also a place where outlanders might find inspiration. The fancy of the narrator, effaced by the pretense of objective realism, has been nourished at one remove by the fancy of the natives. He is not a native, but he breathes again the inspiration of the natives. He needs Jocelyn's island-bred propensity to fantasy to make his own writing possible. That writing will end when the source of inspiration is closed, when Jocelyn simultaneously loses his artistic talent and his infatuation with his well-beloved. When Jocelyn closes the old wells of the island he leaves the narrator with no more story to tell, his own sources of inspiration dried up, but the story once told, written down, printed, and published, perpetuates itself whenever it is read.

Jocelyn can lose his artistic sensibility and his power to love. He can close all the old wells and tear down the stone houses, one above another, which are emblems of his repetitive loves. He will even one day die, though his attempt in the first ending to commit suicide by drowning in the Race fails. The narrator, in his imaginative responses to the story, opens the wells again and keeps them open. He then doubles this reopening by writing the story down. In doing this he demonstrates once more Hardy's abiding insight that nothing can undo the done. Whatever is done leaves traces of itself which have an inexhaustible power of iteration. Jocelyn is right to have an instinctive repugnance for sexual reproduction. His avoidance of marriage does not, however, free him from the perpetuation of the pattern of his life. It is repeated in the imagination of the narrator and in the record of that imagination in the text of the novel.

It would seem that the placement of the "author" should be at the beginning, as the authorizing source. No doubt *The Well-Beloved* obliquely reflects Hardy's relations to his cousin Tryphena Sparks (who matches the Avices) and to his wife Emma Lavinia (who like Marcia was a kimberlin outside the Hardy family). The farm called Talbothays, owned by Hardy's father, had belonged in the sixteenth century to a family named Talbot, "from a seventeenth-century daughter of whom Hardy borrowed the name of Avis or Avice in *The Well-Beloved.*"[15] The novel also, the reader may guess, transposes Hardy's complex shame at his childlessness, his secret joy in that childlessness, his regret, his fear that in one way or another his pedigree would be continued anyhow, his hidden desire that it should be continued, in spite of his childlessness, perhaps through his writing.

Hardy in his life had experienced one version of the story he tells in *The Well-Beloved.* The reader might therefore be tempted to interpret *The Well-Beloved* according to the idea that literature is the self-expression and self-validation of a unique self, the self of the author, in this case Thomas Hardy. The reduction of the author of *The Well-Beloved* to a subsidiary function of the text, made and unmade by it, forbids such an interpretation. The "real" author, Thomas Hardy, attempts to give himself substance in his work. He does this by projecting himself into a fictive narrator who tells a fictive story which is a displacement of Hardy's own story. Instead of providing him with substance, the narrator, by doubling and depersonifying Thomas Hardy and by telling a story about the impossibility of novel or autonomous action, deprives him of originality. The story undermines Hardy's claims to authority as the generating source of the story he writes. The version of the pattern story of *The Well-Beloved* in Hardy's own life was not the "original" one, but a "terribly belated edition" (pt. III, ch. 2), since the pattern, as the novel shows, is one that has occurred over and over from time immemorial, and will go on occurring. Hardy's attempt to possess himself or to found himself securely by telling Jocelyn's story leads to dispossession. The narrator and the story the narrator tells suggest that Hardy is created by the story he has his alter ego tell. The man and author Thomas Hardy becomes within the pages of *The Well-Beloved* subject to the long chain of earlier versions of the story written by the various authors he cites, Plato, Shakespeare, Milton, Crashaw, Shelley. The story he tells repeats with a difference stories they have told. This echoing line of citations shows that this novel is only one more naming of the "one shape of many names." It cannot be appropriated by a single signature, any more than the well-beloved can be incarnated once and for all in a single shell. Thomas Hardy, life story and all, ceases to be the authorizing source and becomes himself only one in the middle of a long row.

The series extends after as well as before. No doubt, for example, Proust would have written *A la recherche du temps perdu* if he had never read *The Well-Beloved* (which he did in 1910), but his novel would not have been quite the same, nor perhaps would his life have been the same. The great scene of the Princesse de Guermantes's matinée at the end of Proust's novel brings together in Odette, Gilberte, and Mlle de Saint-Loup the mother, daughter, and granddaughter whom Marcel has loved or may yet love. Gilberte offers to introduce her daughter to Marcel, just as the second Avice introduces her daughter, the third Avice, to Jocelyn: "I wish you could speak to her—I am sure you would like her" (pt. III, ch. 1). Moreover, the real Marcel Proust loved both Mme Arman de Caillavet and, later, her daughter. He wrote, probably in 1910, the year he read *The Well-Beloved,* a witty impertinent letter to the mother about his love for the daughter. The letter might almost have been written by Jocelyn Pierston to Avice the first about Avice the second, or to Avice the second about Avice the third: "For here I am, in love with your daughter. How naughty of her to be so gracious, for her smile, which has made me fall in love with her, colors her whole personality."[16] Both Proust's life and his novel seem to have been intermittently taken possession of by patterns from Hardy. It is as though Proust had become willy-nilly subject to a compulsion to repeat like that of Jocelyn, like that of the narrator of *The Well-Beloved,* or like that of Hardy himself. Proust perpetuates the pattern of which Hardy's life and writing are further examples, items in the row.

Any reader, or anyone who writes a critical essay on *The Well-Beloved,* is momentarily the last in this line. He is no more able than any of the other links in the chain to put an end to it. He cannot provide a definitive explanation of the novel which will stop the passing on of its compulsion to repeat itself. What the critic says also in its own way keeps the generative force alive. This might be called the aporia of interminability. It is not the encounter with the blank wall beyond which one cannot go, but the failure ever to find an end to the corridors of interpretation. Since no movement backward through the woven lines of the text will reach a starting place with explanatory power to run through the whole chain, it is equally impossible in the other direction ever to reach a definitive explanatory end. Goal vanishes when origin recedes. Each explanation both hides and reveals the lack of sufficient reasonable explanation, the failure of that "principle of reason" which is the basis of metaphysical thinking in the West.

The critic's effort to express his insight puts one more barrier between himself and what he is attempting to express. This parallels the way Hardy is driven to write and rewrite the same episode, providing alternative "endings," none of which "puts an end" to the novel. Or the critic's enterprise is analogous to Jocelyn's effort to gain and lose his individuality by joining himself, in art or in love, to his well-beloved. That effort by writer, artist, lover, or critic would, even if it were successful, lead only to the creation of more works of art, more critical essays, more names for the pedigree, so keeping the immortal germ cell alive and perpetuating what wants to die. Either ending of the novel, or any one of a potentially interminable set of other possible endings, adds itself to the series of episodes. Each makes sense, but none can be the neat denouement which unties all knots and at the same time gathers all loose ends. The double ending in the New Wessex Edition keeps the chain visibly open. It thereby corresponds to the meaning of the novel, which is its lack of definitive meaning. This meaning cannot be reduced to some formula like narcissism, the fear of castration, the death of God, or the death wish, since the sequence of explanations is always open to a further variation, whether inside the novel itself, or in a "creative" extension like Proust's, or in a critical essay. Each of these may take a different form and reinscribe the pattern differently, though each will be, if it is a valid member of the series, a version of this particular pattern.

The aporia of interminability in *The Well-Beloved* is generated by its various forms of interlocking repetition. This impasse is not the confrontation of a definitive obstacle to further thought but a searching for a definite end which can never be found. The repetitions one behind the other in past and in future make it impossible to solve or resolve the story once and for all. The critic can only reformulate the pattern once more in an interpretation which is more or less adequate, though I claim that the interpretation I offer here best accounts for the manifest lack of "organic unity" in the novel as we have it in its double form.

The recurrences for which any reading must account include the different versions of Jocelyn's life in the sequence of episodes and in the inconclusiveness of the double ending. They include the doubling of the hero by the narrator, of the narrator by the author, of earlier authors by the text, of the author by each later novelist or critic who reads *The Well-Beloved.* They include all the other forms of doubling I have identified: the doubling of each Avice by the next, the doubling of Jocelyn by his image in the glass, the doubling of Jocelyn by each of his lunar sister-images, the doubling and redoubling in the stone of the island, layer after layer. All these forms of repetition forbid any closure of the novel in a conclusive reading, though the "reasons" why such a reading is in principle impossible may perhaps be conclusively formulated. In the case of such a text, any new reading, like each of the Avices, is no more than an additional link midway in an endless chain stretching before and behind.

If *Wuthering Heights* manifests the consequences for literary form of the assumption that there must be a transcendent origin but an origin which is in principle incompatible with unequivocal expression in either conceptual or figurative language, *The Well-Beloved*, like *Tess of the d'Urbervilles*, and like Hardy's other work in prose and verse, is an exploration of the consequences for human life and for literary form of the absence of any conscious transcendent mind. The specifically theological or metaphysical aspect of Hardy's thought is his full understanding that only such a transcendent mind would guarantee the possibility of the rational order of beginning, middle, end, and determinate meaning either for human lives or for works of literature. Hardy's lucid recognition of the enormous losses which follow from the vanishing of belief in God motivates his attempts to see ghosts and to talk himself into some form of belief. "I have always wanted to see a ghost," he told a friend. ". . . I would willingly concede ten years of my life if I could see any supernatural thing that could be proved to me to exist by any means within my capacity." [17] All his life Hardy went on looking for God, "as an external personality, of course—the only true meaning of the word,"[18] and he felt that if God existed he would have found him. When we go to church, he wrote, "we have to sing, 'My soul doth magnify the Lord,' when what we want to sing is 'O that my soul could find some Lord that it could magnify!' "[19] The distinction of Hardy's "full look at the Worst" is to have seen so clearly, perhaps most clearly of all in *The Well-Beloved*, the connections among three strata of human life: erotic experience, unfulfilled religious longing, and the making or reading of works of literature. If the transcendent shape named by the various incarnations of the well-beloved is an illusion, a projection, then both human life and works of literature will take the form of a virtually endless series of similar episodes which can be stopped neither by knowing the illusion is an illusion nor by not knowing it. *The Well-Beloved* brilliantly exemplifies a form of repetition growing out of this situation and out of the futile attempt to stop repeating.

7

MRS. DALLOWAY

Repetition as the Raising of the Dead

THE SHIFT FROM THE LATE VICTORIAN or early modern Thomas Hardy to a fully modernist writer like Virginia Woolf might be thought of as the transition to a new complexity and a new self-consciousness in the use of devices of repetition in narrative. Critics commonly emphasize the newness of Virginia Woolf's art. They have discussed her use of the so-called stream-of-consciousness technique, her dissolution of traditional limits of plot and character, her attention to minutiae of the mind and to apparently insignificant details of the external world, her pulverization of experience into a multitude of fragmentary particles, each without apparent connection to the others, and her dissolution of the usual boundaries between mind and world.[1] Such characteristics connect her work to that of other twentieth-century writers who have exploded the conventional forms of fiction, from Conrad and Joyce to French "new novelists" like Nathalie Sarraute. It might also be well to recognize, however, the strong connections of Woolf's work with the native traditions of English fiction. Far from constituting a break with these traditions, her novels are an extension of them. They explore further the implications of those conventions which Austen, Eliot, Trollope, and Thackeray exploited as the given conditions of their craft. Such conventions, it goes without saying, are elements of meaning. The most important themes of a given novel are likely to lie not in anything which is explicitly affirmed, but in significances generated by the way in which the story is told. Among the most important of those ways is Woolf's organizing of her novels around various forms of recurrence. Storytelling, for Woolf, is the repetition of the past in memory, both in the memory of the characters and in the memory of the narrator. *Mrs. Dalloway* (1925) is a brilliant exploration of the functioning of memory as a form of repetition.

The novel is especially fitted to investigate not so much the depths of individual minds as the nuances of relationship between mind and mind. If this is so, then a given novelist's assumptions about the way one mind can be related to others will be a generative principle lying behind the form his or her novels take. From this perspective the question of narrative voice can be seen as a special case of the problem of relations between minds. The narrator too is a mind projected by a way of speaking, a mind usually endowed with special access to other minds and with special powers for expressing what goes on there.

The manipulation of narrative voice in fiction is closely associated with that theme of human time or of human history which seems intrinsic to the form of the novel. In many novels the use of the past tense establishes the narrator as someone living after the events of the story have taken place, someone who knows all the past perfectly. The narrator tells the story in a present which moves forward toward the future by way of a recapitulation or repetition of the past. This retelling brings that past up to the present as a completed whole, or it moves toward such completion. This form of an incomplete circle, time moving toward a closure which will bring together past, present, and future as a perfected whole, is the temporal form of many novels.

Interpersonal relations as a theme, the use of an omniscient narrator who is a collective mind rising from the copresence of many individual minds, indirect discourse as the means by which that narrator dwells within the minds of individual characters and registers what goes on there, temporality as a determining principle of theme and technique—these are, I have argued elsewhere,[2] among the most important elements of form in Victorian fiction, perhaps in fiction of any time, in one proportion or another. Just these elements are fundamental to Virginia Woolf's work too. It would be as true to say that she investigates implications of these traditional conventions of form as to say that she brings something new into fiction. This can be demonstrated especially well in *Mrs. Dalloway.* The novel depends on the presence of a narrator who remembers all and who has a power of resurrecting the past in her narration. In *Mrs. Dalloway* narration is repetition as the raising of the dead.

"Nothing exists outside us except a state of mind"[3]—this seemingly casual and somewhat inscrutable statement is reported from the thoughts of the solitary traveler in Peter Walsh's dream as Peter sits snoring on a bench in Regent's Park. The sentence provides an initial clue to the mode of existence of the narrator of *Mrs. Dalloway.* The narrator is that state of mind which exists outside the characters and of which they can never be directly aware. Though they are not aware of it, it is aware of them. This "state of mind" surrounds them, encloses them, pervades them, knows them from within. It is present to them all at all the times and places of their lives. It gathers those times and places together in the moment. The narrator is that "something central which permeate[s]," the "something warm which [breaks] up surfaces" (p. 46), a power of union and penetration which Clarissa Dalloway lacks. Or, to vary the metaphor, the narrator possesses the irresistible and subtle energy of the bell of St. Margaret's striking half past eleven. Like that sound, the narrator "glides into the recesses of the heart and buries itself." It is "something alive which wants to confide itself, to disperse itself, to be, with a tremor of delight, at rest" (p. 74). Expanding to enter into the inmost recesses of each heart, the narrator encloses all in a reconciling embrace.

Though the characters are not aware of this narrating presence, they are at every moment possessed and known, in a sense violated, by an invisible mind, a mind more powerful than their own. This mind registers with infinite delicacy their every thought and steals their every secret. The indirect discourse of this registration, in which the narrator reports in the past tense thoughts which once occurred in the present moments of the characters' minds, is the basic form of narration in *Mrs. Dalloway.* This disquieting mode of ventriloquism may be found on any page of the novel. Its distinguishing mark is the conventional "he thought" or "she thought," which punctuates the narrative and reveals the presence of a strange one-way interpersonal relation. The extraordinary quality of this relation is hidden primarily because readers of fiction take it so much for granted. An example is the section of the novel describing Peter Walsh's walk from Clarissa's house toward Regent's Park: "Clarissa refused me, he thought"; "like Clarissa herself, thought Peter Walsh"; "It is Clarissa herself, he thought"; "Still the future of civilisation lies, he thought"; "The future lies in the hands of young men like that, he thought" (pp. 74–76)—and so on, page after page. If the reader asks himself where he is placed as he reads any given page of *Mrs. Dalloway,* the answer, most often, is that he is plunged within an individual mind which is being understood from inside by an ubiquitous, all-knowing mind. This mind speaks from some indeterminate later point in time, a point always "after" anything the characters think or feel. The narrator's mind moves easily from one limited mind to another and knows them all at once. It speaks for them all. This form of language generates the local texture of *Mrs. Dalloway.* Its sequential structure is made of the juxtaposition of longer or shorter blocks of narrative in which the narrator dwells first within Clarissa's mind, then within Septimus Smith's, then Rezia Smith's, then Peter's, then Rezia's again, and so on.

The characters of *Mrs. Dalloway* are therefore in an odd way, though they do not know it, dependent on the narrator. The narrator has preserved their evanescent thoughts, sensations, mental images, and interior speech. She rescues these from time past and presents them again in language to the reader. Narration itself is repetition in *Mrs. Dalloway.* In another way, the narrator's mind is dependent on the characters' minds. It could not exist without them. *Mrs. Dalloway* is almost entirely without passages of meditation or description which are exclusively in the narrator's private voice. The reader is rarely given the narrator's own thoughts or shown the way the world looks not through the eyes of a character, but through the narrator's private eyes. The sermon against "Proportion" and her formidable sister "Conversion" is one of the rare cases where the narrator speaks for her own view, or even for Woolf's own view, rather than by way of the mind of one of the characters. Even here, the narrator catches herself up and attributes some of her own judgment of Sir William Bradshaw to Rezia: "This lady too [Conversion] (Rezia Warren Smith divined it) had her dwelling in Sir William's heart" (p. 151).

In *Mrs. Dalloway* nothing exists for the narrator which does not first exist in the mind of one of the characters, whether it be a thought or a thing. This is implied by those passages in which an external object—the mysterious royal motorcar in Bond Street, Peter Walsh's knife, the child who runs full tilt into Rezia Smith's legs, most elaborately the skywriting airplane—is used as a means of transition from the mind of one character to the mind of another. Such transitions seem to suggest that the solid existing things of the external world unify the minds of separate persons because, though each person is trapped in his or her own mind and in his or her own private responses to external objects, nevertheless these disparate minds can all have responses, however different they may be, to the same event, for example to an airplane's skywriting. To this extent at least we all dwell in one world.

The deeper meaning of this motif in *Mrs. Dalloway* may be less a recognition of our common dependence on a solidly existing external world than a revelation that things exist for the narrator only when they exist for the characters. The narrator sometimes moves without transition out of the mind of one character and into the mind of another, as in the fourth paragraph of the novel, in which the reader suddenly finds himself transported from Clarissa's mind into the mind of Scrope Purvis, a character who never appears again in the novel and who seems put in only to give the reader a view of Clarissa from the outside and perhaps to provide an initial demonstration of the fact that the narrator is by no means bound to a single mind. Though she is bound to no single mind, she is dependent for her existence on the minds of the characters. She can think, feel, see only as they thought, felt, and saw. Things exist for her, she exists for herself, only because the others once existed. Like the omniscient narrators of *Vanity Fair*, *Middlemarch*, or *The Last Chronicle of Barset*, the omniscient narrator of *Mrs. Dalloway* is a general consciousness or social mind which rises into existence out of the collective mental experience of the individual human beings in the story. The cogito of the narrator of *Mrs. Dalloway* is, "They thought, therefore I am."

One implication of this relation between the narrator's mind and the characters' minds is that, though for the most part the characters do not know it, the universal mind is part of their own minds, or rather their minds are part of it. If one descends deeply enough into any individual mind one reaches ultimately the general mind, that is, the mind of the narrator. On the surface the relation between narrator and individual goes only one way. As in the case of those windows which may be seen through in a single direction, the character is transparent to the narrator, but the narrator is opaque to the character. In the depths of each individual mind, this one-way relationship becomes reciprocal. In the end it is no longer a relationship, but a union, an identity. Deep down the general mind and the individual mind become one. Both are on the same side of the glass, and the glass vanishes.

If this is true for all individual minds in relation to the universal mind, then all individual minds are joined to one another far below the surface separateness, as in Matthew Arnold's image of coral islands which seem divided, but are unified in the depths.[4] The most important evidence for this in *Mrs. Dalloway* is the fact that the same images of unity, of reconciliation, of communion well up spontaneously from the deep levels of the minds of all the major characters. One of the most pervasive of these images is that of a great enshadowing tree which is personified, a great mother who binds all living things together in the manifold embrace of her leaves and branches. This image would justify the use of the feminine pronoun for the narrator, who is the spokeswoman for this mothering presence. No man or woman is limited to himself or herself, but each is joined to others by means of this tree, diffused like a mist among all the people and places he or she has encountered. Each man or woman possesses a kind of immortality, in spite of the abrupt finality of death: "did it not become consoling," muses Clarissa to herself as she walks toward Bond Street, "to believe that death ended absolutely? but that somehow in the streets of London, on the ebb and flow of things, here, there, she survived, Peter survived, lived in each other, she being part, she was positive, of the trees at home; of the house there, ugly, rambling all to bits and pieces as it was; part of people she had never met; being laid out like a mist between the people she knew best, who lifted her on their branches as she had seen the trees lift the mist, but it spread ever so far, her life, herself" (p. 12; see also pp. 231, 232). "A marvellous discovery indeed—" thinks Septimus Smith as he watches the skywriting airplane, "that the human voice in certain atmospheric conditions (for one must be scientific, above all scientific) can quicken trees into life! . . . But they beckoned; leaves were alive; trees were alive. And the leaves being connected by millions of fibres with his own body, there on the seat, fanned it up and down; when the branch stretched he, too, made that statement" (p. 32). "But if he can conceive of her, then in some sort she exists," thinks the solitary traveler in Peter Walsh's dream, "and advancing down the path with his eyes upon sky and branches he rapidly endows them with womanhood; sees with amazement how grave they become; how majestically, as the breeze stirs them, they dispense with a dark flutter of the leaves charity, comprehension, absolution . . . let me walk straight on to this great figure, who will, with a toss of her head, mount me on her streamers and let me blow to nothingness with the rest" (pp. 85–87). Even Lady Bruton, as she falls ponderously asleep after her luncheon meeting, feels "as if one's friends were attached to one's body, after lunching with them, by a thin thread" (p. 170).

This notion of a union of each mind in its depths with all the other minds and with a universal, impersonal mind for which the narrator speaks is confirmed by those notations in *A Writer's Diary* in which, while writing *Mrs. Dalloway,* Woolf speaks of her "great discovery," what she calls her "tunnelling process,"[5] that method whereby, as she says, "I dig out beautiful caves behind my characters: I think that gives exactly what I want; humanity, humour, depth. The idea is that the caves shall connect" (WD, p. 59).

Deep below the surface, in some dark and remote cave of the spirit, each person's mind connects with all the other minds, in a vast cavern where all the tunnels end. Peter Walsh's version of the image of the maternal tree ends nevertheless on an ominous note. To reach the great figure is to be blown to nothingness with the rest. This happens because union with the general mind is incompatible with the distinctions, the limitations, the definite edges and outlines, one thing here, another thing there, of daylight consciousness. The realm of union is a region of dispersion, of darkness, of indistinction, sleep, and death. The fear or attraction of the annihilating fall into nothingness echoes through *Mrs. Dalloway*. The novel seems to be based on an irreconcilable opposition between individuality and universality. By reason of his or her existence as a conscious human being, each man or woman is alienated from the whole of which he or she is actually, though unwittingly or at best half-consciously, a part. That half-consciousness gives each person a sense of incompletion. Each person yearns to be joined in one way or another to the whole from which he or she is separated by the conditions of existence as an individual.

One way to achieve this wholeness might be to build up toward some completeness in the daylight world, rather than to sink down into the dark world of death. "What a lark! What a plunge!" (p. 3)—the beginning of the third paragraph of *Mrs. Dalloway* contains in miniature the two contrary movements of the novel. If the fall into death is one pole of the novel, fulfilled in Septimus Smith's suicidal plunge, the other pole is the rising motion of "building it up," of constructive action in the moment, fulfilled in Clarissa Dalloway's party. Turning away from the obscure depths within them, the characters, may, like Clarissa, embrace the moment with elation and attempt to gather everything together in a diamond point of brightness: "For Heaven only knows why one loves it so, how one sees it so, making it up, building it round one, tumbling it, creating it every moment afresh"; "what she loved was this, here, now, in front of her"; "Clarissa . . . plunged into the very heart of the moment, transfixed it, there—the moment of this June morning on which was the pressure of all the other mornings, . . . collecting the whole of her at one point" (pp. 5, 12, 54). In the same way, Peter Walsh after his sleep on a park bench feels, "Life itself, every moment of it, every drop of it, here, this instant, now, in the sun, in Regent's Park, was enough" (pp. 119–120). (This echoing from Clarissa to Peter, it is worth noting, is proof that Clarissa is right to think that they "live in each other.")

"The pressure of all the other mornings"—one way the characters in *Mrs. Dalloway* achieve continuity and wholeness is through the ease with which images from their pasts rise within them to overwhelm them with a sense of immediate presence. If the characters of the novel live according to an abrupt, discontinuous, nervous rhythm, rising one moment to heights of ecstasy only to be dropped again in sudden terror or despondency, nevertheless their experience is marked by profound continuities.

The remarkably immediate access the characters have to their pasts is one such continuity. The present, for them, is the perpetual repetition of the past. In one sense the moment is all that is real. Life in the present instant is a narrow plank reaching over the abyss of death between the nothingness of past and future. Near the end of the novel Clarissa thinks of "the terror; the overwhelming incapacity, one's parents giving it into one's hands, this life, to be lived to the end, to be walked with serenely; there was in the depths of her heart an awful fear" (p. 281). In another sense, the weight of all the past moments presses just beneath the surface of the present, ready in an instant to flow into consciousness, overwhelming it with the immediate presence of the past. Nothing could be less like the intermittencies and difficulties of memory in Wordsworth or in Proust than the spontaneity and ease of memory in *Mrs. Dalloway.* Repeatedly during the day of the novel's action the reader finds himself within the mind of a character who has been invaded and engulfed by a memory so vivid that it displaces the present of the novel and becomes the virtual present of the reader's experience. So fluid are the boundaries between past and present that the reader sometimes has great difficulty knowing whether he is encountering an image from the character's past or something part of the character's immediate experience.

An example of this occurs in the opening paragraphs of the

novel. *Mrs. Dalloway* begins in the middle of things with the report of something Clarissa says just before she leaves her home in Westminster to walk to the florist on Bond Street: "Mrs. Dalloway said she would buy the flowers herself" (p. 3). A few sentences later, after a description of Clarissa's recognition that it is a fine day and just following the first instance of the motif of terror combined with ecstasy ("What a lark! What a plunge!"), the reader is "plunged" within the closeness of an experience which seems to be part of the present, for he is as yet ignorant of the place names in the novel or of their relation to the times of Clarissa's life. Actually, the experience is from Clarissa's adolescence: "For so it had always seemed to her, when, with a little squeak of the hinges, which she could hear now, she had burst open the French windows and plunged at Bourton into the open air" (p. 3).

The word "plunge," reiterated here, expresses a pregnant ambiguity. If a "lark" and a "plunge" seem at first almost the same thing, rising and falling versions of the same leap of ecstasy, and if Clarissa's plunge into the open air when she bursts open the windows at Bourton seems to confirm this identity, the reader may remember this opening page much later when Septimus leaps from a window to his death. Clarissa, hearing of his suicide at her party, confirms this connection by asking herself, "But this young man who had killed himself—had he plunged holding his treasure?" (p. 281). If *Mrs. Dalloway* is organized around the contrary penchants of rising and falling, these motions are not only opposites, but are also ambiguously similar. They change places bewilderingly, so that down and up, falling and rising, death and life, isolation and communication, are mirror images of one another rather than a confrontation of negative and positive orientations of the spirit. Clarissa's plunge at Bourton into the open air is an embrace of life in its richness, promise, and immediacy, but it is when the reader encounters it already an image from the dead past. Moreover, it anticipates Septimus's plunge into death. It is followed in Clarissa's memory of it by her memory that when she stood at the open window she felt "something awful was about to happen" (p. 3). The reader is not surprised to find that in this novel which is made up of a stream of subtle variations on a few themes, one of the things Clarissa sees from the window at Bourton is "the rooks rising, falling" (p. 3).

The temporal placement of Clarissa's experiences at Bourton is equally ambiguous. The "now" of the sentence describing Clarissa's plunge ("with a little squeak of the hinges, which she could hear now"), is the narrator's memory of Clarissa's memory of her childhood home brought back so vividly into Clarissa's mind that it becomes the present of her experience and of the reader's experience. The sentence opens the door to a flood of memories which bring that faraway time back to her as a present with the complexity and fullness of immediate experience.

These memories are not simply present. The ambiguity of the temporal location of this past time derives from the narrator's use of the past tense conventional in fiction. This convention is one of the aspects of the novel which Woolf carries on unchanged from her eighteenth- and nineteenth-century predecessors. The first sentence of the novel ("Mrs. Dalloway said she would buy the flowers herself"), establishes a temporal distance between the narrator's present and the present of the characters. Everything that the characters do or think is placed firmly in an indefinite past as something which has always already happened when the reader encounters it. These events are resurrected from the past by the language of the narration and placed before the present moment of the reader's experience as something bearing the ineradicable mark of their pastness. When the characters, within this general pastness of the narration, remember something from their own pasts, and when the narrator reports this in that indirect discourse which is another convention of *Mrs. Dalloway,* she has no other way to place it in the past than some version of the past tense which she has already been using for the "present" of the characters' experience: "How fresh, how calm, stiller than this of course, the air was in the early morning" (p. 3). That "was" is a past within a past, a double repetition.

The sentence before this one contains the "had" of the past perfect which places it in a past behind that past which is the "present" of the novel, the day of Clarissa's party. Still Clarissa can hear the squeak of the hinges "now," and the reader is led to believe that she may be comparing an earlier time of opening the windows with a present repetition of that action. The following sentence is in the simple past ("the air was"), and yet it belongs not to the present of the narration, but to the past of Clarissa's girlhood. What has happened to justify this change is one of those subtle dislocations within the narration which are characteristic of indirect discourse as a mode of language. Indirect discourse is always a relationship between two distinguishable minds, but the nuances of this relationship may change, with corresponding changes in the way it is registered in words. "For so it had always seemed to her"—here the little word "had" establishes three identifiable times: the no-time or time-out-of-time-for-which-all-times-are-past of the narrator; the time of the single day of the novel's action; and the time of Clarissa's youth. The narrator distinguishes herself both temporally and, if one may say so, "spatially," from Clarissa and reports Clarissa's thoughts from the outside in a tense which she would not herself use in the "now" of her own experience. In the next sentence these distances between the narrator and Clarissa disappear. Though the text is still in indirect discourse in the sense that the narrator speaks for the character, the language used is much more nearly identical with what Clarissa might herself have said, and the tense is the one she would use: "How fresh, how calm, stiller than this of course, the air was in the early morning." The "was" here is the sign of a relative identity between the narrator's mind and the character's mind. From the point of view the narrator momentarily adopts, Clarissa's youth is at the same distance from the narrator as it is from Clarissa, and the reader is left with no linguistic clue, except the "stiller than this of course," permitting him to tell whether the "was" refers to the present of the narration or to its past. The "was" shimmers momentarily between the narrator's past and Clarissa's past. The subtly varying tense structure creates a pattern of double repetition in which three times keep moving together and then apart. Narration in indirect discourse, for Woolf, is repetition as distancing and merging at once.

Just as a cinematic image is always present, so that there is difficulty in presenting the pastness of the past on film (a "flash-back" soon becomes experienced as present), so everything in a conventional novel is labeled "past." All that the narrator presents takes its place on the same plane of time as something which from the narrator's point of view and from the reader's is already part of the past. If there is no past in the cinema, there is no present in a novel, or only a specious, ghostly present which is generated by the narrator's ability to resurrect the past not as reality but as verbal image.

Woolf strategically manipulates in *Mrs. Dalloway* the ambiguities of this aspect of conventional storytelling to justify the power she ascribes to her characters of immediate access to their pasts. If the novel as a whole is recovered from the past in the mind of the narrator, the action of the novel proceeds through one day in the lives of its main characters in which one after another they have a present experience, often one of walking through the city, Clarissa's walk to buy flowers, Peter Walsh's walk through London after visiting Clarissa, Septimus and Rezia's walk to visit Sir William Bradshaw, and so on. As the characters make their ways through London the most important events of their pasts rise up within them, so that the day of *Mrs. Dalloway* may be described as a general day of recollection. The revivification of the past performed by the characters becomes in its turn another past revivified, brought back from the dead, by the narrator.

If the pressure of all the other moments lies on the present moment which Clarissa experiences so vividly, the whole day of the action of *Mrs. Dalloway* may be described as such a moment on a large scale. Just as Proust's *A la recherche du temps perdu,* a book much admired by Woolf, ends with a party in which Marcel encounters figures from his past turned now into aged specters of themselves, so the "story" of *Mrs. Dalloway* (for there is a story, the story of Clarissa's refusal of Peter Walsh, of her love for Sally Seton, and of her decision to marry Richard Dalloway), is something which happened long before the single day in the novel's present. The details of this story are brought back bit by bit for the reader in the memories of the various characters as the day continues. At the same time the most important figures in Clarissa's past actually return during the day, Peter Walsh journeying from India and appearing suddenly at her door, then later coming to her party; Sally Seton, now married and the mother of five sons, also coming to her party.

The passage in *A Writer's Diary* about Woolf's "discovery," her "tunnelling process," takes on its full meaning when it is seen as a description of the way *Mrs. Dalloway* is a novel of the resurrection of the past into the present of the characters' lives. The tunnelling process, says Woolf, is one "by which I tell the past by instalments, as I have need of it" (WD, p. 60). The "beautiful caves" behind each of the characters are caves into the past as well as caves down into the general mind for which the narrator speaks. If in one direction the "caves connect" in the depths of each character's mind, in the other direction "each [cave] comes to daylight at the present moment" (WD, p. 59), the present moment of Clarissa's party when the important figures from her past are present in the flesh.

Woolf has unostentatiously, even secretly, buried within her novel a clue to the way the day of the action is to be seen as the occasion of a resurrection of ghosts from the past. There are three odd and apparently irrelevant pages in the novel (pp. 122–124) which describe the song of an ancient ragged woman, her hand outstretched for coppers. Peter hears her song as he crosses Marylebone Road by the Regent's Park Tube Station. It seems to rise like "the voice of an ancient spring" spouting from some primeval swamp. It seems to have been going on as the same inarticulate moan for millions of years and to be likely to persist for ten million years longer:

> ee um fah um so
> foo swee too eem oo

The battered old woman, whose voice seems to come from before, after, or outside time, sings of how she once walked with her lover in May. Though it is possible to associate this with the theme of vanished love in the novel (Peter has just been thinking again of Clarissa and of her coldness, "as cold as an icicle"; pp. 121–122), still the connection seems strained, and the episode scarcely seems to justify the space it occupies unless the reader recognizes that Woolf has woven into the old woman's song, partly by paraphrase and variation, partly by direct quotation in an English translation, the words of a song by Richard Strauss, "Allerseelen," with words by Hermann von Gilm.[6] The phrases quoted in English from the song do not correspond to any of the three English translations I have located, so Woolf either made her own or used another which I have not found. Here is a translation more literal than any of the three published ones I have seen and also more literal than Woolf's version:

> Place on the table the perfuming heather,
> Bring here the last red asters,
> And let us again speak of love,
> As once in May.
>
> Give me your hand, that I may secretly press it,
> And if someone sees, it's all the same to me;
> Give me but one of your sweet glances,
> As once in May.
>
> It is blooming and breathing perfume today on every grave,
> One day in the year is free to the dead,
> Come to my heart that I may have you again,
> As once in May.

Heather, red asters, the meeting with the lover once in May, these are echoed in the passage in *Mrs. Dalloway,* and several phrases are quoted directly: "look in my eyes with thy sweet eyes intently"; "give me your hand and let me press it gently"; "and if some one should see, what matter they?" The old woman, there can be no doubt, is singing Strauss's song. The parts of the song not directly echoed in *Mrs. Dalloway* identify it as a key to the structure of the novel. "One day in the year" is indeed "free to the dead," "Allerseelen," the day of a collective resurrection of spirits. On this day the bereaved lover can hope that the beloved will return from the grave. Like Strauss's song, *Mrs. Dalloway* has the form of an All Souls' Day in which Peter Walsh, Sally Seton, and the rest rise from the dead to come to Clarissa's party. As in the song the memory of a dead lover may on one day of the year become a direct confrontation of his or her risen spirit, so in *Mrs.*

Dalloway the characters are obsessed all day by memories of the time when Clarissa refused Peter and chose to marry Richard Dalloway, and then the figures in those memories actually come back in a general congregation of persons from Clarissa's past. The power of narrative not just to repeat the past but to resurrect it in another form is figured dramatically in the action of the novel.

Continuity of each character with his own past, continuity in the shared past of all the important characters—these forms of communication are completed by the unusual degree of access the characters have in the present to one another's minds. Some novelists, Jane Austen or Jean-Paul Sartre, for example, assume that minds are opaque to one another. Another person is a strange apparition, perhaps friendly to me, perhaps a threat, but in any case difficult to understand. I have no immediate knowledge of what he is thinking or feeling. I must interpret what is going on within his subjectivity as best I can by way of often misleading signs—speech, gesture, and expression. In Woolf's work, as in Trollope's, one person often sees spontaneously into the mind of another and knows with the same sort of knowledge he has of his own subjectivity what is going on there. If the narrator enters silently and unobserved into the mind of each of the characters and understands it with perfect intimacy because it is in fact part of her own mind, the characters often, if not always, may have the same kind of intimate knowledge of one another. This may be partly because they share the same memories and so respond in the same way to the same cues, each knowing what the other must be thinking, but it seems also to be an unreflective openness of one mind to another, a kind of telepathic insight. The mutual understanding of Clarissa and Peter is the most striking example of this intimacy: "They went in and out of each other's minds without any effort," thinks Peter, remembering their talks at Bourton (p. 94). Other characters have something of the same power of communication. Rezia and Septimus, for example, as he helps her make a hat in their brief moments of happiness before Dr. Holmes comes and Septimus throws himself out of the window: "Not for weeks had they laughed like this together, poking fun privately like married people" (p. 217). Or there is the intimacy of Clarissa and her servant Lucy: " 'Dear!' said Clarissa, and Lucy shared as she meant her to her disappointment (but not the pang); felt the concord between them" (p. 43).

In all these cases, there is some slight obstacle between the minds of the characters. Clarissa does after all decide not to marry Peter and is falling in love with Richard Dalloway in spite of the almost perfect communion she can achieve with Peter. The communion of Rezia and Septimus is intermittent, and she has little insight into what is going on in his mind during his periods of madness. Clarissa does not share with Lucy the pang of jealousy she feels toward Lady Bruton. The proper model for the relations among minds in *Mrs. Dalloway* is that of a perfect transparency of the minds of the characters to the mind of the narrator, but only a modified translucency, like glass frosted or fogged, between the mind of one character and the mind of another. Nevertheless, to the continuity between the present and the past within the mind of a given character there must be added a relative continuity from one mind to another in the present.

The characters in *Mrs. Dalloway* are endowed with a desire to take possession of these continuities, to actualize them in the present. The dynamic model for this urge is a movement which gathers together disparate elements, pieces them into a unity, and lifts them up into the daylight world in a gesture of ecstatic delight, sustaining the wholeness so created over the dark abyss of death. The phrase "building it up" echoes through the novel as an emblem of this combination of spiritual and physical action. Thinking of life, Clarissa, the reader will remember, wonders "how one sees it so, making it up, building it round one" (p. 5). Peter Walsh follows a pretty girl from Trafalgar Square to Regent Street across Oxford Street and Great Portland Street until she disappears into her house, making up a personality for her, a new personality for himself, and an adventure for them both together: "it was half made up, as he knew very well; invented, this escapade with the girl; made up, as one makes up the better part of life, he thought—making oneself up; making her up" (p. 81). Rezia's power of putting one scrap with another to make a hat or of gathering the small girl who brings the evening paper into a warm circle of intimacy momentarily cures Septimus of his hallucinations and of his horrifying sense that he is condemned to a solitary death: "For so it always happened. First one thing, then another. So she built it up, first one thing and then another . . . she built it up, sewing" (pp. 219, 221). Even Lady Bruton's luncheon, to which she brings Richard Dalloway and Hugh Whitbread to help her write a letter to the *Times* about emigration, is a parody version of this theme of constructive action.

The most important example of the theme is Clarissa Dalloway's party, her attempt to "kindle and illuminate" (p. 6). Though people laugh at her for her parties, feel she too much enjoys imposing herself, nevertheless these parties are her offering to life. They are an offering devoted to the effort to bring together people from their separate lives and combine them into oneness: "Here was So-and-so in South Kensington; some one up in Bayswater; and somebody else, say, in Mayfair. And she felt quite continuously a sense of their existence; and she felt what a waste; and she felt what a pity; and she felt if only they could be brought together; so she did it. And it was an offering; to combine, to create" (pp. 184–185). The party which forms the concluding scene of the novel does succeed in bringing people together, a great crowd from poor little Ellie Henderson all the way up to the Prime Minister, and including Sally Seton and Peter Walsh among the rest. Clarissa has the "gift still; to be; to exist; to sum it all up in the moment" (p. 264).

Clarissa's party transforms each guest from his usual self into a new social self, a self outside the self of participation in the general presence of others. The magic sign of this transformation is the moment when Ralph Lyon beats back the curtain and goes on talking, so caught up is he in the party. The gathering then becomes "something now, not nothing" (p. 259), and Clarissa meditates on the power a successful party has to destroy the usual personality and replace it with another self able to know people with special intimacy and able to speak more freely from the hidden depths of the spirit. These two selves are related to one another as real to unreal, but when one is aware of the contrast, as Clarissa is in the moment just before she loses her self-consciousness and is swept up into her own party, it is impossible to tell which is the real self, which the unreal: "Every time she gave a party she had this feeling of being something not herself, and that every one was unreal in one way; much more real in another . . . it was possible to say things you couldn't say anyhow else, things that needed an effort; possible to go much deeper" (pp. 259–260).

An impulse to create a social situation which will bring into the open the usually hidden continuities of present with past, of person with person, of person with the depths of himself, is shared by all the principal characters of *Mrs. Dalloway.* This universal desire makes one vector of spiritual forces within the novel a general urge toward lifting up and bringing together.

This effort fails in all its examples, or seems in part to have failed. It seems so implicitly to the narrator and more overtly to some of the characters, including Clarissa. From this point of view, a perspective emphasizing the negative aspect of these characters and episodes, Peter Walsh's adventure with the unknown girl is a fantasy. Lady Bruton is a shallow, domineering busybody, a representative of that upper-class society which Woolf intends to expose in her novel. "I want to criticise the social system," she wrote while composing *Mrs. Dalloway,* "and to show it at work, at its most intense" (WD, p. 56). Rezia's constructive power and womanly warmth does not prevent her husband from killing himself. And Clarissa? It would be a mistake to exaggerate the degree to which she and the social values she embodies are condemned in the novel. Woolf's attitudes toward upper-class English society of the nineteen-twenties are ambiguous, and to sum up the novel as no more than negative social satire is a distortion. Woolf feared while she was writing the novel that Clarissa would not seem attractive enough to her readers. "The doubtful point," she wrote in her diary a year before the novel was finished, "is, I think, the character of Mrs. Dalloway. It may be too stiff, too glittering and tinselly" (p. 60). There is in fact a negative side to Clarissa as Woolf presents her. She is a snob, too anxious for social success. Her party is seen in part as the perpetuation of a moribund society, with its hangers-on at court like Hugh Whitbread and a Prime Minister who is dull:

"You might have stood him behind a counter and bought biscuits," thinks Ellie Henderson, "—poor chap, all rigged up in gold lace" (p. 261).

Even if this negative judgment is suspended and the characters are taken as worth our sympathy, it is still the case that, though Clarissa's party facilitates unusual communication among these people, their communion is only momentary. The party comes to an end; the warmth fades; people return to their normal selves. In retrospect there seems to have been something spurious about the sense of oneness with others the party created. Clarissa's power to bring people together seems paradoxically related to her reticence, her coldness, her preservation of an area of inviolable privacy in herself. Though she believes that each person is not limited to himself, but is spread out among other people like mist in the branches of a tree, with another part of her spirit she contracts into herself and resents intensely any invasion of her privacy. It almost seems as if her keeping of a secret private self is reciprocally related to her social power to gather people together and put them in relationship to one another. The motif of Clarissa's frigidity, of her prudery, of her separateness runs all through *Mrs. Dalloway.* "The death of her soul," Peter Walsh calls it (p. 89). Since her illness, she has slept alone, in a narrow bed in an attic room. She cannot "dispel a virginity preserved through childbirth which [clings] to her like a sheet" (p. 46). She has "through some contraction of this cold spirit" (p. 46) failed her husband again and again. She feels a stronger sexual attraction to other women than to men. A high point of her life was the moment when Sally Seton kissed her. Her decision not to marry Peter Walsh but to marry Richard Dalloway instead was a rejection of intimacy and a grasping at privacy. "For in marriage a little licence, a little independence there must be between people living together day in day out in the same house; which Richard gave her, and she him . . . But with Peter everything had to be shared; everything gone into. And it was intolerable" (p. 10). "And there is a dignity in people; a solitude; even between husband and wife a gulf," thinks Clarissa much later in the novel (p. 181). Her hatred of her daughter's friend Miss Kilman, of Sir William Bradshaw, of all the representatives of domineering will, of the instinct to convert others, of "love and religion" (p. 191), is based on this respect for isolation and detachment: "Had she ever tried to convert any one herself? Did she not wish everybody merely to be themselves?" (p. 191). The old lady whom Clarissa sees so often going upstairs to her room in the neighboring house seems to stand chiefly for this highest value, "the privacy of the soul" (p. 192): "that's the miracle, that's the mystery; that old lady, she meant . . . And the supreme mystery . . . was simply this: here was one room; there another. Did religion solve that, or love?" (p. 193).

The climax of *Mrs. Dalloway* is not Clarissa's party but the moment when, having heard of the suicide of Septimus, Clarissa leaves her guests behind and goes alone into the little room where Lady Bruton has a few minutes earlier been talking to the Prime Minister about India. There she sees in the next house the old lady once more, this time going quietly to bed. She thinks about Septimus and recognizes how factitious all her attempt to assemble and to connect has been. Her withdrawal from her party suggests that she has even in the midst of her guests kept untouched the privacy of her soul, that still point from which one can recognize the hollowness of the social world and feel the attraction of the death everyone carries within him as his deepest reality. Death is the place of true communion. Clarissa has been attempting the impossible, to bring the values of death into the daylight world of life. Septimus chose the right way. By killing himself he preserved his integrity, "plunged holding his treasure" (p. 281), his link to the deep places where each man or woman is connected to every other man or woman. For did he not in his madness hear his dead comrade, Evans, speaking to him from that region where all the dead dwell together? "Communication is health; communication is happiness" (p. 141)—Septimus during his madness expresses what is the highest goal for all the characters, but his suicide constitutes a recognition that communication cannot be attained except evanescently in life. The only repetition of the past that successfully repossesses it is the act of suicide.

Clarissa's recognition of this truth, her moment of self-condemnation, is at the same time the moment of her greatest insight:

> She had once thrown a shilling into the Serpentine, never anything more. But he had flung it away. They went on living . . . They (all day she had been thinking of Bourton, of Peter, of Sally), they would grow old. A thing there was that mattered; a thing, wreathed about with chatter, defaced, obscured in her own life, let drop every day in corruption, lies, chatter. This he had preserved. Death was defiance. Death was an attempt to communicate; people feeling the impossibility of reaching the centre which, mystically, evaded them; closeness drew apart; rapture faded, one was alone. There was an embrace in death. (Pp. 280–81)

From the point of view of the "thing" at the center that matters most, all speech, all social action, all building it up, all forms of communication, are lies. The more one tries to reach this centre through such means the further away from it one goes. The ultimate lesson of *Mrs. Dalloway* is that by building it up, one destroys. Only by throwing it away can life be preserved. It is preserved by being laid to rest on that underlying reality which Woolf elsewhere describes as "a thing I see before me: something abstract; but residing in the downs or sky; beside which nothing matters; in which I shall rest and continue to exist. Reality I call it" (WD, pp. 129–130). "Nothing matters"—compared to this reality, which is only defaced, corrupted, covered over by all the everyday activities of life, everything else is emptiness and vanity: "there is nothing," wrote Woolf during one of her periods of depression, "—nothing for any of us. Work, reading, writing are all disguises; and relations with people" (WD, p. 141).

Septimus Smith's suicide anticipates Virginia Woolf's own death. Both deaths are a defiance, an attempt to communicate, a recognition that self-annihilation is the only possible way to embrace that center which evades one as long as one is alive. Clarissa does not follow Septimus into death (though she has a bad heart, and the original plan, according to the preface Woolf wrote for the Modern Library edition of the novel, was to have her kill herself). Even so, the words of the dirge in *Cymbeline* have been echoing through her head all day: "Fear no more the heat o' th' sun/Nor the furious winter's rages." Clarissa's obsession with these lines indicates her half-conscious awareness that in spite of her love of life she will reach peace and escape from suffering only in death. The lines come into her mind for a last time just before she returns from her solitary meditation to fulfill her role as hostess. They come to signify her recognition of her kinship with Septimus, her kinship with death. For she is, as Woolf said in the Modern Library preface, the "double" of Septimus. In *Mrs. Dalloway,* Woolf said, "I want to give life and death, sanity and insanity" (WD, p. 56). The novel was meant to be "a study of insanity and suicide; the world seen by the sane and the insane side by side" (WD, p. 51). These poles are not so much opposites as reversed images of one another. Each has the same elemental design. The death by suicide Woolf originally planned for Clarissa is fulfilled by Septimus, who dies for her, so to speak, a substitute suicide. Clarissa and Septimus seek the same thing: communication, wholeness, the oneness of reality, but only Septimus takes the sure way to reach it. Clarissa's attempt to create unity in her party is the mirror image in the world of light and life of Septimus's vigorous appropriation of the dark embrace of death in his suicide: "Fear no more the heat of the sun. She must go back to them. But what an extraordinary night! She felt somehow very like him—the young man who had killed himself. She felt glad that he had done it; thrown it away" (p. 283). For Woolf, as for Conrad, the visible world of light and life is the mirror image or repetition in reverse of an invisible world of darkness and death. Only the former can be seen and described. Death is incompatible with language, but by talking about life, one can talk indirectly about death.

Mrs. Dalloway seems to end in a confrontation of life and death as looking-glass counterparts. Reality, authenticity, and completion are on the death side of the mirror, while life is at best the illusory, insubstantial, and fragmentary image of that dark reality. There is, however, one more structural element in *Mrs. Dalloway,* one final twist which reverses the polarities once more, or rather which holds them poised in their irreconciliation. Investigation of this will permit a final identification of the way Woolf brings into the open latent implications of traditional modes of storytelling in English fiction.

I have said that *Mrs. Dalloway* has a double temporal form. During the day of the action the chief characters resurrect in memory by bits and pieces the central episode of their common past. All these characters then come together again at Clarissa's party. The narrator in her turn embraces both these times in the perspective of a single distance. She moves forward through her own time of narration toward the point when the two times of the characters come together in the completion of the final sentences of the novel, when Peter sees Clarissa returning to her party. Or should one say "almost come together," since the temporal gap still exists in the separation between "is" and "was"? "It is Clarissa, he said. For there she was" (p. 296).

In the life of the characters, this moment of completion passes. The party ends. Sally, Peter, Clarissa, and the rest move on toward death. The victory of the narrator is to rescue from death this moment and all the other moments of the novel in that All Souls' Day at a second power which is literature. Literature for Woolf is repetition as preservation, but preservation of things and persons in their antithetical poise. Time is rescued by this repetition. It is rescued in its perpetually reversing divisions. It is lifted into the region of death with which the mind of the narrator has from the first page been identified. This is a place of absence, where nothing exists but words. These words generate their own reality. Clarissa, Peter, and the rest can be encountered only in the pages of the novel. The reader enters this realm of language when he leaves his own solid world and begins to read *Mrs. Dalloway.* The novel is a double resurrection. The characters exist for themselves as alive in a present which is a resuscitation of their dead pasts. In the all-embracing mind of the narrator the characters exist as dead men and women whose continued existence depends on her words. When the circle of the narration is complete, past joining present, the apparently living characters reveal themselves to be already dwellers among the dead.

Clarissa's vitality, her ability "to be; to exist," is expressed in the present-tense statement made by Peter Walsh in the penultimate line of the novel: "It is Clarissa." This affirmation of her power to sum it all up in the moment echoes earlier descriptions of her "extraordinary gift, that woman's gift, of making a world of her own wherever she happened to be": "She came into a room; she stood, as he had often seen her, in a doorway with lots of people round her . . . she never said anything specially clever; there she was, however; there she was" (pp. 114–115); "There she was, mending her dress" (p. 179). These earlier passages are in the past tense, as is the last line of the novel: "For there she was." With this sentence "is" becomes "was" in the indirect discourse of the narrator. In that mode of language Clarissa along with all the other characters recedes into an indefinitely distant past. Life becomes death within the impersonal mind of the narrator and within her language, which is the place of communion in death. There the fragmentary is made whole. There all is assembled into one unit. All the connections between one part of the novel and another are known only to the agile and ubiquitous mind of the narrator. They exist only within the embrace of that reconciling spirit and through the power of her words.

Nevetheless, to return once more to the other side of the irony, the dirge in *Cymbeline* is sung over an Imogen who is only apparently dead. The play is completed with the seemingly miraculous return to life of the heroine. In the same way, Clarissa comes back from her solitary confrontation with death during her party. She returns from her recognition of her kinship with Septimus to bring "terror" and "ecstasy" to Peter when he sees her (p. 296). She comes back also into the language of the narration where, like Imogen raised from the dead, she may be confronted by the reader in the enduring language of literature.

It is perhaps for this reason that Woolf changed her original plan and introduced Septimus as Clarissa's surrogate in death. To have had a single protagonist who was swallowed up in the darkness would have falsified her conceptiion. She needed two protagonists, one who dies and another who dies with his death. Clarissa vividly lives through Septimus's death as she meditates alone during her party. Then, having died vicariously, she returns to life. She appears before her guests to cause, in Peter Walsh at least, "extraordinary excitement" (p. 296). Not only does Clarissa's vitality come from her proximity to death. The novel needs for its structural completeness two opposite but similar movements, Septimus's plunge into death and Clarissa's resurrection from the dead. *Mrs. Dalloway* is both of these at once: the entry into the realm of communication in death and the revelation of that realm in words which may be read by the living.

Though *Mrs. Dalloway* seems almost nihilistically to recommend the embrace of death, and though its author did in fact finally take this plunge, nevertheless, like the rest of Woolf's writing, it represents in fact a contrary movement of the spirit. In a note in her diary of May 1933, Woolf records a moment of insight into what brings about a "synthesis" of her being: "how only writing composes it: how nothing makes a whole unless I am writing (WD, p. 201). Or again: "Odd how the creative power at once brings the whole universe to order" (p. 213). Like Clarissa's party or like the other examples of building it up in *Mrs. Dalloway,* the novel is a constructive action which gathers unconnected elements into a solidly existing object. It is something which belongs to the everyday world of physical things. It is a book with cardboard covers and white pages covered with black marks. This made-up thing, unlike its symbol, Clarissa's party, belongs to both worlds. If it is in one sense no more than a manufactured physical object, it is in another sense made of words which designate not the material presence of the things named but their absence from the everyday world and their existence within the place out of place and time out of time which are the space and time of literature. Woolf's writing has as its aim bringing into the light of day this realm of communication in language. A novel, for Woolf, is the place of death made visible. Writing is the only action which exists simultaneously on both sides of the mirror, within death and within life at once.

Though Woolf deals with extreme spiritual situations, her work would hardly give support to a scheme of literary history which sees twentieth-century literature as more negative, more "nihilistic," or more "ambiguous" than nineteenth-century literature. The "undecidability" of *Mrs. Dalloway* lies in the impossibility of knowing, from the text, whether the realm of union in death exists, for Woolf, only in the words, or whether the words represent an extralinguistic realm which is "really there" for the characters, for the narrator, and for Woolf herself. Nevertheless, the possibility that the realm of death, in real life as in fiction, really exists, is more seriously entertained by Woolf than it is, for example, by Eliot, by Thackeray, or by Hardy. The possibility that repetition in narrative is the representation of a transcendent spiritual realm of reconciliation and preservation, a realm of the perpetual resurrection of the dead, is more straightforwardly proposed by Virginia Woolf than by most of her predecessors in English fiction.

8

BETWEEN THE ACTS

Repetition as Extrapolation

IF *MRS. DALLOWAY* CONCENTRATES for the most part on various ways in which recollection by a character or by the narrator is a form of repetition, Virginia Woolf's last work, *Between the Acts*, published posthumously in 1941, has a wider scope. It focuses more explicitly on the ways human history and literary history may be forms of repetition. *Between the Acts* makes explicit the way the question about the grounding or lack of ground in a repetitive series (my two forms of repetition), is related not only to the activity by which the mind makes sense of the past but also to the question of how it moves into the future, attempting to build the new on the ground of the old. In its exploration of the way the writer in his or her constructive activity with words, the way human beings in their living together, and the way the mind in its solitary thinking from moment to moment move forward uncertainly into a precarious future, *Between the Acts* dramatizes not so much the problem of interpreting a repetitive sequence which already exists as the problem of adding new elements to such a sequence and so keeping the human story from disintegrating into unconnected fragments. The abiding question for this activity is another form of the question raised by kinds of repetition in fiction examined in earlier chapters of this book: What are the grounds for evaluating another element added to a series? How can one know the new element is a valid repetition of the old ones, extending and continuing them? A passage late in *Between the Acts* is a good starting place for investigating this. It formulates neatly the question of extrapolation in human history or in literary history in terms of the question of whether the different can or cannot be another version of the same:

> "Did you feel," [Mrs. Swithin] asked, "what he said: we act different parts but are the same?"
> "Yes," Isa answered. "No," she added. It was Yes, No. Yes, yes, yes, the tide rushed out embracing. No, no, no, it contracted. The old boot appeared on the shingle.
> "Orts, scraps, and fragments," she quoted what she remembered of the vanishing play.[1]

Yes, no; sameness, difference; "*Unity—Dispersity . . . Un . . dis . . .*" (as Miss La Trobe's gramophone gurgles at the end of her play; BA, p. 201)—these are the alternatives proposed in *Between the Acts.* Almost any passage contains some version of this opposition. Each bit acts a different part in the economy of the whole, but each is the same. Stamped with the same genetic pattern, each may be taken as an emblem of the whole. The opposition between yes and no, continuity and discontinuity, sameness and difference, is tied to a tangle of related themes which branch out to include problems of origin and end, of temporality, of history, of literary history, of representation, of the nature of the mind, of the ground of the mind, of the relation of the mind's energy to nature's energy, and so on. Woolf's subject in *Between the Acts,* as in her previous work, is the activity of the mind. How does the mind continue? How does it get from here to there? How does it link the orts, scraps, and fragments of its experience into a valid unity? How does it express itself, its difference, in terms of the same, that is, in terms of words, figures, rhythms which have come down from the past?

To say that each fragment of *Between the Acts* is stamped with the genetic pattern common to the whole, and so may be taken as an emblem of that whole, begs the question raised by that pattern. Each fragment, it would be better to say, is marked with the question of its relation to the whole. The novel constantly interrogates its own order, in a self-reflective reversal of which it contains many examples on a small and large scale. In this turning back, oneness becomes duplicity, in a defiance of representational logic which some critics have compared to a Möbius strip. A given passage functions as the fictional representation of a reality that fiction speaks of as lying outside itself and as being only named by its language. At the same time, the passage calls attention to itself as part of a design of words which generates its own intrinsic meaning. A Möbius strip, however, like the image of the *mise en abîme,* or like Jacques Derrida's image of "double invagination" for such structures in fiction,[2] is no more than a spatial and perceptual image for something which is a property of language, not a property of the visual world. Such images are not more than approximate, or even misleading, metaphors. Each is inappropriate insofar as it implies that such linguistic structures can be visualized, in however paradoxical a form, and so comprehended at a glance.

In any case, such passages in *Between the Acts* as the one I have quoted, in their echo of motifs which recur throughout the novel, raise the question of difference and sameness for the texture of event and verbal detail in the novel itself thought of as a fabric of words. Is the difference of each fragment intrinsic and essential? Does difference go all the way down to the bottom, so to speak, so that each fragment remains an ort, and old boot on the shingle, and the whole a dispersed collection of scraps with gaps between? Or is the difference only superficial? Do the fragments join one another at some deep level, or do they allow their particularity to be embraced by some all-engulfing tide of unity saying yes, yes, yes? What would be the source of such a principle of continuity? Is it natural, or mental, or perhaps in some way metaphysical? Or is there for Woolf some third, perhaps unnamed, possibility, neither yes nor no, neither unity nor dispersity, but the echoing of elements which remain at a distance? In this case sameness would arise from differences which do not vanish in their resonance. This resonance might be that "sort of humming noise, not articulate, but musical, exciting," which, according to Woolf in *A Room of One's Own,* charged the air in the time of Tennyson and Christina Rossetti and "changed the value of the words themselves," though people spoke the same things then as now, at an Oxbridge luncheon party.[3]

Everything important, for Woolf, is at stake in these questions. At stake is the power of the mind to continue, to establish a valid order within itself. The alternative possibility is that the mind may move randomly from experience to experience according to the accidents of external stimuli or according to some mechanical principle of association. The conversation at Pointz Hall moves from fish to Wells's *An Outline of History,* to dentists, to Pharaohs (BA, pp. 30–31). In the same way, Lucy Swithin, believer though she is in unity, "skipped, sidelong, from yeast to alcohol; so to fermentation; so to inebriation; so to Bacchus; and lay under purple lamps in a vineyard in Italy, as she had done, often" (p. 34).

At stake also is the question of the validity of relations among people, Giles and Isa, Lucy and old Bart, Mrs. Manresa, and the rest. A novel, after all, even a novel by Virginia Woolf, deals with relations among people. Are these relations merely factitious, each family a congregation of isolates, or is genuine community possible?

I have just said a novel deals with relations among people, while a few paragraphs ago I was emphasizing the way it is made of words. These are two surfaces of the same continuum, and the competent reader of a novel moves easily back and forth between attention to complexities of verbal texture and thinking of the characters as if they were real people among whom there are relations of one sort or another. As everyone knows, though as all readers often forget, a novel can deal with relations among people only by representing those people and their interrelations in words. In *Between the Acts* this relation between words and minds is another question that is explicitly asked. What does it say about minds that they can be represented in words, and is it the case that the mind can only continue through time by means of words or other signs?

At stake also in *Between the Acts* is the continuity of history, the power of the present to renew, prolong, and repeat the past. The novel traces a sequence leading from Wells's prehistoric man, "half-human, half-ape," when there were "mammoths in Piccadilly" and "no sea at all between us and the continent" (pp. 218, 30, 29), through the Elizabethan, Restoration, and Victorian parodies of Miss La Trobe's pageant, to the similar drama of love enacted in the present by the inhabitants of Pointz Hall. This present drama is enacted in the shadow of the Second World War and the possible destruction of civilization. Similar these five stories are, but is their difference more important than their sameness? Does the present truly continue the past? Might the sequence break off in silence or dispersal, the wall of civilization crumble?

At stake, finally, is the power of the mind to construct itself and its concomitant power to construct a proper work of art. Such a work will have an intrinsic unity and a corresponding ability to order the minds of its readers. Is *Between the Acts* a collection of fragments stitched haphazardly together, "a cloud that melted into other clouds on the horizon," "a failure," as Miss La Trobe judges her pageant to have been (p. 209)? Or does it have that "integrity" and "truth," ensuring survival, which Woolf in *A Room of One's Own* ascribes to the greatest novels, such as *War and Peace*? ("What one means by integrity, in the case of the novelist, is the conviction that he gives one that this is the truth"; p. 75.)

Woolf has no doubt of the mind's power to continue. She has no doubt that relations among people will continue, no doubt of the mind's power to express itself outside itself in works of art. The question is whether there are grounds for these continuities and, if so, what those grounds are. The danger is that the mind's verve will lead it to rush off into an escapist singsong which has not assimilated enough solid facts. This danger is exemplified, in *Between the Acts*, in Isa's "abortive" poetry:

> "Where we know not, where we go not, neither know nor care," she hummed. "Flying, rushing through the ambient, incandescent, summer silent . . ."
>
> The rhyme was "air" . . . "With a feather, a blue feather . . . flying mounting through the air . . . there to lose what binds us here . . ." The words weren't worth writing in the book bound like an account book in case Giles suspected. "Abortive," was the word that expressed her. (BA, p. 15)

If one penchant of Woolf's mind is toward an embracing tidal unity, toward the creation of assimilating form (given here in the elemental example of rhyme), the other penchant is toward the inclusion of as much as possible of the recalcitrant particularity of life. This includes the particularity of mental life, random and haphazard as it may be, the particularity of social behavior and custom, and the particularity of events in nature, the old boot on the shingle, the habits of goldfish in a pond. In this last characteristic Woolf's work may be seen as firmly committed to traditional principles of "realism" in the novel, in spite of its apparently experimental and expressionistic quality. Though her subject may be the mind's activity, this subject is dispersed among the various realistically presented characters in *Between the Acts.* The novel tells a straightforwardly mimetic story about a group of people in an English country house on the day when a village pageant is given to benefit the local church. The reader comes to have as much confidence in the accuracy of Woolf's social notations as in those of Austen or Eliot. The space given to the registering of subjective experience, of what people think and feel, is also an entirely traditional part of the English novel. Moreover, Woolf does not tamper with the chronological sequence in *Between the Acts,* nor in fact in most of her other work. She tells things, for the most part, in the order in which they happen.

Between the Acts, finally, exploits throughout that basic technical resource of the English novel through more than three centuries, the omniscient narrator. Such a narrator can enter at will into the minds and feelings of the characters. He knows more than any one of them separately and is able to remain hovering above them all at a more or less perceptible ironic distance. This distance is present throughout *Between the Acts* in the discrepancy between what the characters think and feel and the slightly acerb reporting of this by the narrative voice. *Between the Acts,* in short, like *Mrs. Dalloway,* is an admirable confirmation of the continuity of technique and subject matter of the English novel from the eighteenth through the twentieth centuries.

This fidelity to the mimetic tradition is confirmed in Woolf's criticism, for example when she says, in *A Room of One's Own,* using the most traditional of metaphors: "If one shuts one's eyes and thinks of the novel as a whole, it would seem to be a creation owning a certain looking-glass likeness to life, though of course with simplifications and distortions innumerable" (p. 74). Not less faithful to representational realism is her notion that the goal of women's liberation, in the area of writing, would be "the development by the average woman of a prose style completely expressive of her mind" (p. 99). This assumes that the woman's mind is there before the expression of it. Objective realism, the imitation of "life"; subjective realism, the imitation of the mind—these two goals have been those of the English novel since Fielding and Sterne, and before.

On the other hand, both in her practice and in her theoretical statements Woolf recognizes a contrary intention, the attempt to create an intrinsic, musical, architectural form. She also sees that these two intentions interfere with each other. They are to some degree incompatible. If the novel, in one direction, "own[s] a certain looking-glass likeness to life," in the other direction "it is a structure leaving a shape on the mind's eye, built now in squares, now pagoda shaped, now throwing out wings and arcades, now solidly compact and domed like the Cathedral of Saint Sophia at Constantinople." This shape "is not made by the relation of stone to stone, but by the relation of human being to human being." One emotion is generated by the reader's sense of the correspondence of the novel to life. A different emotion is generated by the reader's response to the intrinsic shape of the novel, its self-contained harmonies and recurrences. Each of those emotions may be thought of as having its individual rhythm, the rhythm of the novel's correspondence to life, the rhythm of its internal echoes and cross-references. The two rhythms interfere. They splash against each other like two waves intersecting. "Thus," as Woolf says, "a novel starts in us all sorts of antagonistic and opposed emotions. Life conflicts with something that is not life" (*Room,* p. 74).

In *Between the Acts* this interference of two rhythmical emotions is present in the contradiction between the reader's sense, on the one hand, that the narrator has told the reader what in fact happened on these two days at Pointz Hall, in all its diversity and irrelevance,[4] so that, within the fiction, the novel is an imitation of the writing of a historical account, with all its random contingencies, and his sense, on the other hand, that certain images, motifs, phrases recur. A pattern bit by bit emerges through these recurrences. The reader gradually comes to suspect that each of these apparently irrelevant details may be significant, perhaps somehow "symbolic," as the "tree . . . pelted with starlings" (p. 212) becomes an allegory of the continuing life force and of the participation in that life force of artistic creativity. Since the key to the overall pattern remains veiled, the reader is kept on the stretch between the "realistic" and the "symbolic" ways of reading this text. The ability to generate an unusual degree of tension between these two ways of reading especially characterizes *Between the Acts.* Each passage is an exact notation of what happened to be there for the narrator to see or hear. At the same time it is part of a larger musical or architectural design. The verbal texture of the novel combines oneness and twoness in a single surface.

Another version of this in *Between the Acts* is Woolf's special use of the traditional device of the play within the play. Miss La Trobe's pageant, with its stylized parodies of Elizabethan, Restoration, and Victorian modes, is clearly "artifice," "fiction." This tends to reinforce the reader's conviction of the reality of the first level of the narration, the story of Giles, Isa, Lucy, Bart, and the others at Pointz Hall. A chain of increasing fictionality is set up leading from the reader to the audience at the play to the play itself. At the same time, in a way entirely traditional and by no means a challenge to the metaphysical assumptions underlying mimetic realism, the audience is in various ways assimilated to the play:[5] by the occurrence in their thoughts of motifs which appear in the play; in the role of nature, the "yearning bellow" of the cows (p. 140), in filling a gap in the play; in the incorporation of the audience into the pageant at its end when the "ten mins. of present time" (p. 179) are followed, after a sudden shower ("Nature once more had taken her part"; p. 181), by the actors holding many dancing mirrors up to the audience so that they behold themselves in this present time as the ultimate goal, so far, of English history; in the mingling of the actors and actresses, still in their costumes, with the audience when the play is over. Those in the pageant and those in the audience are all actors in a play which is the reality of English history. The distinction between players and audience, fiction and reality, is obliterated. As the

Reverend Streatfield says in his interpretation of the pageant: "We act different parts; but are the same" (p. 192), or as Lucy Swithin praises Miss La Trobe: "What a small part I've had to play! But you've made me feel I could have played . . . Cleopatra!" (p. 153).

This presenting a fiction within a fiction functions here, as it does traditionally in English drama and fiction, both to represent the role of fictions in human life (when the reader suspends his knowledge that *Between the Acts* is a fiction and takes it as though it were the account of events that "really happened"), and at the same time to invite the reader to reflect that *Between the Acts* too is a fiction and has the same relation to his own life as the pageant does to the lives of the main characters in *Between the Acts.* Most readers of novels, like spectators of *Hamlet,* are adept at moving back and forth from one of these levels to another, keeping separate the nature and function of each, even though the "first level" of the narrative functions simultaneously as a represented reality and as something which for the reader is already a fiction itself.

The climactic use of the device of the play within a play in *Between the Acts,* however, does make the text as a whole an illogical combination of singleness and dissimulation. In this alternation the text has two levels, the fictive and the real, and at the same time it has only one surface. This surface is both fictive and real at once. After the failure, as she thinks, of her pageant, Miss La Trobe goes to the local pub to find forgetfulness in drink. There the first words of a new play arise from the depths of her mind, like goldfish rising from the mud at the bottom of a pool: "There was the high ground at midnight; there the rock; and two scarcely perceptible figures . . . She heard the first words" (p. 212). A few pages later, in the drawing room at Pointz Hall, after Lucy and Bart have gone to bed, Isa and Giles are left alone for the first time that day: "Alone, enmity was bared; also love. Before they slept, they must fight; after they fought, they would embrace. From that embrace another life might be born" (p. 219). The play they are about to enact is the elemental one of hatred and love which has been performed over and over since there were mammoths in Piccadilly and rhododendrons in the Strand. It is the ur-drama of which the episodes of Miss La Trobe's pageant have been repetitions in the decor of this or that age. It is also the new play which Miss La Trobe is about to write. Just beyond the margin of the text, in an extrapolation into the void where there are not yet more words, Miss La Trobe's fiction and the reality of the life of Isa and Giles will become indistinguishable. The text the reader would be reading then would be simultaneously Woolf's novel and a fiction created by one of the characters in that novel. In its end, or just beyond its end, *Between the Acts* becomes a single verbal surface which merges the two levels of "real" people and play kept separate earlier in the novel:

> The great hooded chairs had become enormous. And Giles too. And Isa too against the window. The window was all sky without colour. The house had lost its shelter. It was night before roads were made, or houses. It was the night that dwellers in caves had watched from some high place among rocks.
>
> Then the curtain rose. They spoke. (P. 219)

In a brilliant essay, "Virginia's Web," Geoffrey Hartman recognizes that Virginia Woolf's subject is the mind's activity. He defines that activity as a work of "interpolation."[6] Behind Hartman's essay, referred to briefly in passing, are the lifelong meditations of Paul Valéry on the mind's work of extending its range, taking possession of its domain, reducing that domain to order, filling in blank spaces, like some tireless spider weaving its web in the brain.[7] For Valéry the means of this extension and reduction to order are chiefly three: hypothesis, rhythm, and figure. The three turn out to be different versions of the same act. Hypothesis makes a statement which assumes that something valid here will still be valid over there. A hypothesis presupposes that conditions are similar in two regions occupied by the mind, so that, for example, formulations worked out for architecture will apply in music. Rhythm is the establishment of a proportion or ratio which can assimilate new material and accommodate it to the same harmony.[8] For Valéry a poem usually begins with a rhythm which is carried as far as it will go in the reduction to its special order of alien material, the stubborn particularity of words. Figure includes not only metaphor but also the other master tropes: metonymy, synecdoche, irony, hyperbole, chiasmus, catachresis, metalepsis, and the rest. Figure in this inclusive sense is the hypothetical affirmation of the similarity of the dissimilar. *Between the Acts* sustains itself by the extensions of figure, as when Woolf compares the mind's production of phrases, images, and rhythms to the rising of goldfish from a pond, or as when she metaleptically replaces late with early and has Giles and Isa about to enact a prehistoric drama, the drama of which all the episodes of Miss La Trobe's pageant are reincarnations. This reversal apparently confirms Lucy Swithin's disbelief in history: " 'The Victorians . . . I don't believe,' she said with her odd little smile, 'that there ever were such people. Only you and me and William dressed differently.' 'You don't believe in history,' said William" (pp. 174–175).

Hartman is right to see Woolf as essentially an affirmative writer. For her there is a creative power in the mind which thrusts itself forward, in spite of obstacles and hesitations. This energy pushes out to fill in gaps and pauses, to weave a web which ties this to that, one thing to another, in the assertion of a continuous power of production. This affirmative power expresses itself through the projections of figure, through the sustaining and prolonging of rhythm, and through the major hypothesis of the sameness of the different: "we are members of one another. Each is part of the whole . . . Scraps, orts, and fragments! Surely, we should unite?" (p. 192).[9]

The creative energy, for Woolf, participates in a similar power in nature. It is perhaps a displaced, differentiated, or deferred version of the generative élan of nature. Miss La Trobe takes heart, after her despair over her play, when a flock of starlings lands in a tree. Her own creativity is initiated by her sense of the vitality of nature: "The tree became a rhapsody, a quivering cacophony, a whizz and vibrant rapture, branches, leaves, birds syllabling discordantly life, life, life, without measure, without stop devouring the tree" (p. 209). In a passage from *A Room of One's Own* on which Hartman comments, the view out Woolf's window of the traffic passing in a London street leads her to a vision of "a force in things which one had overlooked," "a river, which flowed past, invisibly, round the corner, down the street, and took people and eddied them along, as the stream at Oxbridge had taken the undergraduate in his boat and the dead leaves." The sight of "a girl in patent leather boots, and then a young man in a maroon overcoat" caught up in this stream of life, meeting, taking a taxi which then "glided off as if it were swept on by the current elsewhere" produces in Woolf's mind a rhythm participating in the rhythm of nature: "The sight was ordinary enough; what was strange was the rhythmical order with which my imagination had invested it" (*Room*, p. 100). This "rhythmical order" is the force that leads her, through its power to assimilate whatever it encounters, like a stream sweeping all before it, to the creation of works of literature.

A final example, often quoted, of the cooperation of the energy of nature with the artist's creative energy occurs when Miss La Trobe's play breaks down. The words sung by the chorus of villagers are inaudible; the illusion fails; her power leaves her. In the nick of time the cows in the neighboring field begin to moo: "All the great moon-eyed heads laid themselves back. From cow after cow came the same yearning bellow. The whole world was filled with dumb yearning. It was the primeval voice sounding loud in the ear of the present moment . . . The cows annihilated the gap; bridged the distance; filled the emptiness and continued the emotion." It is no accident that this bellow is female, initiated by a cow who "had lost her calf." This primeval voice is Demeter calling for Persephone, Io's cry, the bellow of animals moonstruck or maddened by love, "as if Eros had planted his dart in their flanks and goaded them to fury" (pp. 140–141). This bellow is an expression of an especially female power of generation, of bridging abysses and maintaining continuities.

The writer's creativity is, it seems, an extension of the creativity of nature. It takes what is given, the orts and fragments of reality, and fills the spaces between them with the intrinsic rhythmical order of the mind. Is this activity so certain and so unambiguous for Virginia Woolf? Two recent commentators on the form of fiction, Wolfgang Iser and Frank Kermode, have given oddly contradictory explanations for the fact that interpretations of a given novel often differ wildly from one another.[10] On the one hand, according to Iser, however abundant the effort by a novelist to spell out all the connections, a novel is still to some degree indeterminate. Not enough is given for the reader to be sure what relations to make between this detail and that detail or how to order the details into a whole. A more or less large region is left for the reader's activity of filling gaps. The data given may allow for a large number of valid alternative ways of doing this. Kermode, on the other hand, presents a picture of novels as characteristically "overdetermined." The reader's problem is having too much data, not too little. A novel presents a superabundance of perhaps contradictory material which is impossible to order in a single comprehensive pattern. If the critic presents one interpretation he will have used certain data from the text but left other data out. That other material would contradict what he said about the novel. Another critic will make another pattern using different data and ignoring some used by the first critic. The meaning of a novel is uncertain not because too little is given but because the reader is given too much.

How can this be? Does *Between the Acts* provide simultaneously too little and too much, so that Woolf has failed by not drawing all the lines between the notations she gives, and at the same time has presented too many contradictory hints for interpretation? Perhaps the seeming paradox of a simultaneous overdetermination and indetermination arises from the fact that the activity of interpolation is not complete. Insofar as the text is orts, scraps, and fragments not wholly assimilated into unity, it presents simultaneously too little and too much, too many fragments, too little rhythmical assimilation of them. Or perhaps there is something wrong with the models presented by Hartman, Iser, and Kermode for the form of a novel and for the reader's activity of interpreting it.

What is misleading in these models (which I have of course oversimplified to make my point) is their implication that a literary work is made of fixed pieces which can be fitted together like a jigsaw puzzle. A text is not such a puzzle, since it is made of words, not of spatially contiguous objects. Nor is a work of literature like a set of motionless points between which one could draw lines to make a duck or a rabbit, as one connects the numbered dots in a child's game. Even the smallest unit of a novel or poem is both overdetermined and indeterminate. The gaps between units of a text are not capable of being filled by some fluid medium, consciousness as unifier. The mind is neither a space nor a substance but a function of its own sign-making, sign-made activity. There is no rhythm without embodiment, so rhythm as such, disembodied rhythm, is not a means of filling the spaces between signs, or out beyond the last one. The gaps between words could only be filled by more words. The gaps, in fact, are not between the words at all but within them, for example in alternations between possible literal meanings and possible figurative meanings, between straight and ironic senses, of a given word. Such gaps are impossible to fill by any act of extrapolation. Anything put in the gap could only be more words. These would contain their own gaps and indeterminacies. No literary work can give exactly enough. Such an ideal text would be "full" but not too full, and so altogether determinate, its meaning able to be fixed exactly. Even the shortest poem, say Wordsworth's "A Slumber Did My Spirit Seal" or "The Boy of Winander," gives at once too little and too much. As a result it is virtually inexhaustible to criticism. Adding more and more to such a brief poem until the poet has fashioned something as long as *The Prelude* makes a work which is neither more nor less ambiguous but only produces more of the same problems of interpretation, such as the problems of understanding repetition in narrative.

In place of Hartman's image of interpolation it might be better to put the image of extrapolation. This image is closer both to Woolf's activity of creation and to the reader's activity of interpreting *Between the Acts.* Extrapolation, not interpolation, is Valéry's subject in the meditations to which Hartman refers. Valéry's problem is not how one weaves a web between two known points in the mind but how one moves out into the void from the known to the unknown, enlarging the compass of the mind toward that universality which he hypothesizes. This universality is defined by the assumption that whatever one reaches will be somehow like what one has already reached. This hypothesis can never be verified. It remains figurative not literal, poetic not scientific.

Woolf's interest too is in extrapolation rather than in interpolation. The passage about the cows bellowing describes the projection into a not yet existent future of an emotion which has failed, for the moment, to continue. The passage cited above from *A Room of One's Own* describes events in the present generating a rhythmical order projecting itself into the as yet unknown future. The starlings whizzing in the tree initiate in Miss La Trobe's mind a movement toward the play she has not yet written. It is true that the text of *Between the Acts* takes place "between the acts." It is an entr'acte, a filling in of space between parts of the main drama with a masque or pageant.[11] The abortive dalliances of Giles, Isa, Bart, and even Lucy with their guests Mrs. Manresa, William Dodge, and the man in the gray suit are as much between the acts as Miss La Trobe's play. The real "acts" are not given in the novel: the primeval drama which presumably began it all and the love battle of Giles and Isa from which another life might be born. These interchangeable events, an early and a late, that which has always already occurred and that which has always not quite yet occurred, take place in the margins of the novel, outside its bounds. They remain problematic, uncertain, impossible to present directly.

The event which cannot be presented directly, which has always not quite yet occurred because it has always already occurred, is death. Love and creativity are the reversed images of death. Isa's attraction to the man in the gray suit matches in reverse her love for her husband. The drowning of the Lady Ermyntrude is a mirror of Miss La Trobe's new play. One descends into the pool. The other rises from its mud. If *Between the Acts* as a whole is a blank space filled by Woolf's creative activity spinning a web of words, that web is hung not from the known to the known but from the unknown to the unknown, or between points which can be named and known only figuratively, by way of the hypothetical extension of the rhythms and proportions of the known.

All the thematic questions dramatized by *Between the Acts* are questions not about the establishing of connections between things already known but about the extension of the known into the unknown. Will the continuity of history be prolonged beyond the present moment or will the war destroy civilization? Will the continuity of the Oliver family be maintained by the marriage of Giles and Isa or will that marriage break down in extramarital philanderings? Will Miss La Trobe be able to write another play, after the failure, as she sees it, of her pageant? Will that new play be a genuine continuation of the tradition of English literature, the tradition of Shakespeare, Wycherley, Congreve, the Victorians, to whom she has done homage through parody in her play? Such a genuine extension of the English literary sensibility would have to be continuous with that tradition and at the same time add to it something so far unexpressed.

The same question is raised by the fragmentary images, rhythms, rhymes which run through Isa's head all day. These are examples of poetry in the act of being written, with all its hazards and uncertainties. The intermingling of echoes of earlier English poetry—Shakespeare, Keats, Swinburne—with Isa's improvisations suggests the way in which the new must grow out of the old. Perhaps Isa's reveries are the covert presentation of genuine creativity in *Between the Acts,* or perhaps, as she herself thinks, her attempts are only abortive, doomed never even to be written down. Her feminine sensibility has, it may be, been overwhelmed and quenched by the alien rhythms of the male tradition in literature. *A Room of One's Own* presents the pathos of the woman writer in this way.

All of these questions remain unanswered in *Between the Acts,* or are answered only projectively, hypothetically. Perhaps it is appropriate in this context to remember that *Between the Acts* was left incomplete by its author's death, "the one experience," as she said, "I shall never describe."[12] "She would not, I believe," says Leonard Woolf in his headnote to *Between the Acts,* "have made any large or material alterations in it, though she would probably have made a good many small corrections or revisions before passing the final proofs." Even in its textual state *Between the Acts* remains projective, hypothetical, incomplete. It possesses unknown gaps or frayed edges.

The two figures, interpolation and extrapolation, in fact involve a similar uncertainty. The same unverifiable hypothesis is necessary to the assumption that the space between two known points is homogeneous with those points as is necessary to the assumption that in moving out into the unknown I shall encounter something in harmony with what I already know. The first of these two kinds of incompletion makes it easier to take for granted the assumption that the space between is homogeneous, while the second makes that appear less certain. If the space is homogeneous the reader needs only to draw the lines, fill the gaps correctly. The indeterminacy is apparent rather than real. The necessary information is there, but it has not all been given, or it has been displaced, given elsewhere or indirectly. The clues for a coherent reading are present if the reader knows where to look for them. Perhaps they are there in the suggestions of an aboriginal pattern—a man and a woman in a cave on a hilltop looking out at the darkness. All the dramas of history are the displaced repetitions of this drama in the costumes of different eras. The other possibility is that something is really missing. The elements are open to alternative patternings no one of which would include everything in a satisfactory way. This possibility is inscribed in *Between the Acts* in the incompatible interpretations of Miss La Trobe's play expressed by the members of the audience and in the insistence on the diverse subjectivities of the characters. Old Bart is a man of reason, a "separatist," who believes that the orts and fragments remain orts and fragments, while Lucy is a "unifier." If there is something missing in the text, then there may be no center, no ur-pattern, just echoing differences. This second possibility is easiest to see if the reader thinks of the text in terms of extrapolation rather than interpolation. In this case there is no fixed point on the other side of the gap to convince the interpreter that he has got it right.

Between the Acts alternates between these two possibilities. Their conflict establishes the intimate rhythm of the novel, as of Woolf's other work. One force is the powerful affirmative energy which Hartman has recognized. This energy sweeps all before it like a great wave, incorporating diverse details in the rhythmical order of the whole. One figurative expression of this unifying drive in *Between the Acts* is music, especially the music which punctuates Miss La Trobe's play, scraped out on the gramophone hidden in the bushes:

> Like quicksilver sliding, filings magnetized, the distracted united. The tune began; the first note meant a second; the second a third. Then down beneath a force was born in opposition; then another. On different levels they diverged . . . The whole population of the mind's immeasurable profundity came flocking; . . . from chaos and cacophony measure; but not the melody of surface sound alone controlled it; but also the warring battle-plumed warriors straining asunder: To part? No. Compelled from the ends of the horizon; recalled from the edge of appalling crevasses; they crashed; solved; united. (P. 189)

At the same time, *Between the Acts* is full of breaks in that rhythm, interruptions, silences, gaps, cacophonies, incompletions, as though the author were unwilling for some reason to trust her own verve and go all the way in the direction her creative energy leads her. She is, it seems, driven to mar the perfection of her work. She reduces it periodically back to an arhythmical collection of scraps and orts. As the anonymous voice from the bushes at the end of the pageant says: "Let's break the rhythm and forget the rhyme" (p. 187).[13] In *Between the Acts* the rhythm always breaks before the goal is reached. The reader remains at the end between the acts, after any previous act of unification and prior to the next hypothetical one.

This breaking of rhythm takes several forms. The narrative of *Between the Acts* is continuous enough. All events of importance during the time of the action are presented. Nevertheless, that narrative, in the sections before and after the pageant, is presented in short blocks of language. These are often unified around a single image or theme. Between the blocks there are blank spaces on the page. The text starts and then stops, leaves a blank, and then starts again. Moreover, the novel constantly presents small-scale notations of continuities which begin and then are broken off. The wind blows away the words of Miss La Trobe's play. The actors forget their lines. The right gramophone record cannot be found. The lady and the gentleman in the two paintings at Pointz Hall do not look at each other across the silence of the dining room. In any case, "in real life they had never met . . . The lady was a picture . . . ; the man was an ancestor" (p. 36). Isa is never able to complete the poem which runs in her head: "She waited for a rhyme, it failed her, but somewhere surely one sun would shine and all, without a doubt, would be clear" (p. 61). The constant reiteration of the themes of failure and discord produces a slight feeling of frustration, as if one were being blocked from completing a familiar sequence. The effect is like the irritating search for a word one cannot quite remember, or like being prevented from carrying to its conclusion a well-known tune: " 'expatriated' was more like it, but not the right word, which he had on the tip of his tongue, but couldn't get at" (p. 40).

These small-scale cacophonies and incompletions are matched by the large-scale theme of failure which runs through the novel: the abortive flirtations of Giles and Isa, Miss La Trobe's sense that her play has failed. In *Mrs. Dalloway* and *To the Lighthouse* movements toward dispersal are countered by affirmations "building it up." Septimus's suicide is countered by Clarissa's party, though which is failure, dispersal, and which a plunge toward unity, remains uncertain. Mrs. Ramsay's death is followed at last by the trip to the lighthouse. Lily Briscoe puts the finishing stroke on her painting. In *Between the Acts* the movements up and down, building up and dispersing, are joined. Dispersal, the dispersal of the audience, Isa's final no against her yes, the withdrawal of the tide leaving the old boot on the shingle, has, the reader may feel, the final say, at least on this side of the silence which lies beyond the text, in the next act of the play.

It seems as though Woolf may be putting in question, in this last work, the ability of art to create an other than factitious stay against fragmentation. It may be that the most important moment in *Between the Acts,* truest to Woolf's sense of life, is not the final harmonious melody on the gramophone, but the next to the last tune, with its broken harshness and its mocking grating singsong rhymes and half-rhymes. This tune is followed by the holding of the looking-glasses up to the audience, and then by the medley of all the actors from the times of Queen Bess, Queen Anne, and Queen Victoria, each "declaim[ing] some phrase or fragment from their parts," in a hodgepodge of Shakespeare, nursery rhymes, popular songs, Tennyson, and Dante (p. 185):[14]

> The tune changed; snapped; broke; jagged. Foxtrot, was it? Jazz? Anyhow the rhythm kicked, reared, snapped short. What a jangle and a jingle! . . . What a cackle, a cacophony! Nothing ended. So abrupt. And corrupt. Such an outrage; such an insult; and not plain. Very up to date, all the same. What is her game? To disrupt? Jog and trot? Jerk and smirk? Put the finger to the nose? Squint and pry? Peek and spy? O the irreverence of the generation which is only momentarily—thanks be—"the young." The young, who can't make, but only break; shiver into splinters the old vision; smash to atoms what was whole. (P. 183)

It is easy to see the reasons for this penchant toward discord, toward breaking the rhythm and mocking the rhyme. It is equally easy to see the need for the grand affirmative order which breaks against that cacophony and strives to master it. A genuine rhythm, though it must be continuous with the old, must be a new rhythm, the unique rhythm of Woolf's particular woman's sensibility. Any familiar rhythm will continue some rhythm used before in the English novel or rhythms used before by Shakespeare, Keats, Tennyson, or some such male writer. Such a rhythm is not a means of extrapolating out into the unknown and so must be broken. Only an unrecognizable rhythm can reach and express the unknown, the heretofore unexpressed. An unrecognizable rhythm is, however, unthinkable, a contradiction in terms. It would be like a metaphor in which the two terms are wholly dissimilar, or like a hypothesis using no terms drawn from the familiar and verified. Between these two irreconcilable necessities Woolf is caught, though her work is an admirable articulation of her predicament.

Virginia Woolf's anxiety of influence is the anxiety of the woman writer in relation to all the previous generations of male writers—her father, all those fathers, grandfathers, great-grandfathers, extending back in a continuous line through Shakespeare, through Dante, to Aeschylus and Homer. These men have wielded most of the power for millennia—social power, power of appropriation and possession, power to earn a private income and have a room of one's own, sexual power, power of the pen, power to determine the rhythms of the language. On the other hand, "we think back through our mothers if we are women" (*Room,* p. 79). Those mothers were, for the most part, mute, dispossessed, too poor, almost, even to buy a few quires of paper on which to write *Pride and Prejudice* or *Jane Eyre.* They were prevented by a thousand circumstances of centuries of enslavement from developing their own feminine rhythms of style. Only such a woman's style would be "completely expressive of her mind" (p. 99), for the "creative power" in women, says Woolf, "differs greatly from the creative power of men" (p. 91). Her anxiety is therefore a determination not to write like all those fathers—Shakespeare, Johnson, Carlyle, and the rest. She must be an Iphigenia in reverse. She must sacrifice the father for the health of the community. Woolf's thinking about the special role of women, as writers and simply as women, is as contradictory as Nietzsche's complex of attitudes toward women. Allowing for the change of sexual perspective, Woolf repeats Nietzsche's contradictions on this subject.[15] This is scarcely surprising, since in both cases what is in question is the traditional repertoire of figures and concepts about women and about the sameness and difference of the sexes.

If Woolf's effort as a writer is the filling of gaps and the extension of her mind into the unknown, two possibilities determine this enterprise. The gap may be really there, the unknown an emptiness. On the other hand, there may be a hidden presence behind the apparent gap, a pre-existing goal the extrapolation might reach. Woolf's work, as *A Room of One's Own* explicitly affirms, is conducted under the traditional aegis of questions of "the truth" and of the possibility of a true representation of this truth. In a literary work of "integrity," that is, of "truth," what, for Woolf, is being expressed? Is it reality—physical, social, and psychological things as they are? Is it the life force of nature, of which the writer's creative energy is a displacement? Is it the mind of the writer, with its intrinsic rhythms and sensibility? Is it the collective mind of the previous writers, the tradition incarnated in the already existing rhythms and figures of the language? The notion of a historical evolution of sensibility is as important in *Between the Acts* as it is in *Orlando* or in Woolf's literary criticism. Or is it some "source" which is expressed in the genuine work, the ground rhythm behind all the rhythms, some ontological energy behind nature and behind the mind, the heart of darkness at the bottom of the pool in which the Lady Ermyntrude drowned herself? Or does a work of literature express only language? Does it weave a fictive covering over an abyss, veil an absence, those "appalling crevasses" (BA, p. 189) over which the final music of the pageant is suspended? All these possibilities are threaded through the text of *Between the Acts* in multicolored diversity, here a green strand, there a red, there a black.

If the gap, the something missing, is "the truth," then the proper work of the writer would be to make that gap appear. The vacancy can be revealed by breaking the rhythm, by sudden sinkings, open places in the text, incompletions, vertigoes. This movement of the mind, a drop in the text, is the sinking into death, the breaking of the illusion, the drowning of the Lady Ermyntrude: "It was in that deep centre, in that black heart, that the lady had drowned herself" (BA, p. 44). In the same way, the lady in the painting in the dining room at Pointz Hall leads the beholder "into the heart of silence" (p. 49):

> She led the eye up, down, from the curve to the straight, through glades of greenery and shades of silver, dun, and rose into silence. The room was empty.
>
> Empty, empty, empty; silent, silent, silent. The room was a shell, singing of what was before time was; a vase stood in the heart of the house, alabaster, smooth, cold, holding the still, distilled essence of emptiness, silence. (Pp. 36–37)

Men, according to Woolf, are everlasting sterile egotists. They believe in some original column of meaning from which all meanings have descended. They refuse to accept the silence and emptiness which is there, the hollow vase. Their sexual, stylistic, and rhythmical affirmations have covered this vacancy. They have covered it with the factitious constructions of the male ego. In *A Room of One's Own* Woolf opposes the dry self-assertions in a new novel by "Mr. A" to the broken rhythms of "Mary Carmichael's" *Life's Adventure.* Woolf's analysis may be taken as an oblique description of her own stylistic rhythms. It is a remarkable act of self-interpretation. Like the bold self-assertion of the male "ancestor" in the painting facing the one of the lady in the Hall (BA, p. 36), Mr. A's writing is entirely self-confident and free: "Indeed, it was delightful to read a man's writing again. It was so direct, so straightforward after the writing of women. It indicated such freedom of mind, such liberty of person, such confidence in himself. One had a sense of physical well-being in the presence of this well-nourished, well-educated, free mind, which had never been thwarted or opposed, but had had full liberty from birth to stretch itself in whatever way it liked" (*Room,* p. 103). But this self-affirmation is ultimately arid. Mr. A is cut off from the truth of things by the shadow of his ego: "after reading a chapter or two a shadow seemed to lie across the page. It was a straight dark bar, a shadow shaped something like the letter 'I.' One began dodging this way and that to catch a glimpse of the landscape behind it" (p. 103). Mr. A's self-confidence hides a secret fear of his impotence, of his exclusion from the truth. This fear expresses itself, in his novel, by repetitive and ultimately boring scenes in which the hero asserts his male ego by sexual assaults on the heroine, "protesting against the equality of the other sex by asserting his own superiority" (p. 105).[16] "But why was I bored?" asks Woolf. "Partly because of the dominance of the letter 'I' and the aridity, which, like the giant beech tree, it casts within its shade. Nothing will grow there. And partly for some more obscure reason. There seemed to be some obstacle, some impediment of Mr. A's mind which blocked the fountain of creative energy and shored it within narrow limits" (p. 104). The male writer, says Woolf, for all his arrogance and sexual athleticism, is impotent. His pen is an arid beak or scimitar, death-dealing not lifegiving, drawing whatever life it may have from women. Mr. Ramsay, in *To the Lighthouse,* returns continually to Mrs. Ramsay to be restored. Peter Walsh, in *Mrs. Dalloway,* must flourish his penknife in a futile effort to prove that he is a man.

Mary Carmichael's problem is different. She has no male illusions. She dwells near the truth. She knows silence and emptiness. She finds, however, that the large and small rhythms of the traditional literary language, constructed as they have been by male writers, will not allow her to express her insight:

> Lamb, Browne, Thackeray, Newman, Sterne, Dickens, De Quincey—whoever it may be—never helped a woman yet, though she may have learnt a few tricks of them and adapted them to her use. The weight, the pace, the stride of a man's mind are too unlike her own for her to lift anything substantial from him successfully. The ape is too distant to be sedulous. Perhaps the first thing she would find, setting pen to paper, was that there was no common sentence ready for her use . . . It was a sentence that was unsuited for a woman's use . . . Indeed, since freedom and fullness of expression are of the essence of the art, such a lack of tradition, such a scarcity and inadequacy of tools, must have told enormously upon the writing of women. Moreover, a book is not made of sentences laid end to end, but of sentences built, if an image helps, into arcades and domes. And this shape too has been made by men out of their needs for their own uses. (Pp. 79–80)

Mary Carmichael's solution to this problem is the same as Virginia Woolf's. It is eloquently expressed in Woolf's ironically bewildered reaction to her reading of *Life's Adventure*. Nietzsche, in *The Gay Science*, sees belief in the magical power of rhythm as a relic of the ages of superstition: "even now, after men have fought against such superstitions for thousands of years, the wisest among us are still occasionally fooled by rhythm—if only insofar as we sometimes consider an idea truer simply because it has a metrical form and presents itself with a divine skip and jump [*göttlichen Hopsassa*]."[17] Like Woolf herself, Mary Carmichael shares Nietzsche's suspicion of the magical force of rhythm. She takes her revenge on the traditional rhythms in the same way that Woolf does in *Between the Acts*, by initiating them and then breaking them off. The reader's expectations are defrauded, and he sinks. In his fall he has, it may be, a glimpse of the abyss, the truth that there is no truth, the truth veiled by all those factitious constructions of the male ego. "I tried a sentence or two on my tongue," says Woolf of her attempt to decide whether Mary Carmichael "has a pen in her hand or a pickaxe":

> Soon it was obvious that something was not quite in order. The smooth gliding of sentence after sentence was interrupted. Something tore, something scratched; a single word here and there

> flashed its torch in my eyes. She was "unhanding" herself as they say in the old plays.[18] She is like a person striking a match that will not light, I thought . . . Alas, I sighed, that it should be so. For while Jane Austen breaks from melody to melody as Mozart from song to song, to read this writing was like being out at sea in an open boat. Up one went, down one sank . . . I am almost sure, I said to myself, that Mary Carmichael is playing a trick on us. For I feel as one feels on a switchback railway when the car, instead of sinking, as one has been led to expect, swerves up again. Mary is tampering with the expected sequence. First she broke the sentence; now she has broken the sequence . . . Perhaps she had done this unconsciously, merely giving things their natural order, as a woman would, if she wrote like a woman. But the effect was somehow baffling; one could not see a wave heaping itself, a crisis coming round the next corner. Therefore I could not plume myself either upon the depths of my feelings and my profound knowledge of the human heart. For whenever I was about to feel the usual things in the usual places, about love, about death, the annoying creature twitched me away, as if the important point were just a little further on. (Pp. 84–85, 95)

The special genius of the woman writer, Woolf suggests, may be for shivering into splinters the old vision for the sake of offering insight, in the silence left, of the true vacancy behind. On the other hand, Woolf says of Mary Carmichael's tamperings with the sentence and with the sequence that "she has every right to do both these things if she does them not for the sake of breaking, but for the sake of creating" (p. 85). Though the gap may really be there, the talent of women, as writers and simply as women, may be for creative veiling of the emptiness. They are adepts at weaving a web of illusion. They can heal wounds, send out a great tide of emotion to engulf every scrap, ort, and fragment in an ocean of unity. There is an odd adverb, "out" where one would expect "in," in the citation describing Isa's reverie with which I began this chapter: "Yes, yes, yes, the tide rushed out embracing" (BA, p. 215). This suggests that the source of the tide is not the impersonal sea over there but the personal power here, the female creative energy of Isa, old Lucy, or Miss La Trobe. Men are dry, impotent, paralyzed by a fear of castration, the fear of vacancy. They are unable ever to finish the constructions their wills to power have initiated. Like Mr. Ramsay in *To the Lighthouse,* they can never get all the way from A to Z. Each man must constantly return to some woman, as Mr. Ramsay returns to his wife, to have his power renewed by immersion in female fountains of creativity:

> And I looked at the bookcase again. There were the biographies: Johnson and Goethe and Carlyle and Sterne and Cowper and Shelley and Voltaire and Browning and many others. And I began thinking of all those great men who have for one reason or another admired, sought out, lived with, confided in, made love to, written of, trusted in, and shown what can only be described as some need of and dependence upon certain persons of the opposite sex . . . What they got, it is obvious, was something that their own sex was unable to supply; and it would not be rash, perhaps, to define it further, without quoting the doubtless rhapsodical words of the poets, as some stimulus, some renewal of creative power which is in the gift only of the opposite sex to bestow. (P. 90)

This womanly power, it may be, is only a power of fiction-making. Miss La Trobe, for example, thinks of her power over her audience as a power of maintaining the "illusion": "This is death, death, death, she noted in the margin of her mind; when illusion fails" (BA, p. 180). Men continue a search for "the truth." They try to extrapolate all the way out to Z. They believe in the existence, somewhere, of an original or conclusive head meaning, an ur-word or an end word. They are inveterately logocentric, "phallogocentric," in their thinking, though this belief is undermined by their fear that behind the last veil there may be nothing. Women know that death, emptiness, silence underlie every surface. They are therefore mistresses of illusion known to be illusion, manipulators of surface, denouncers of "depth of feelings." Theirs is an art of dissimulation. Their parodies of the old male masters both continue the traditional rhythms and at the same time undercut them, show them, through hyperboles and ironies, as fictions. Their genuine quality, their integrity or truth, in an odd reversal of the terminology of the authentic and proper I have been using, becomes their manifestation of untruth.

Between the Acts is throughout, especially in the pageant, a work of outrageous and hilarious parody, parody of Shakespeare, of Congreve, of the Victorians. The novel is full of literary allusions, quotations, and echoes. Parody is repetition as praise, but it is destruction too. One effect of *Between the Acts* is to kill off the father writers by hyperbolic imitation of them. Woolf's parody shows them up as the collection of stylized conventions they are. One can never take Shakespeare's late romances, or *The Country Wife,* or *The Way of the World* in quite the same way again.

The final possibility, in this triplet of possibilities for the role of the woman writer, is that the gap may hide a positive truth, an ontological principle, "being," the "heart of darkness." Women may be especially able to reach down through the false veils woven by male egoism to get at this truth and express it, as words, for example, rise up from the mud to initiate Miss La Trobe's new play. In a hypothetical conversation, in *A Room of One's Own,* between a male writer and a woman to whom he has come for renewal, "there would follow, even in the simplest talk, such a natural difference of opinion that the dried ideas in him would be fertilised anew; and the sight of her creating in a different medium from his own would so quicken his creative power that insensibly his sterile mind would begin to plot again, and he would find the phrase or the scene which was lacking when he put on his hat to visit her" (p. 90).

If women have special access to that "force in things which one had overlooked" (p. 100), then women should not so much reject the male enterprise as complete it. The reader will note the reversal in the passage just quoted. It is the female who has the power of "fertilization." If so, women should wrest the pen from the hands of the father writers in the name of their more genuine access to a positive truth. This act would not so much break the rhythm to reveal an absence as destroy the old false male rhythm and replace it with an authentic female rhythm. This new rhythm would be capable of filling the spaces and going out into the unknown, making the unknown into the known. Such a writer would be that androgyne of whom Woolf dreamed, possessed of male power and female sensitivity. In such an androgyne, the male and the female would "live in harmony together, spiritually cooperating . . . the mind . . . fully fertilised" (p. 102).

This androgyne is an ideal, not yet a reality. The present relation of the sexes is not the tranquil harmony of male and female, "naturally creative, incandescent and undivided" (p. 102). It is rather the sexual and spiritual battle presented in Woolf's novels: "Love and hate—how they tore her asunder!" (BA, p. 215). An example is that primordial plot of *Between the Acts,* about to be enacted once more by Giles and Isa: "But first they must fight, as the dog fox fights with the vixen, in the heart of darkness, in the fields of night" (p. 219). This sexual battle would be particularly without quarter if the destiny of the woman writer were to take over the enterprise of writing as it has been defined by men. The woman writer would then join in the search for the truth, rather than reveal its absence or weave a fictive veil over the place where it is not.

Among these possibilities *Between the Acts,* like Woolf's other work, alternates, just as each of the novels interpreted in this book alternates in its own way among different possibilities of meaning. *Between the Acts* affirms now one possibility, now another, now all three at once, in a rotation which Woolf does not master and could not master, since each possibility contains the others and calls them up. Nor can the reader master this oscillation in the text. The novel renders impossible of solution the problem of the truth behind the words, the problem of "truth" as such. The critic can only in one way or another restate the alternatives without resolving them into unity, moving back and forth from one to another as one passage or another in the text is stressed as evidence. This constant reversal is analogous to that in Walter Benjamin's figure of the sock, which I discussed in Chapter 1.

In this analogy, my book comes full circle. Is this analogy between beginning and ending an example of the first kind of repetition or of the second? The same question may be asked of the many other echoes from one chapter to another in this book. It remains, after all my exploration, still an open question. It has been my intention to open this and other questions about repetition in fiction, not to answer them definitively, though my aim has been to show with as much exactness and completeness as possible just how repetition functions in each of the seven novels. My fundamental premise in this book is that the specific heterogeneity of a given text can be exactly defined, even though a univocal meaning cannot be justified by the text, at least not by the ones discussed here. As I said initially, how far this can and should be universalized to apply to all literary texts remains to be seen. *Between the Acts* in any case makes explicit the way each new work in one way or another is a repetition of the long row of previous ones. Most of the modes of repetition which function in English fiction are not only present in *Between the Acts* but made overtly matters of interrogation. In these ways, as well as in its openness to an uncertain future, beyond even the death of its author, *Between the Acts* is a good place to end this investigation of the relation between fiction and repetition in the English novel.

NOTES

1. Two Forms of Repetition

1. Thomas Hardy, *Tess of the d'Urbervilles: A Pure Woman Faithfully Presented,* New Wessex Edition (London: Macmillan, 1974), ch. 5. Further citations from the novel will be identified by chapter number from this edition.

2. Cited by Claude Lévi-Strauss in "Introduction à l'oeuvre de M. Mauss," in Marcel Mauss, *Sociologie et anthropologie* (Paris: Presses Universitaires de France, 1950), p. xli; my translation.

3. I have had this broad context in mind as a background for my seven interpretations. A more immediate context of previous secondary work has also been presumed at every point, though I have not wished to disrupt unnecessarily my focus on the texts of the seven novels by manifold indications of indebtedness, agreement, or disagreement. Here and there, however, for example in a summary of the wildly divergent readings of *Wuthering Heights* in Chapter 3, it has seemed appropriate to bring in previous criticism.

This context of previous work can be divided roughly into three categories, for each of which an extensive bibliography could be provided of work which has been useful to me, not to speak of the indefinitely long lists of work actually existing of each kind which could be made. One category is critical or biographical writing on each of my five authors. For each author the list would be a long one, even if it were limited to work relevant to my chapters here. A second category is recent work specifically on repetition. Again a long list could be given. It would include not only work by those authors listed already—Lacan, Deleuze, Eliade, and Derrida—but also, to give a few examples out of many, Walter Benjamin, Edward Said, Bruce Kawin, Peter Garrett, and Jeffrey Mehlman. A third category would be even larger: recent work on the theory of fiction generally and, more particularly, on the question of whether or not determinate or univocal readings of works of literature are in principle possible.

In one way or another useful to me, even if sometimes only to help me work out my own different conclusions, has been work by the "new critics" on literary form and ambiguity, especially Kenneth Burke and William Empson; work by Wayne Booth on the rhetoric of fiction and on irony; work by Wolfgang Iser and Stanley Fish proposing in different ways a "reader response" theory of criticism; work by a large number of critics in America and Europe developing in one way or another structuralist theories of fiction, for example Gérard Genette, Tzvetan Todorov, Jonathan Culler, and, with particular reference to the question of ambiguity, Shlomith Rimmon-Kenan; work explicitly in a "deconstructionist" mode or related kinds of criticism, not only by Derrida and Paul de Man, but also by younger critics. There is much diversity among the latter, but work by the following has been especially valuable to me: Cynthia Chase, Michal Peled Ginsburg, Joseph Riddel, John Romano, Ramón Saldívar, Homer Brown, Sharon Cameron, Philippe Lacoue-Labarthe, Jean-Luc Nancy, Samuel Weber, and Edgar Dryden. To this may be added work of a Marxist structuralist or semiotic sort, for example that of Fredric Jameson. My thinking has been aided, finally, by work developing theories of disunity, disparity, incongruity, and incoherence, or arguing against these, books or essays, for example, by John Bayley, James Kincaid, Frank Kermode, Gerald Graff, and Frank Lentricchia.

The ongoing debate in these areas may be followed in the pages of many journals, but five may be singled out as especially important for my enterprise here, since essays published in them often bear directly on the criticism of prose fiction: *Poetics Today, New Literary History, Critical Inquiry, Poétique,* and *Diacritics.*

My interpretations here would have been impossible without these previous writers, even when my conclusions differ. I am anxious at the outset to acknowledge an indebtedness which extends far beyond the titles actually mentioned in any of my chapters. This book will I hope take its place in the context of these manifold arguments about literary criticism generally, about the criticism of fiction in particular, and, more narrowly, about the work of the five authors discussed here.

4. (Paris: Les Editions de Minuit, 1969), p. 302; my translation.

5. Christopher Devlin, ed., *The Sermons and Devotional Writings of Gerard Manley Hopkins* (London: Oxford University Press, 1959), p. 100.

6. *Illuminations,* trans. Harry Zohn (New York: Schocken, 1969), p. 202. For the German original, see *Illuminationen* (Frankfurt am Main: Suhrkamp Verlag, 1969), pp. 355–356.

7. *Illuminations,* p. 204; German text, *Illuminationen,* p. 358.

8. See Cynthia Chase's admirable discussion of this in relation to Freud's interpretation of Sophocles' *Oedipus the King:* "Oedipal Textuality: Reading Freud's Reading of *Oedipus,*" *Diacritics,* 9, no. 1 (Spring 1979), 54–68, esp. 57–58.

9. *Illuminations,* pp. 204–205; German text, *Illuminationen,* pp. 358–359.

10. (Frankfurt am Main; Suhrkamp Verlag, 1969); this has been translated by John Osborne as *The Origin of German Tragic Drama* (London: New Left Books, 1977).

11. My translation; German text, *Illuminationen,* pp. 100–101.

12. "Aesthetic Poetry," *Appreciations* (London: Macmillan, 1889), pp. 213–214.

13. Pt. III, ch. 1, New Wessex Edition (London: Macmillan, 1975), p. 139. The pagination of the hardcover version of the New Wessex Edition of Hardy's works differs from that of the paperback version.

14. Trans. Walter Kaufmann (New York: Vintage, 1967), pp. 90–91; German text, *Werke in Drei Bänden,* ed. Karl Schlecta, I (Munich: Carl Hanser Verlag, 1966), 79–80.

15. See "The Linguistic Moment in 'The Wreck of the Deutschland,' " *The New Criticism and After,* ed. T. D. Young (Charlottesville: University Press of Virginia, 1976), pp. 47–60.

16. "Nothing Fails Like Success," *Deconstructive Criticism: Directions: SCE Reports,* 8 (Fall 1980), 9–10.

17. See "On Edge: The Crossways of Contemporary Criticism," *Bulletin of the American Academy of Arts and Sciences,* 32, no. 4 (Jan. 1979), 13–32; "The Function of Rhetorical Study at the Present Time," *The State of the Discipline: 1970s–1980s, ADE Bulletin,* no. 62 (Sept.-Nov. 1979), pp. 10–18; "The Critic as Host," *Deconstruction and Criticism* (New York: Seabury Press, 1979), pp. 217–253; "Theory and Practice: A Response to Vincent Leitch," *Critical Inquiry,* 6 (Summer 1980), 609–614.

18. Gerald Graff, "Who Killed Criticism?" *American Scholar,* 49, no. 3 (Summer 1980), 337–355.

2. *Lord Jim:* Repetition as Subversion of Organic Form

1. Wallace Stevens, *The Collected Poems* (New York: Knopf, 1951), p. 443.

2. Letter to Joseph Cottle, 1815, in *Unpublished Letters of Samuel Taylor Coleridge, Including Certain Letters Republished from Original Sources,* ed. Earl Leslie Griggs, II (New Haven: Yale University Press, 1933), 128.

3. Ibid., p. 129.

4. Letter of Dec. 20, 1897, in *Joseph Conrad's Letters to R. B. Cunninghame Graham,* ed. C. T. Watts (Cambridge: Cambridge University Press, 1969), pp. 56–57.

5. Ibid., p. 57.

6. *Youth and Two Other Stories* (Garden City, N.Y.: Doubleday, Page, 1925), p. 48.

7. *Lord Jim, A Tale* (London: Dent, 1948), ch. 5. Further quotations from *Lord Jim* will be identified by chapter number from this edition.

8. In *The Form of Victorian Fiction* (Notre Dame, Ind.: University of Notre Dame Press, 1968).

9. "The New Novel" (1914), in *Notes on Novelists* (London: Dent, 1914), p. 276.

10. (Cambridge: Cambridge University Press, 1966), pp. 41–170; (Berkeley: University of California Press, 1979), pp. 259–269.

11. Sherry, *Conrad's Eastern World,* pp. 299–309.

3. *Wuthering Heights:* Repetition and the "Uncanny"

1. Emily Brontë, *Wuthering Heights,* Clarendon Edition, ed. Hilda Marsden and Ian Jack (Oxford: Clarendon Press, 1976), II, ch. 20. Further citations from the novel will be identified by volume and chapter number from this edition, or by page number in the case of Charlotte Brontë's prefatory essays. The epigraph for this chapter is from volume I, chapter 2.

2. See Robert C. McKibben, "The Image of the Book in *Wuthering Heights,*" *Nineteenth-Century Fiction,* 15 (1960), 159–169.

3. The review is reprinted in *Emily Brontë: A Critical Anthology,* ed. Jean-Pierre Petit (Harmondsworth, Middlesex: Penguin, 1973), pp. 38–39.

4. See Dorothy Van Ghent, *The English Novel: Form and Function* (New York: Rinehart, 1953), pp. 153–170; C. P. Sanger, *The Structure of Wuthering Heights* (London: Hogarth Press, 1926); Thomas Moser, "What is the Matter with Emily Jane?" *Nineteenth-Century Fiction,* 17 (June 1962), 1–19; David Cecil, *Early Victorian Novelists* (London: Constable, 1948), pp. 136–182; Mark Schorer, "Introduction" to *Wuthering Heights* (New York: Holt, Rinehart and Winston, 1950), pp. iv–xvii; J. Hillis Miller, *The Disappearance of God* (Cambridge, Mass.: Harvard University Press, 1963), pp. 157–211; Georges Bataille, *La Littérature et le mal* (Paris: Gallimard, 1957), pp. 11–31; Camille Paglia, *Sexual Personae: The Androgyne in Literature and Art,* Diss. Yale 1974, pp. 321–333; Frank Kermode, *The Classic* (New York: Viking, 1975), pp. 117–141: Margaret Homans, "Repression and Sublimation of Nature in *Wuthering Heights,*" *PMLA,* 93, no. 1 (Jan. 1978), 9–19; Leo Bersani, *A Future for Astyanax: Character and Desire in Literature* (Boston: Little, Brown, 1976), pp. 197–223; David Wilson, "Emily Brontë, First of the Moderns," *Modern Quarterly Miscellany,* no. 1 (1947), pp. 94–115; Arnold Kettle, "*Wuthering Heights,*" in *Introduction to the English Novel,* I (London: Hutchinson University Library, 1965), pp. 139–155; Terry Eagleton, *Myths of Power: A Marxist Study of the Brontës* (London: Macmillan, 1975), pp. 97–121.

5. See paragraph 59 of Kant, *Critique of Judgment,* trans. J. H. Bernard (New York: Hafner, 1951), pp. 196–198. See also Paul de Man's discussion of this paragraph in "The Epistemology of Metaphor," *Critical Inquiry,* 5, no. 1 (Autumn 1978), 26–29.

6. The uncanny in literature is firmly opposed by Freud to situations in real life which are uncanny. Nevertheless, the uncanny, both in literature and in life, is defined by Freud as "nothing else than a hidden, familiar thing that has undergone repression and then emerged from it." Sigmund Freud, "The 'Uncanny' " (1919), *Collected Papers,* IV (New York: Basic Books, 1959), p. 399. This

familiar thing is, in the definition from Schelling which Freud recalls, not just anything hidden which reappears, but "something which ought to have been kept concealed but which has nevertheless come to light" (p. 394). If it ought to have been kept hidden it ought also to be brought to light, or at any rate there is a compulsion to bring it to light, even if only in disguised forms. Freud therefore connects the uncanny with the repetition-compulsion, *der Wiederholungszwang.*

4. *Henry Esmond:* Repetition and Irony

1. See Gordon N. Ray, *The Buried Life: A Study of the Relation between Thackeray's Fiction and his Personal History* (Cambridge, Mass.: Harvard University Press, 1952), pp. 78–96: "as Thackeray wrote the last eight chapters of the first book of *Esmond* and the first two chapters of the second, he again lived through the whole course of the Brookfield affair and made it a part of his novel. In the six months that followed, as he wrote the rest of *Esmond,* he sketched out in fantasy the way his relation with Mrs. Brookfield might have developed under other circumstances" (p. 86).

2. "L'Anti-histoire de Henri Esmond," *Poétique,* no. 9 (1972), pp. 61–79.

3. Quotations from *Henry Esmond* will be identified by book and chapter numbers, so the reader may refer to any edition at hand. I have used the text in William Makepeace Thackeray, *Works,* Centenary Biographical Edition, X (London: Smith, Elder, 1910–1911; rpt. New York: AMS Press, 1968).

4. Letter of Nov. 1851, *The Letters and Private Papers of William Makepeace Thackeray,* ed. Gordon N. Ray, II (Cambridge, Mass.: Harvard University Press, 1945), 815.

5. *The Book of Snobs, Works,* IX, 3.

6. By René Girard, in *Mensonge romantique et vérité romanesque* (Paris: Grasset, 1961). The concept derives from Jean-Paul Sartre. See, for example, his *Saint Genet: Comédien et martyr* (Paris: Gallimard, 1952).

7. Thackeray, *Letters and Private Papers,* II, 309. The phrase comes from Ephesians 2:12.

8. See Nietzsche, "European Nihilism," *The Will to Power,* trans. Walter Kaufmann and R. J. Hollingdale (New York: Random House, 1967), pp. 5–82.

9. *Vanity Fair, Works,* II, vol. II, ch. 32, p. 431; ch. 67 in those editions in which the chapters are numbered consecutively.

10. I am indebted here to an unpublished paper by Anne Clendenning.

11. Thackeray's wife was named Isabella. She went mad in 1842, a decade before the publication of *Henry Esmond,* and was permanently confined to a sanitorium. Is that relevant to the reader's understanding of the character named Isabella in *Henry Esmond,* and if so, just how?

12. Letter to his mother, Nov. 1851, *Letters and Private Papers,* II, 815.

13. Letter to Lady Stanley, Oct. 1851, ibid., p. 807.

14. Friedrich Schlegel, *Kritische Ausgabe,* ed. Ernst Behler, XVIII (Munich:

Verlag Ferdinand Schöningh; Zürich: Thomas Verlag, 1963), p. 85: "Die Ironie ist eine permanente Parekbase." Sören Kierkegaard, *The Concept of Irony*, trans. Lee M. Capel (Bloomington: Indiana University Press, 1968), p. 271. Kierkegaard borrows his formulation from Hegel's *Philosophy of Fine Art*.

15. As Stephen Bann has argued on pp. 62–63, 72–75, 79 of "L'Anti-histoire de Henri Esmond."

16. For example by John Carey in *Thackeray: Prodigal Genius* (London: Faber and Faber, 1977). I much admire Carey's enthusiastic appreciation of Thackeray's exuberant early work, but the weakness of his thesis of a decline in Thackeray's later work into sentimentality and snobbish respectability is indicated by the fact that it depends on taking *Henry Esmond* as without irony against its narrator. Carey reads the novel as a straightforward endorsement of Henry's values and of Henry's portrait of himself. The young Thackeray, hater of humbug, is still present in *Henry Esmond*, as this chapter attempts to show.

17. See Cynthia Chase, "Oedipal Textuality: Reading Freud's Reading of *Oedipus*," *Diacritics*, 9, no. 1 (Spring 1979), pp. 54–68.

18. Walter Benjamin, "The Image of Proust," *Illuminations*, trans. Harry Zohn (New York: Schocken Books, 1969), p. 204.

5. *Tess of the d'Urbervilles:* Repetition as Immanent Design

1. Thomas Hardy, *Tess of the d'Urbervilles: A Pure Woman Faithfully Presented*, New Wessex Edition (London: Macmillan, 1974), ch. 11. Further citations from the novel will be identified by chapter number from this edition. For a discussion of the revisions of *Tess of the d'Urbervilles* from the manuscript through the successive printed editions, see J. T. Laird, *The Shaping of Tess of the d'Urbervilles* (Oxford: Clarendon Press, 1975). I am also grateful to the authorities of the British Library for allowing me to examine the manuscript itself, BL Additional MS. 38182. In a few places I have indicated readings from the manuscript. See the opening pages of Chapter 1 above for a preliminary identification of repetitive elements in *Tess*.

2. Thomas Hardy, *The Complete Poems*, New Wessex Edition, ed. James Gibson (London: Macmillan, 1976), p. 177.

3. According to *The American Heritage Dictionary of the English Language*, "hieroglyphic" comes from the Greek words *hiero*, meaning sacred or holy, plus *gluphe*, meaning carving or engraving, while "graft" comes from the Greek *graphein*, to write. The root of "glyph" is *gleubh*, to cut, cleave, the origin of words like cleave, clove, cleft, clever, while the root of "graphein" is *gerebh*, to scratch.

4. "To Meet or Otherwise," *Complete Poems*, p. 310.

5. Florence Emily Hardy, *The Life of Thomas Hardy: 1840–1928* (London: Macmillan; New York: St. Martin's Press, 1965), p. 244.

6. See Plato, *Symposium*, 191, a-d, trans. Michael Joyce, in *The Collected Dialogues*, ed. Edith Hamilton and Huntington Cairns, Bollingen Series, LXXI (Princeton: Princeton University Press, 1973), pp. 543–544.

7. Trans. James Strachey, *Complete Psychological Works,* Standard Edition, XVIII (London: Hogarth Press, 1955), see pp. 57–58.

8. A parallel for Hardy's insight into the effect of "points" or of emphases in determining meaning is to be found in *A Midsummer Night's Dream,* V, 1. (I am indebted to René Girard for calling my attention to this passage in conversation.) After Quince has said the correct words in the prologue, but with the pauses and emphases in the wrong places, so that it says the opposite of what its author meant, the gentlefolk comment on this error:

THESEUS.	This Fellow does not stand upon points.
LYSANDER.	He hath rid his prologue like a rough colt; he knows not the stop. A good moral, my lord: it is not enough to speak, but to speak true.
HIPPOLYTA.	Indeed he hath played on his prologue like a child on a recorder; a sound, but not in government.
THESEUS.	His speech was like a tangled chain; nothing impaired, but all disordered.

9. *The Life of Thomas Hardy,* p. 153.

6. *The Well-Beloved:* The Compulsion to Stop Repeating

1. *A Map of Misreading* (New York: Oxford University Press, 1975), p. 23.

2. New Wessex Edition (London: Macmillan, 1975), p. 233 and pt. III, ch. 8. Further references to this novel will be by part and chapter number in this edition, or in the case of citations from the 1892 version of the novel, by page number in the hardcover version of the New Wessex Edition.

3. *The Complete Poems* (London: Macmillan 1976), p. 320, my italics. Henceforth cited as CP.

4. Thomas Hardy, "In Tenebris," II, 14, CP, p. 168.

5. Marcel Proust, *A la recherche du temps perdu,* III (Paris: Bibliothèque de la Pléiade, 1954), 376–377; my translation.

6. *Middlemarch,* III, *The Works of George Eliot,* Cabinet Edition (London: Blackwood, n.d.), p. 455.

7. (New York: New American Library, 1970), p. 318.

8. "Emily Brontë," in *The Disappearance of God* (Cambridge, Mass.: Harvard University Press, 1963), pp. 157–211.

9. Thomas Hardy, *The Return of the Native,* New Wessex Edition (London: Macmillan, 1974), bk. VI, ch. 3.

10. "The Pedigree," CP, p. 460.

11. Notebook entry of 1889: "Love lives on propinquity, but dies of contact," in Florence Emily Hardy, *The Life of Thomas Hardy: 1840–1928* (London: Macmillan; New York: St. Martin's Press, 1965), p. 220. Henceforth cited as *Life.*

12. "To Meet, or Otherwise," CP, p. 310.

13. *Life*, p. 217.

14. J. O. Bailey, *The Poetry of Thomas Hardy: A Handbook and Commentary* (Chapel Hill: University of North Carolina Press, 1970), p. 348.

15. *Life*, p. 6.

16. Marcel Proust, *Letters*, trans. Mina Curtis (New York: Random House, 1949), p. 205.

17. Hermann Lea, *Thomas Hardy Through the Camera's Eye*, p. 30, cited in Bailey, *The Poetry of Thomas Hardy*, p. 85. I have been unable to consult Lea's book.

18. H. C. Duffin, *Thomas Hardy: A Study of the Wessex Novels, the Poems, and The Dynasts* (Manchester: The University Press, 1967), p. 196.

19. *Life*, p. 332.

7. *Mrs. Dalloway:* Repetition as the Raising of the Dead

1. See, for one well-known example of this, "The Brown Stocking," an essay on a passage in *To the Lighthouse*, in Erich Auerbach, *Mimesis*, trans. Willard R. Trask (Princeton: Princeton University Press, 1953), pp. 525–553.

2. In *The Form of Victorian Fiction* (Notre Dame, Ind.: University of Notre Dame Press, 1968).

3. Virginia Woolf, *Mrs. Dalloway* (New York: Harcourt, Brace, 1925), p. 85. Further citations from this novel will be identified by page number from this edition.

4. See "Written in Butler's Sermons" and "To Marguerite—Continued," *The Poems of Matthew Arnold*, ed. Kenneth Allott (London: Longmans, Green, 1965), pp. 51–52, 124–125.

5. *A Writer's Diary* (New York: Harcourt, Brace, 1954), p. 60. Henceforth cited in the text as WD.

6. Opus 10, no. 8. For the score and von Gilm's text see Richard Strauss, *Lieder für Mittlere Stimme mit Klavierbegleitung*, Universal Edition, III (Leipzig: Jos. Aibl-Verlag; London: Boosey and Hawkes, 1907), 9–11.

8. *Between the Acts:* Repetition as Extrapolation

1. Virginia Woolf, *Between the Acts* (New York: Harcourt, Brace, 1941), p. 215. Henceforth cited in the text as BA. The working title of *Between the Acts*, "Pointz Hall," may be a pun combining orts and scraps (Pointz/points) and unity (Hall/all).

2. In "Living On: Border Lines," *Deconstruction and Criticism* (New York: Seabury, 1979), pp. 100–101.

3. Virginia Woolf, *A Room of One's Own* (New York: Harcourt, Brace and World, n.d.), p. 12. Henceforth cited in the text as *Room*.

4. On the function of "irrelevant details" in fiction, see Roland Barthes, "L'Effet du réel," *Communications*, no. 11 (1969), pp. 84–89, and Martin Price,

"The Irrelevant Detail and the Emergence of Form," in *Aspects of Narrative*, ed. J. Hillis Miller (New York: Columbia University Press, 1971), pp. 69–91.

5. See Jackson I. Cope's comprehensive discussion of this trope in *The Theater and the Dream: From Metaphor to Form in Renaissance Drama* (Baltimore: Johns Hopkins University Press, 1973).

6. See Geoffrey Hartman, "Virginia's Web," in *Beyond Formalism* (New Haven: Yale University Press, 1970), pp. 71–84.

7. I am indebted here to an admirable unpublished discussion of the first paragraph of Valéry's "Introduction à la méthode de Léonardo da Vinci" by Hans-Jost Frey of the University of Zürich.

8. See the essay by Emile Benveniste on the etymology of the word "rhythm" and on the history of the concept it expresses: "La Notion de 'rhythme' dans son expression linguistique," in *Problèmes de linguistique générale* (Paris: Gallimard, 1966), pp. 327–335.

9. This hypothesis of homogeneity is the same one Valéry makes in the "Introduction à la méthode de Léonardo da Vinci."

10. See Wolfgang Iser, *The Implied Reader* (Baltimore: Johns Hopkins University Press, 1974); *The Act of Reading* (Baltimore: Johns Hopkins University Press, 1978; and "Indeterminacy and the Reader's Response in Prose Fiction," in *Aspects of Narrative*, ed. Miller, pp. 1–45. For an essay on this topic by Frank Kermode see his discussion of *Wuthering Heights* in *The Classic* (New York: Viking Press, 1975), pp. 117–141.

11. Cf., as well as Hartman's essay, two essays on *Between the Acts* by Avrom Fleishman: one in *The English Historical Novel: Walter Scott to Virginia Woolf* (Baltimore: Johns Hopkins University Press, 1971), pp. 245–255, and the other in *Virginia Woolf: A Critical Reading* (Baltimore: Johns Hopkins University Press, 1975), pp. 202–219.

12. Quentin Bell, *Virginia Woolf: A Biography* (New York: Harcourt Brace Jovanovich, 1972), p. 226.

13. Cf. the notation for Dec. 2, 1939, in Virginia Woolf, *A Writer's Diary* (New York: Harcourt, Brace, 1954), p. 309: "Began reading Freud last night; to enlarge the circumference: to give my brain a wider scope: to make it objective; to get outside. Thus defeat the shrinkage of age. Always take on new things. Break the rhythm, etc."

14. See Fleishman's essay in *Virginia Woolf: A Critical Reading* for an identification of the sources of most of these fragments.

15. For Nietzsche's images of woman, see Jacques Derrida, *Spurs: Nietzsche's Styles*, trans. Barbara Harlow (Chicago: University of Chicago Press, 1979). I am not claiming, of course, that Virginia Woolf was in her feminism influenced by Neitzsche.

16. This sexuality, like the arid male reason it affirms, is, in a way entirely traditional, placed under the aegis of the sun, prime sign, since Plato and before, of reason, the *logos*, Apollo, the head signifier, or, as the French Freudians might say, the phallogocenter himself. (For this word, see Derrida, *Spurs*, p. 97.) The hero of Mr. A's novel commits the gross impropriety of asserting, in pub-

lic, his proprietorship over another person: "And then Alan, I thought, has passions; and here I turned page after page very fast, feeling that the crisis was approaching, and so it was. It took place on the beach under the sun. It was done very openly. It was done very vigorously. Nothing could have been more indecent . . . When Alan approaches what can he do? Being honest as the day and logical as the sun, there is only one thing he can do. And that he does, to do him justice, over and over (I said, turning the page) and over again" (*Room*, pp. 104–105). The woman, by contrast, exists under the aegis of Diana, moon goddess, goddess of night mists, of veiled modesty, propriety, and decent obscurity. The lady in the picture at Pointz Hall is presented "in her yellow robe, leaning, with a pillar to support her, a silver arrow in her hand, and a feather in her hair" (BA, p. 36).

17. *The Gay Science*, trans. Walter Kaufmann (New York: Vintage, 1974), paragraph 84, p. 140; for the German, see *Werke*, ed. Karl Schlechta, II (Munich: Carl Hanser Verlag, 1966), p. 94.

18. An odd locution! "Taking her hands off herself?" "Depriving herself of hands?" In any case, in some way dismantling some unity or action.

INDEX